A Natural History Guide

GRAND CANYON NATIONAL PARK

Jeremy Schmidt

HOUGHTON MIFFLIN COMPANY
Boston   New York
1993

For information about permission to reproduce
selections from this book, write to Permissions,
Houghton Mifflin Company, 215 Park Avenue South,
New York, New York 10003

Library of Congress Cataloging-in-Publication Data

Schmidt, Jeremy, 1949–
     The Grand Canyon / Jeremy Schmidt.
           p.   cm. — (National parks natural history series)
     Includes bibliographical references.
     ISBN 0-395-59931-8 (cl.) — ISBN 0-395-59932-6 (pa.)
     1. Natural history—Arizona—Grand Canyon. 2. Natural history—
Arizona—Grand Canyon National Park. I. Title. II. Series.
QH105.A65S36 1993
508.791'32—dc20   92-45805
                                                                 CIP

Printed in the United States of America

AGM 10 9 8 7 6 5 4 3 2 1

PHOTO CREDITS: Color photos in center insert (pages numbered here
for reference) by Jeremy Schmidt except:
     David Edwards — Deer Creek (p. 1 bottom), ocotillo (p. 16 bottom),
bighorn sheep (p. 17 top), Elves Chasm (p. 20 top), storm clouds (p. 24, bottom), Lava Falls (p. 25 top and bottom), snow on cacti (p. 27), tamarisk (p. 29
top), Anasazi basket (p. 30 bottom), Anasazi granaries (p. 31).
     Michael Collier — limestone (p. 1 top), bee on mesquite (p. 22 bottom),
Anasazi bridge (p. 30 top).
     National Park Service — air quality at Grand Canyon (p. 32 top and bottom).

Acknowledgments

F irst thanks must go to Wendy and Kestrel, cheerful appreciators of natural landscapes and my best travel buddies. Also to Paul Schullery; had he not involved me in this project, Grand Canyon geology would still be an impenetrable mystery to me. Continuing thanks go to Dave Edwards, whose understanding of the canyon's meaning — and whose ability to articulate that meaning — is unsurpassed.

At Grand Canyon National Park, I owe thanks to Carl Bowman for his views on the canyon's complex geology and just about any other subject you want to raise; to John Ray for biological insights; to Ellis Richard for his encouragement and help in tracking down sources of information within the Park Service; to Tim and Charissa Reid and Chris Brickley for hospitality in inclement weather; to the staff in Special Collections for their good-natured help with the vertical files; and to Pam Frasier of the Grand Canyon Natural History Association for perspectives on canyon publications.

Without scientific research, our knowledge of the canyon would be far less rich. Anyone who writes a book like this owes a great debt to the biologists, geologists, archaeologists, and others who do the hard work of systematic study, but who generously share what they have learned. So much of this story is theirs.

Finally, for generous help with photographs and illustrations, thanks to Michael Collier, David Edwards, W. K. Hamblin, Rich Hereford, Bill Leibfried, Diana Lubick, Dee Morris, Sue Priest, Stephen Reynolds, Valerie Saylor, and Cathy Steffens.

To my father and my mother,
Who showed me
Respectively
But not exclusively
How to see a landscape
And how to feel its spirit.

CONTENTS

KEY TO SYMBOLS

Throughout this book, symbols in the margins will help you quickly find information on the subjects that interest you most. Watch for symbols for the following subjects:

 Birds

 Trees

 Wildflowers

 Reptiles and amphibians

 Fish

 Insects

 Fungi

 Geology

Introduction

We know the Grand Canyon is an improbable landscape, but consider this: 4,000 feet below the rim, three miles from the river, up a side canyon of a side canyon, there is a deep pool of clear water fed by a long slender waterfall. Ferns grow in abundance. Columbines bob in gentle canyon breezes. Treefrogs cling to the damp sandstone walls.

Treefrogs?

From a vantage point on the parched South Rim, wet-skinned frogs are the last things you'd expect to see in the canyon. From here, it appears to contain little more than open space and hot, glaring desert. Your thoughts are of rattlesnakes, prickly-pear cactus, yucca, blackbrush, and something cold to drink.

In summer, temperatures of 100 degrees occur often on the rim. It gets hotter as you go down, although to do so — to go walking on, say, the Tonto Platform in the noonday July sun — is to defy common sense. Down there, even the snakes hide from the sun, beneath rocks too hot to sit on.

How could treefrogs fit into that scene — delicate moisture-loving creatures with soft amphibian skin, webbed hind feet, and front digits that look like human fingers?

This is the magic of the Grand Canyon: its vast layered depth. Standing on the edge, looking into that great blue and red space, you see it all — and you see very little. So much is hidden. The scale is too big even for imagination, much less reality. The Colorado River, thundering in the bottom of the mile-deep gorge it has built, appears even through binoculars as a thin green ribbon. Visitors peering down over sheer cliffs have been heard to say, "That little creek is the Colorado? Impossible."

Yet from the rims to that "little creek," there lies so much more than empty space. Rock formations tell a geologic story that began two billion years ago. Although abandoned for 800 years or more, Anasazi Indian dwellings appear perfectly preserved by the desert climate. Deer, bighorn sheep, mountain lions, coyotes, and many other animals thrive at various levels in the canyon, along with more than 1,500 species of plants, only two dozen of which are cacti. Intimate shaded side canyons drip with spring water and fill with the soft fragrance of wildflowers. On the North Rim, dense forests of spruce, fir, and aspen resemble those found in well-watered northern lands. At river level, especially in the Canyon's western reaches, are found the plants and animals of southern Arizona's Sonoran desert.

The place names alone are wonderful. There are rocks called Hermit, Watahomigi, Tapeats, Unkar, Coconino, Kaibab, and Vishnu. Side canyons go by names like Matkatamiba, Bright Angel, Hakatai, Malgosa, Nankoweap, and Elves Chasm. Rising above these places, but below the rim, are structures like Wotan's Throne, Shiva Temple, Shanub and Paguekwash points, Mount Sinyala, Osiris Temple, and King Arthur Castle. With a little time and a map, you soon learn to recognize the Great Unconformity (which has nothing to do with politics), the Grand Canyon Supergroup (nothing to do with music), and the superb Redwall Limestone, one of the Canyon's most visible and endearing landmarks.

There is an old saying about California redwood trees: they are so tall it takes one person a week to see to the top (although working together, seven people can do it in a single day). As folk wisdom, this holds a grain of truth, whether applied to redwoods or the Grand Canyon. You can see, but you cannot quickly know. What the eyes record, the brain does not entirely comprehend.

It takes at least a week, and maybe much longer, to see into the canyon. The first view is overwhelming. Then, after days of looking and reading and listening and walking, something happens. You start seeing new things that were there all along but essentially invisible. Patterns emerge. You begin to recognize rock layers. Some small geological item strikes home and you understand how it got there. A previously blank wall reveals an Anasazi granary. You see a particular landmark from several angles and elevations, and it becomes familiar, like a friend's face in a sea of strangers. In this way, one piece at a time, the canyon landscape begins to make sense.

Let's consider some numbers. The Grand Canyon lies just above 36 degrees latitude, roughly the same as Fresno, California; Memphis, Tennessee; the Straits of Gibraltar; and Tokyo, Japan. Its particular section of North America is called by geologists the Colorado Plateau, 130,000 square miles of canyons and mesas and colored sedimentary rock that is arguably the most scenic desert region in the world.

How long is the canyon? Measured at river level, the Canyon is 277 miles from start to finish. It begins at Lees Ferry below Lake Powell and ends beneath the waters of Lake Mead at the Grand Wash Cliffs near the Arizona-Nevada border. The first 61.5 miles (to the Little Colorado River) are contained in a narrow gorge that John Wesley Powell named Marble Canyon in 1869 when he and his exploration party first floated the river. The name derives from limestone walls that have been carved by the river into wavy shapes that resemble polished marble. Topographically, Marble Canyon is considered part of the Grand Canyon. Beyond Nankoweap Creek, things open up somewhat, until in the center of Grand Canyon (the part most people see) the rims stand about 10 miles apart, and the canyon is roughly a mile deep. This profile changes considerably from one end to the other. The rims vary from four to fifteen miles apart; the depth ranges from 3,500 to 6,000 feet, not including Lees Ferry, where the walls begin to rise from river level. Although the central part of the canyon boasts the grandest proportions, it is difficult to label any one section as the scenic climax. Every turn of the trail, the road, or the river brings something new and astonishing into view.

In those 277 miles, the Colorado River drops 2,215 feet over more than 150 rapids, some of which are among the most challenging whitewater runs in the country. Hance Rapid falls 30 feet in a half mile. Sockdolager drops 19 feet in a shorter distance. Granite drops 17 feet, as does Crystal, currently considered the toughest run on the river. Lava Falls, the biggest of all, drops 37 feet. Historic floods on the river include one of 300,000 cubic feet per second (estimated from driftwood lines above the river) and 200,000 cfs as recorded in 1921 at Phantom Ranch. Over a year, typical flows ranged between 90,000 and 4,000 cubic feet per second before Glen Canyon Dam was built; since then, spring flooding has been essentially curtailed.

How deep is the canyon? At Bright Angel Point, the North Rim is 8,145 feet above sea level. Twelve air miles away on the South Rim, Grand Canyon Village is just under 7,000 feet elevation. Between the two, at river level, Phantom Ranch breathes the relatively thick air at 2,400 feet. This makes the canyon, along this transect, 4,600 feet deep if measured from the South Rim, and almost 5,800 feet deep if measured from the North. The difference in height between the North and South rims is due to the slope of the Kaibab Plateau, which the Grand Canyon cuts through. An annual average of about 27 inches of water falls on the North Rim. Winter snowfall can exceed 200 inches. The South Rim is drier, receiving an average of about 15 inches precipitation per year, including usually less than 60 inches total snowfall. Down at Phantom Ranch, rainfall (it rarely snows at this level of the canyon) averages around seven inches per year, and sometimes much less.

Elevation differences and the shape of the canyon have an impact on temperatures. Average January lows on the North Rim are 20 degrees Fahrenheit; at Phantom Ranch, 36°F. The recorded extremes for the North Rim are a low of minus 26°F and a high of 91°F; at Phantom Ranch, a low of minus 9°F and a high of 120°F.

In its 1,904 square miles (1.2 million acres), Grand Canyon National Park contains most of the canyon below the rims as well as portions of the plateau surfaces. Its neighbors to the north are the Kaibab National Forest, lands owned by the Bureau of Land Management, and Lake Mead National Recreation Area. To the south, neighbors include the Kaibab National Forest and two Indian reservations belonging to the Hualapai and Havasupai tribes. To the east is the Navajo Reservation, and to the west is Lake Mead National Recreation Area.

As big as the canyon appears, it is still a pretty small place when compared with mountain ranges or really big river valleys like the Mississippi. There are few places on Earth where such a range of geographic and climatic conditions can be found in such a compact area. Alpine fir and ocotillo? Treefrogs and cacti? Why not?

1
Pages From the Past

It feels good to sit out on the end of Horseshoe Mesa with my feet dangling off the edge of the cliff. Dinner time: cold chili on a buck knife (I forgot a spoon) and scotch whiskey from a plastic flask. The sun is setting. Scattered clouds throw scattered shadows across the canyon. From those black shadows, mesas and pinnacles emerge in explosions of light, then disappear again. Overhead, jets leave glowing contrails as they scrape and boom their way to California. They've got a good view up there, and they've also got whiskey, but none of those passengers is as free as I. I have nothing to do but sit here and swing my feet; no decision to make except how much scotch I should drink, perched as I am on the edge of a very large space with nothing but my sense of balance between the cliff edge and a long drop.

If I did something clumsy I would land on the Tonto Platform, a broad shelf more than a thousand feet below. Bushes and trees down there appear as speckles. Erosion lines run like muscle striations across the stony gray surface. I can just make out a foot trail that zigzags down a break in the mesa wall. Farther out, where the Inner Gorge cuts a ragged slash through the heart of the canyon, short sections of the river are visible. They glint when the sun shines, then disappear in the black gorge when clouds extinguish the light.

Getting here involved about two hours of walking and a descent of 2,000 feet. I left my car at Grandview Point on the South Rim, which now glows in the sunset behind me, and then walked a mile out to the tip of this interior mesa. I am far below the canyon rims, yet despite that I feel elevated, exposed, lifted up as if the whole world were at my feet. In fact it is: 93 million miles of space lie between me and the setting sun. The universe begins right here, beyond the soles of my boots waving in the air at the edge of the cliff.

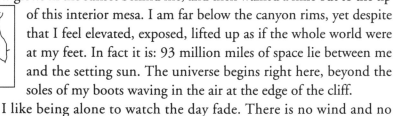

Grandview Point

I like being alone to watch the day fade. There is no wind and no sound save the distant rumble of the Colorado River. It rumbles out of the blackness of the Inner Gorge, carrying to my ears the voices of wild rapids: Sockdolager, Grapevine, Hance. I can't see them from where I sit, but they tell me cold stories, and I shiver at the thought of icy waves pounding the rocks in the deepening February night.

The higher reaches of the canyon look more hospitable, but in an unreal, miragelike way. In the distance, all features but the largest are beyond the resolution power of my human retinas. There are no bushy speckles visible, no erosional striations, just the mass presence of butte and mesa and gorge fading off into twilight's haze, as if an artist were trying to camouflage a museum diorama. Seated on this promontory, it's easy to pretend that I'm looking through clear glass at a landscape from the imagination. If I look carefully, I ought to be able to find where the three-dimensional foreground blends into the painted background.

I let my eyes trace the contours of side canyons, starting near and working out. Mentally I measure the distances: How long would it take me to walk from here to there, and from there to farther yet? I locate potential hiking routes through cliff bands. I recognize major features, and run their names through my mind: Cape Royal, Palisades of the Desert, Wotan's Throne, and others. Knowing those things is important. To smell the air, to recognize the plants, to feel the cold rock under my butt, to know which star is rising over Desert View, or what birds are calling from the juniper (pinyon jays, sounding like a chorus of manic cats and giggling over the success of their imitation), gives me a foothold in the landscape.

And yet a tiny foothold. It is true that knowledge leads to a sense of belonging, but there is so much to learn about the Grand Canyon.

It strikes me that the canyon has two natures. Look at it one way and it's as pure as a crystal, all facets perfectly in line, symmetrically elegant, comprehensible in one glance. Seen this way, the Grand Canyon is a testament to the power of large-scale design, and its geologic story is easily told.

Then turn it sideways, or peer more closely, and the monolith becomes an intricate puzzle, enormously complicated. You could spend lifetimes learning about it; and people have done just that.

Let's take the simple story first. Start with layers of rock laid down over hundreds of millions of years — collecting on ocean floors, along sea coasts, or in the dunes of ancient deserts. The sediments pile up, layer upon layer; then the earth buckles and blisters and heaves its rocky hide into the air, and the upthrust layers start to melt away under the forces of gravity and erosion. Meanwhile the earth keeps moving. The land changes shape. Territory to the west drops away while territory to the east rises. Finally, born among the Rocky Mountains, helped in its task by a second river working its way up from the Gulf of California, the Colorado River slashes down through the old sediments and carves out this big open space.

It's just an erosion channel. A big gully. A drainage ditch.

Now tilt the crystal a fraction. Seen from this angle, my solid perch becomes a rock a thousand feet above the river; tilt the crystal a bit more and my perch is a rock thousands of feet below the ancient waters of an inland sea, but my rock was once thousands of feet below those same waters, and the space in which I sit has been, at various times, solid rock, unstable mud crawling with creatures whose fossils I sit upon, warm shallow ocean, sand dunes, and air. It has been these things at various times over millions of years, millions of millennia, untold rotations of the Earth around its wobbly axis, all echoing across the uncountable vacuum of time. Not so simple a story after all.

A Journey Through Time?

They say — poets, that is, and writers and naturalists — that a walk through the canyon is a journey through time. As if you could experience

David Edwards

River runners camp near Clear Creek beneath steep walls of Vishnu Schist, the oldest rock in the Grand Canyon.

the Proterozoic Era, or the red, oxidizing world of the Permian.

Not me. I'm in the rock-bound present. The canyon's trilobites are fossils, long dead every one of them. It's a desert here now. It's dry. The rock that used to be mud powders when I kick it. I feel the desert heat, and it would never occur to me to think I'm standing at the bottom of a shallow ocean.

Then there's the matter of time itself. I have trouble getting a grasp on centuries, much less millennia. And in the Canyon, we're talking about thousands of millennia, millions of millennia. The oldest rock layer here is 1.7 billion years old. That's 17 million centuries. Sixty million human generations — as if there had been people living way back then, which there weren't.

In trying to get a grip on the scale of time, I think of a common vole, a mouselike creature who lives an unassuming life in the shadows of meadow grass, a timid animal who never sees the horizon and whose sense of cosmology is no doubt less than well developed. His average life span is two or three months, and I imagine his concept of a century is about equivalent to my mental grip on a billion of anything, much less years.

So let the poets have their walks through time. I prefer what geologists say about this place, perhaps because they (most of them) stay away from airy self-analytical rhapsodizing. Geologists work with rocks. They speak in a language that's hard like concrete, and although the images they conjure from their studies come to us from a world that seems as remote as Alpha Centauri, those images are strong enough to break your bones.

Geologists sometimes compare studying the canyon to reading a great book. This, I think, is a truly useful metaphor. I understand reading history in a book. I understand how old stories can give rise to fresh mental images.

Granted, it's a complicated book, one not easily opened, and etched in strange languages that have been only partly deciphered. On top of that, it's been damaged over millions of years of existence — tossed around, overheated,

Vishnu Schist began as ocean sediments interspersed with lava flows and ash layers. With time, it became a beautiful, fine-grained black rock.

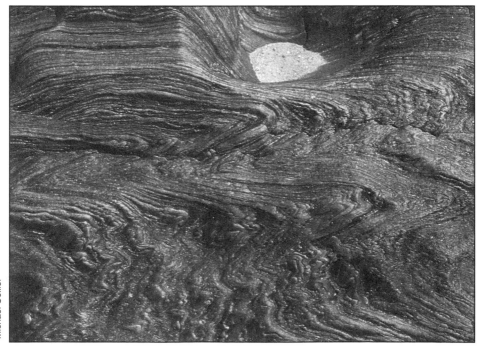

Michael Collier

bent, and cracked. There are pages stuck together, whole chapters torn out, and sometimes new pages stuffed in between older pages. But despite all its injuries, and in some cases because of them, the old book is a treasure house of information, a 1.7-billion-year history of the planet, told from the perspective of one spot on its surface.

This "spot," this particular place on this piece of the Earth's crust that we call North America, is an unstable platform that's done a lot of moving around over the ages, seen many changes, and felt the impact of vast events. The book of the canyon can be read as the sailing log of a continent as it drifted across the planet's surface. Recorded here are such events as the birth of the Pacific Ocean and a mighty collision between North America and Africa. The book tells the stories of seas and mountain ranges and great deserts. It preserves, like flowers pressed between the pages, the fossil remains of things that lived long ago, things of which we would be ignorant without the opportunity to read about them in the rocks. In its first chapters, it describes a time when there was no life on the land, when the atmosphere was far different, and the oceans supported nothing more complex than algae. In the most recent chapters we find dinosaurs (although these rock layers are almost gone from Grand Canyon National Park, they are still present nearby).

Covering huge areas of western North America with its telltale rock layers, the book was once much larger than it is now. What we have at the canyon is a fragment resting on relatively stable ground. The foundation of the continent here is solid, unlike the territory to the west, where the Great Basin is a jumble of broken, tilted pieces; and unlike the Rocky Mountains to the east, where mountain-building and erosion and volcanic eruptions have made a spectacular mess of things.

This fragment, this land of canyons and flat-topped mesas, is called the Colorado Plateau, an area unusual for having flat layers so high above sea level. Its stability is due in part to the unusually thick crust that underlies it — it is about 19 to 25 miles thick. Compare that to the Great Basin, where the crust is about 15 miles thick.

Located on the edge of the Colorado Plateau, the canyon ends where the Great Basin begins. It occupies a transition area between the two provinces. As a result, there are more faults in the western end of the canyon than in the east. This is reflected by the temperature of spring water: If you put a thermometer in several canyon springs, you'll find

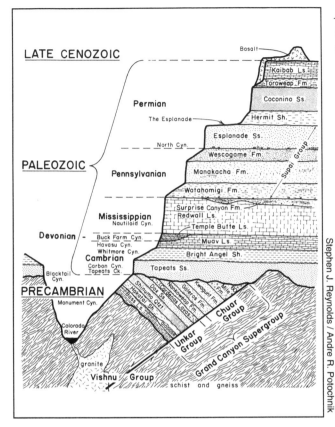

An idealized cross-section view of the Grand Canyon's rock layers.

that the temperature gets slightly and progressively warmer (but not hot) toward the western part of the canyon. Nor is it a surprise to find that volcanic activity in the canyon is confined to its western half, where the crust is thinner and more broken, therefore allowing deep heat to rise nearer to the surface.

If these rock layers form a book, however, it's a closed book, lying flat. It would be unreadable were it not for the canyon, which provides a cross-section through the layers — although it has done this in a clumsy, violent way. It's as if some post-apocalyptic brute stumbled across a great tome of the Earth's ancient wisdom and, perplexed by the strange object, beat on it with his club, knocking off the front cover and damaging the first few pages, but was unable to actually open it; still curious, he takes out his jagged stone knife. He slashes at the book, gouging deeply into the old brittle paper, revealing splendid illuminations and the shiny edges of great secrets, but none of this means anything to him, and he abandons it there for others to discover and attempt to read.

A geologist might prefer a clean incision made by a scalpel-sharp knife. In fact one of the major activities of geologists is the production of diagrams that look like clean slices of the Earth's surface. Yet however imperfect the canyon cross-section might be, it's the best one we have — a trench cut across the plateau with smaller trenches branching to the sides. The main trench exposes the big story, while the side trenches provide additional details. Some of the stories are wonderful to hear.

Picture this: A coastal plain, eroded nearly flat. The ocean pounds black rock into coarse, barren rock with no plants or animals present. There is nothing present but wind and sky and sea and stone. An empty world, unlike anything existing on Earth today.

Another image, many millions of years later: Volcanos erupt on the rim of the canyon in its lower reaches. Lava pours into the gorge, great viscous blobs of it spilling over the rim, sliding into the river, turning water to steam. In a matter of weeks — maybe days — the lava piles up to a depth of 2,300 feet and hardens. The river is stopped. A huge lake forms, eventually reaching the upper end of what is now Lake Powell. It takes 22 years for the river to fill the lake, overtop the dam, and begin cascading down the other side. A few thousand years later, the cascade becomes a sheer waterfall over 2,000 feet high. Yet another few thousand years, and the whole thing is gone, like a waking dream.

There are many such geologic stories. The stones that comprise the canyon reveal their histories bit by bit, in little pieces, many of them not yet incorporated into the larger view of how things happened, many of them not yet understood. For example, there is a small rounded structure in the Nankoweap Formation, a billion years old. One opinion calls it the fossil of a stranded jellyfish. A burrowing annelid, says another. A gas bubble, according to a third. There are shales at the bottom of the canyon that have 10,000 of a particular fossil per cubic centimeter. Also tiny mystery orbs: Are they trilobite eggs? Algal cysts? No one knows for sure, but geologists are continually trying to piece all these bits of data into one comprehensive, epic tale.

The Course of the River

Beginning in north central Colorado, the Colorado River traverses four major physiographic provinces: the Rocky Mountains, the Colorado Plateau, the Transition Zone, and the Basin and Range country centered on Nevada. The Grand Canyon occupies the Transition Zone between the stable, horizontal platform of the Colorado Plateau and the extensively faulted, much rearranged territory of the Basin and Range.

By current definition, the canyon is 277 miles long, as measured along the river from Lees Ferry to the Grand Wash Cliffs. The last 40 miles or so is now the upper end of Lake Mead. The first 61.5 miles is called Marble Canyon; it was considered by John Wesley Powell, leader of the first river expedition through the canyon, as distinct from the Grand Canyon, but now both are recognized as a single geographic unit.

From its beginning at Lees Ferry, it takes the canyon over 50 miles to reach one mile in depth; when it finishes, it ends suddenly. At the Grand Wash Cliffs, the river leaves high walls behind and emerges into the glaring flatness of Lake Mead.

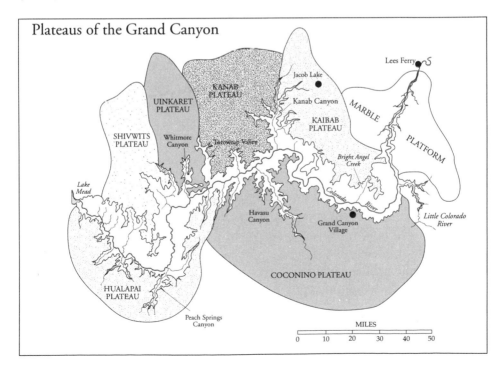

Plateaus of the Grand Canyon

In its course through the canyon, the Colorado River drops 1,900 feet over nearly 200 rapids. The drop was higher, and there were more rapids, before Lake Mead invaded the lower section of the canyon. River runners generally do not float all the way to the lake, choosing instead to pull out at Diamond Creek, which is 227 miles from Lees Ferry and 1,780 feet below it. Along the way, they pass innumerable tributaries in side canyons branching out from the main stem. At least a dozen of these tributaries possess permanent water, and some have carved impressive canyons in their own right — notably the Little Colorado River, Bright Angel Creek, Nankoweap Creek, Kanab Creek, and Havasu Creek.

Dozens of others possess intermittent, or seasonal streams. They flow in the spring when snow melts on the rims, or in late summer when thunderstorms are common. Some flow year round at one level in the canyon, only to dry up at another — or go underground. A watercourse without water is not necessarily a dead creek. A mile upstream or downstream, you might find it flowing merrily.

The least reliable sources of water are drainages that flow only during or just after rainstorms. These are called ephemeral streams. It's impossible to know how many of these there are until a heavy summer thunderstorm soaks the canyon, and they all spring to life.

Most side canyons follow natural lines of weakness — faults, fractures, areas of soft rock and so forth. This is to be expected and is worth noting only because the main canyon does not. On the contrary, for much of its length it runs across fault lines and against the tilt of strata. In doing so, it seems to defy both physics and logic. It approaches the great upwarp of the Kaibab Plateau, and instead of flowing around it, taking what would seem the easy path, the river cuts through it at nearly its highest point. Rivers don't normally do this, and geologists have spent considerable effort trying to explain how the Colorado achieved this feat. Their work is the subject of Chapter 2, "Old River, Young Canyon."

For now, it's worth pointing out that the river cuts through an extensive highland comprising several distinct, adjoining plateaus — all of them sections of the much larger Colorado Plateau, and all of them separated by fault lines. On the North Rim, moving from east to west, are the Kaibab, Kanab, and Uinkaret plateaus. Because they are less distinct on the South Rim, these three are lumped together and called the Coconino Plateau. Back on the North Rim, the plateau farthest to the west is called the Shivwits. It too extends across to the South Rim, but there it is called the Hualapai. I get the feeling someone is trying to confuse us.

The Kaibab is the highest plateau, rising to a maximum of 9,200 feet outside the park in the Kaibab National Forest. The highest point on the North Rim within the park is 8,801 feet, at Point Imperial. The Canyon width from rim to rim varies depending on where you measure, but an average of ten miles seems reasonable. The depth is also variable, but averages 4,000 to 5,000 feet from rim to river. Because the Kaibab Plateau slopes down toward the south, and the river cuts across that slope, the South Rim in the center of the park is lower than the North Rim. Bright Angel Point, for example, is 8,145 feet high; ten air miles away, Grand Canyon Village is 1,180 feet lower at 6,965 feet elevation.

The Dating Game

At the South Rim one June day, I heard this conversation:

"So that's the big ditch."

"Sure is."

"I come all the way from California just to see that."

"California? Where you from?"

They were two couples from southern California, and they talked a bit about it being a small world before they turned their attention back to the canyon.

"They say it was made by an earthquake," said one of the men.

"I heard it was a meteor," answered his friend.

"Must've been an awful big meteor. It'd have to have come in at an angle, you know, shootin' across like that...ba-WHAM!"

The origins of the Grand Canyon are not a matter of common sense. Whatever we know on the subject we owe to the work and insights of geologists, and once we hear their interpretations of ancient events, it all seems sensible. Or at least believable. But it's not intuitive.

The first geologist to visit the area specifically to investigate the canyon was John Strong Newberry, a member of the Ives expedition, an attempt in 1857 to ascertain the possibilities of navigating the river in steamboats.

Newberry was impressed, and said the Grand Canyon was a wonderful place with lots of rocks exposed, but he never came back. By not returning, he missed an opportunity for fame, but at least he avoided the snorts and giggles that have been directed over the years at his boss. It was Lt. Joseph Ives who wrote:

> "The region is, of course, altogether valueless. It can be approached only from the south, and after entering it there is nothing to do but leave. Ours has been the first, and will doubtless be the last, party of whites to visit this profitless locality. It seems intended by nature that the Colorado River, along the greater portion of its lonely and majestic way, shall be forever unvisited and undisturbed."

Like Newberry, John Wesley Powell also saw the geologic potential of studying the Grand Canyon, and Powell was a born self-promoter. He built himself a name as both an adventurer and a geologist with his expeditions on the Colorado River. Afterwards, he helped establish the U.S. Geological Survey, served for a time as its director, and greatly advanced the scientific understanding of the West in general and the Grand Canyon in particular. Ives's "profitless locality" became a proving ground for American geologists at a time when the science, still in its infancy, was dominated by Europeans. It was also a testing ground for some daring new ideas — for example, that rivers carve their valleys, instead of simply being channeled by them.

Perhaps most important, the canyon played a role in developing principles of stratigraphy — the reading of geologic history by interpreting successive rock layers. The basic concept is very simple: Younger rocks lie on top of older rocks. If you have three layers, and you know the ages of the bottom and the top layers, you can approximate the age of the middle one. Or if you know that a lava flow occurred 10 million years ago, you also know that the gravel deposit under the lava must be at least 10 million years old.

In practice, stratigraphy is complicated by missing layers, folded layers, intermittent layers, fault lines, rocks that can't be dated, volcanic disruptions, and a hundred other factors that challenge those who try to

Shivwitz Plateau

Cataract Cr.

U.S. Air Force

High altitude (U2) photograph of the Grand Canyon looking west from above the forested Kaibab Plateau. In the middle of the picture is Great Thumb Mesa; in the distance, Shivwitz Plateau; beyond that, not visible, lies Lake Mead.

solve the puzzle. But it remains a critical key to deciphering geologic history. Basically, it's a matter of putting numbers on the pages of the ancient book.

Some of the numbers can be gotten directly by measuring radioactive isotopes. The carbon dating technique is well known, but it measures ages less than 40,000 years, making it more useful in archeology than geology. Better for canyon studies is potassium/argon (K/Ar) dating, which is considered accurate for rocks older than two million years. When it decays, potassium becomes argon. With time, the proportion of one to the other changes.

That is, as the rock ages, more argon is present. This constantly changing proportion is like a ticking clock, which provides a good method for long-term dating. But argon is a gas, and if for some reason it escapes from the rock, the clock is reset. Heating or fracturing resets the clock. This is a problem but also an opportunity. It means that we can specify the date of significant heating or fracturing but not the absolute age of the altered material itself.

Isotopic data tell us more than mere age. For example, water temperatures in the ancient sea can be determined by isotope levels in fossil seashells, because in forming the shells, organisms grab a different isotope in cold water than in warm.

Another method involves paleomagnetism, a concept based on the movement of the north magnetic pole over millions of years. Like tiny compasses, iron molecules in molten rock tend to orient themselves with the Earth's magnetic field. It also happens when tiny iron-bearing particles settle in very still water. When the rocks later harden into shale, the iron molecules and particles are frozen in position. Even after the magnetic pole has migrated to a different location, these tiny compasses point to where it was in some distant age.

If only there were a map charting the movements of the pole over the past few billion years, it would be a fairly simple matter to check the iron molecules in a given sample of rock, refer to the chart, and attach a date to the rock. But there is no such chart, and besides that, the rocks themselves have been moving around the planet as the continents drift, and that tends to complicate matters. The logic here can become circular, using magnetic data to chart the pole's movements, then using the pole's movements to date the rocks. If you knew for certain the age of the rocks, you could use those data to locate the pole at that time; and vice versa. It's a bit like the chicken and the egg. Each points at the other. Clearly, it takes a great volume of data, along with corroborative evidence, to make sense of all this.

Fossils provide yet another indicator. Living communities change over time, and once their fossils have been dated, so can the rock in which they are found. This principle can aid researchers in widely separated places. For example, there is a rock layer in Petrified Forest National Park (east of Grand Canyon), that is not amenable to direct dating. The fossils within them are clear, but how old are they? And how old is the rock?

Luckily for those who want to know, it happens that on the East Coast, the same fossils are found sandwiched between lava flows that can be dated. Assuming that the animals or plants lived at the same time in both locations, a reasonable assumption when we're talking in units of a million years at a time, the dates indicated by the East Coast fossils must apply also to the ones at Petrified Forest.

It is this sort of cross-referencing that the Grand Canyon helped geologists develop into a fine art. Rock strata here are correlated with strata and geologic events all around the world. Information from one place can be applied to other places. The importance of these seemingly repetitive layers of sediment goes way beyond this local peculiarity called the Grand Canyon. The rocks tell much bigger stories, global stories.

The result is a long history, the story of a continent taken chapter by chapter, rock layer by rock layer. It is a history still being written — or should we say, being read. Undoubtedly some interpretations will change as new evidence comes to light. And gaps, especially in the early chapters, will be filled. Nonetheless, in broad outline, as seen currently, the history of Grand Canyon rocks is as follows.

Two Billion Years on a Drifting Continent

Two billion years ago, the Earth's surface was very different from what we now know. The continents were scrambled, their shapes were unrecognizable, and their locations were elsewhere.

Like dumplings in a hot stew, continents drift according to currents in the Earth's semiliquid core. The sea floor acts like a conveyor, new material pushing out of a central ridge, and moving back down in deep sea trenches. Therefore, the sea floor continually renews itself and stays young, less than 200 million years old. Continents, in contrast, are of lighter material. They float, getting older and more battered with time.

Two billion years ago, North America was already old. On that portion of it that would someday be home to the Grand Canyon, there was a shallow sea with occasional lava flows. Evidence for this comes from the sediment types that make up over 50 percent of the Vishnu Schist.

What changed the sediment to schist? Something took the sea bed and crunched it. Likely, it was a collision with an island arc similar in size and

A trilobite fossil in Bright Angel Shale. Trilobites, once one of the most abundant creatures on earth, scavenged the floor of an ancient sea during Cambrian times.

Grand Canyon National Park

origin to Japan. The arc, now part of North America, is found in Precambrian rocks in central Arizona. This could sound preposterous unless we remember that the continents were drifting. They still are. India is currently colliding with Asia. The resultant crumpled fender is a feature we call the Himalaya Mountains.

Likewise here. The event (it would be wrong to call it a mishap) caused extensive damage in the form of heating, contorting, and mountain building. The faults visible now in the canyon, and there are many of them, occur along lines created in that ancient disturbance.

Even as the collision messed things up, the Earth naturally sought equilibrium. Some land went up, while other land was pushed down, partially melted, metamorphosed, or forced upward again as a liquid. It was then that the already old layers of sediments and volcanic rock were metamorphosed and became Vishnu Schist. Also, the schist was shattered and shot through with the lighter-colored material called Zoroaster Granite. It makes for a lovely combination of pink granite veins marbling nearly black schist. (Not all Zoroaster is light, nor is all the Vishnu dark, but this is generally the case.)

The metamorphosis happened 1.7 billion years ago. How do we know? Through radioactive dating methods including the decay processes of potassium/argon, uranium/lead, and rubidium/strontium. As we have seen, these methods reflect not the time the rock was deposited in the first place, but the time of metamorphosis — specifically the time when the rock reached a threshold temperature, just one moment in the long process of metamorphosis. Of course this moment could not have been the same for all the schist, at every point within the schist, nor was the degree of metamorphosis consistent throughout. But the figure is close enough when we're measuring in millions of years.

Skip ahead 500 of those millions. Erosion has now cut the mountains down to a plain. We can picture a flat land 1.3 billion years ago. Again the Earth moves, and a basin subsides, perhaps a rift valley cutting through the area. Like East Africa's Great Rift Valley, it is the sort of crack that splits continents and gives birth to new oceans, but this one apparently fails to keep opening. No ocean appears. The rift stagnates and eventually fills with 13,000 feet of sediment — sand, mud, and limestone — a series of mostly soft rocks that form the Grand Canyon Supergroup. They show up along a narrow line confined mostly to the eastern part of the canyon, beneath the Kaibab Plateau.

Let events take their course for another 500 million years, and look again. Now, 830 million years ago, there is another episode of uplifting, tilting, mountain building, maybe more rifting to the west. Here is another good example of potassium/argon dating: From various evidence, we know that Cardenas Lava was extruded one billion years ago, yet the K/Ar age of the lava is 830 million years. Why is it 170 million years off? Because 830 million years ago there occurred a cataclysmic event that reset the clock. Something big split off from North America in an event that had a wide impact, leaving geologic evidence in many places beyond the Grand Canyon. Was it Siberia? Australia? Antarctica? At this time, votes are piling up for Antarctica, but there is still no consensus. Whatever it was, something did cut loose and mountains were built here, and although the event seems far removed from the Grand

Canyon as we see it today, the story was nonetheless written in the Cardenas Lava.

With the new mountains came faster erosion. Erosion knows only one trick, and it would have had great force in this era, which was still before the existence of terrestrial vegetation as we think of it today. Erosion smoothed out the landscape once again. Mountains became mere hills separated by shallow valleys. These hills, made from Shinumo Quartzite of the Grand Canyon Supergroup, stood for a time above the ocean as it advanced, bringing the next layer of deposition—the Tapeats Sandstone.

The point of contact between the Tapeats and the older layers beneath it represents a time gap hundreds of millions of years wide. During this time there were other mountains, other uplifts, and repeated cycles of erosion. There was deposition of layers that have since disappeared entirely, but we have no clear record of those events, and so geologists have given the gap a pleasing name, the Great Unconformity.

It is an easy feature to see, even from viewpoints along the rim. The Tapeats is the layer of brown stone that forms the cliff-edged rim of the inner gorge. It lies flat, like the layers above it, but it sits on the twisted and folded and much darker Vishnu Schist—and the colorful strata of the Grand Canyon Supergroup where those layers occur. It looks like someone plastered over an old rough surface, and this is essentially what happened, except that in places the plaster was not thick enough to cover in one coat. If you go to the right places in the canyon, you can find beach lines around the low Shinumo hills mentioned above. You can see boulders that fell from those hills into the wet sands and were buried. You can read in the turbulent bedding lines of the sandstone around the boulders that a surf pounded here, and imagine a landscape of cliff-rimmed islands in a shallow sea.

The Boring Era

In speaking about what follows, some geologists stifle a yawn. Others yawn openly. There began a long deposition period, the Paleozoic Era, with no exciting earth movements. The sea came in, the sea went out, and layers of rock tell the story of every cycle.

Grand Canyon National Park

At that time, the continent was near the equator, lacking California and Florida, drifting toward what is now the east, which was then south because the continent was oriented differently. Remember that what's here now wasn't here then. Continents were floating around. They still are. There was a tropical climate "here" millions of years ago, but back then, "here" wasn't 37 degrees north latitude, as it is today. "Here" was at the equator.

In addition to direct fossil remains, so-called trace fossils like these vertebrate tracks in sandstone, have helped scientists understand conditions in the ancient world.

So we need to picture the continent on its side, drifting south. What is now the north coast of the continent was pointing west. The area that would become the Grand Canyon rode on the trailing edge of the continent — the quiet edge, not subject to much activity. It was a coastal shelf, rising and falling a bit, flooded now and dry later, erosion carrying loads of sediment from neighboring higher areas and dumping them here.

Whenever the sea went out, there was erosion; when the sea came back, there was deposition. Sand and mud came from the erosion of land — mountains, hills, plateaus, whatever there was to cut down and

Grand Canyon National Park

The Great Unconformity, where basement rocks of the inner gorge meet overlying horizontal strata, is easily recognized thoughout the central part of Grand Canyon.

carry away. Limestone came from the ocean in the form of shells and other products of sea creatures. As a rule, an encroaching ocean deposits layers in a characteristic sequence. First, sand collects on the beach, where wave action carries away the lighter material. Tapeats Sandstone, for example, was deposited in a zone of turbulence — the beach of an encroaching ocean.

As an ocean rises, the shoreline moves inland, building a new sandy beach. The former beach now lies beyond the waves in relatively calm water, allowing fine-grained silt to settle over the sands. Therefore, where we find siltstone or shale on top of sandstone, we infer that the sea was encroaching. Conversely, if sandstone lies on siltstone, the reverse is true.

The sea went out, the sea came back. There was deposition, there was erosion, and there wasn't much else happening for about 250 million years. Two oceanic transgressions that happened between 360 and 325 million years ago laid down the Redwall Limestone, a formation found as far north as Montana.

On top of the Redwall, there came the Watahomigi Formation. Then the Manakacha and Wescogame formations, and the Esplanade Sandstone, all of which are bunched together in the Supai Group, which is good because to the untrained eye they are almost as difficult to distinguish as they are to pronounce.

Suddenly, North America hits Africa, the one event that enlivens the Boring Period. All hell breaks loose. Mountains are jammed upward: the ancestral Rockies and the Appalachians wrinkle into existence. Eroded materials from them come this way — sand, mud, silt, new materials, not just the same old variations of limestone. These new layers were the Upper Supai group, a mixed collection of deposits from stream beds and estuaries, and from sand dunes in a coastal desert.

Then came Hermit Shale, brought as mud from rivers. It made a great swamp similar to the Mississippi River delta of modern times; but the swamp dried out and was covered with sand. By then, North America was sitting in the trade belt, where winds blew from east to west. As the winds came over the ancestral Rockies, the air dropped its moisture, and the winds drove hard and dry across the region that would become Grand Canyon. Vast Saharalike deserts covered the old shale beds. Instead of mud there was now sand. Dune sand: the Coconino Sandstone.

Yet again the land fell, and the sea advanced across Arizona like some old army conquering, retreating, and reconquering, leaving behind the detritus of its action — in this case, the Toroweap Formation, a mixture of gray limestone, siltstone, and sandstone loaded with fossils.

The next time it was the Kaibab, a light gray limestone that forms the rims of the canyon and virtually all of the land surface in the immediate vicinity. Everyone who stands on either rim has touched the Kaibab Limestone.

We come finally to the end of the Paleozoic Era, 250 million years ago, and geologic history takes a turn. The giants shift in their sleep. There is revolution underfoot. The ponderous old continent reverses course. North America changes its drift toward the west: The trailing edge becomes the leading edge, where things happen. The first big event occurs when the continent runs into a series of banks and shoals we now call California. The collision builds mountains that rise like a floodwall to finally block the oceans from the west. But not from the east; the middle part of the continent still experiences the continual advance and retreat of shallow oceans.

That was not the end of deposition. There were more layers, beginning with the Moenkopi Formation, a soft, reddish brown mix of siltstone, shale, and mudstone. But the Moenkopi is gone from the canyon area. So are the layers that came after the Moenkopi — something like 5,000 vertical feet of sandstone and shale melted away by erosion. They are gone, leaving the canyon rims stripped down to the Kaibab Limestone, and so with the Kaibab we can stop this recitation of canyon layers.

We are nearing the end of the Mesozoic Era, the Age of Dinosaurs, and the beginning of the Laramide Orogeny, a delightful name for a period of uplift that lasted from 75 to 50 million years ago. For some time, the Farallon Plate (part of the Pacific sea floor) has been slipping beneath North America. Now for some reason its dive gets shallower. The Pacific plate starts dragging on the underside of North America — it lifts and compresses the continent, causing bulges in the surface. One such bulge is the Rocky Mountain Range. Another is the Kaibab Plateau.

One last important event: The subduction of the Farallon Plate ends and the continent comes under the influence of a new plate moving northwest along California's San Andreas fault. Compression is relieved, resulting in both tensional force and a collapse. The effects are felt across Nevada and parts of neighboring states, where mountain blocks rise and valley blocks fall. The Colorado Plateau remains stable, but to the west is born a new topography called Basin and Range.

The future site of Grand Canyon is now too high for oceans. All the major sediments are in place, from Vishnu Schist and the Grand Canyon Supergroup, up past the Great Unconformity and through the many Paleozoic (Boring) Era layers. The scene is set for the origins of the Colorado River and eventually, its grand canyon.

2
Old River, Young Canyon

They call it the Muddy Creek Formation, and you might not think anything of it except it makes a mighty bumpy road. You notice the bumps on the way to Pearce Ferry at the far western end of the Grand Canyon. The road goes down a long grade to the still waters and silty banks of Lake Mead. The light-colored dust kicked up by bouncing tires — the same stuff settling on the dashboard and collecting in your lungs — is part of the Muddy Creek Formation.

Aside from the lake and its margin of greenery, the most noticeable feature of the landscape is a line of high cliffs facing west — the Grand Wash Cliffs, which mark the edge of the Colorado Plateau and the end of the Grand Canyon. The cliffs were formed by movement along a fault zone, in which the block to the west subsided, creating a long trough at the base of high cliffs.

The trough is important to our story because since it was formed (less than 17 million years ago) it has collected a series of sediments and volcanic material that make up the Muddy Creek Formation. These materials came from nearby sources. The manner of their deposition shows that for a long time the trough was an interior basin with no outlet — and no Colorado

River emptying into it. Furthermore, there is a small canyon in the Grand Wash Cliffs just north of Pearce Ferry that, during the course of its erosion, built a debris fan that ran across the mouth of the present Grand Canyon. If the canyon had been there at the time, this could not have happened.

With these facts in mind, the age of the Muddy Creek Formation becomes of great interest — especially the top and youngest deposit, a layer of limestone that collected at the bottom of a shallow salt lake. Like the other bits of evidence, the lake could not have existed at the same time as the through-flowing Colorado River. So how old is the limestone? Fortunately, it includes deposits of volcanic tuff that can be dated by isotopic means at five to six million years of age.

Pearce Ferry

Five to six million years ago, there was no Colorado River flowing through a Grand Canyon in its current location.

Does this mean that the Colorado River is less than six million years old? Not exactly. The Muddy Creek Formation answers one question and poses several others. To understand why, consider these two facts: First, the Kaibab Plateau was uplifted in Laramide times, when the Rockies first rose above the plains. That happened about 70 million years ago.

Second, the Colorado River approaches the plateau from the north-east, runs along its flank for a while, and then does something truly unexpected. Turning toward the west, it cuts a broad curve directly through the heart of the upland.

Any way you look at it, this is strange behavior. Rivers usually avoid mountain ranges, plateaus, and other high places. How could this happen?

For about 60 years after John Wesley Powell floated the river, the answer was thought to be simple — the river must have existed before the plateau. As the plateau rose beneath it, the river cut down through it. It was like lifting a chunk of wood beneath a stationary saw.

Rivers have done this in many parts of the world. The most dramatic examples are found in the Himalaya Mountains, where a number of major rivers originate on the north slope in Tibet but turn south and, cutting their way through the mountains, empty into the Bay of Bengal or the Arabian Sea. These rivers include the Indus, the Brahmaputra, the Karnali, the Arun, and others. The gorges they have carved between Himalayan giants are in places over 20,000 feet deep. Their rate of

The Grand Canyon ends where the Colorado River cuts through the high rampart of the Grand Wash Cliffs, seen here from the west at Pearce Ferry on Lake Mead.

descent is steep, and the resulting cascades are frightening to behold.

Such rivers are called antecedent rivers, because they existed before the land began to rise. The process is almost self-regulating. If the land rises gradually, the rivers flow gently and cut slowly. If the land rises quickly, as the Himalaya have done, the rivers pick up speed and cut faster.

When it comes to the Grand Canyon, however, there are problems with this theory. One early sticking point is that during its course across the southwest, the Colorado River cuts through several uplifts, not just one. And it's not just the Colorado. Other rivers in the region perform similar feats. The San Juan River, for example, slices a canyon through the heart of the Monument Upwarp. The Green River bores through the Uinta Mountains. The Dolores and San Miguel rivers cut at right angles across major anticlines. This is how most of the famous canyons of the Southwest came to be.

It did not seem reasonable that all these rivers could have experienced the same conditions of uplift and erosion. Further, evidence began to

Michael Collier

The East Kaibab Monocline rises in a dramatic curve some 3,000 feet high, stretching about 150 miles from the San Francisco Peaks to southern Utah.

show that the rivers were younger than the highlands. There had to be another explanation.

Around the turn of the century, geologists began probing a theory of superposition. They suggested that a great thickness of sediments had buried a system of existing highlands — in effect providing a flat plain on top of the old warped surface. If that were the case, rivers could have gotten their start on the elevated landscape and then, having established their positions, they could cut down through whatever lay beneath — plateaus, ridges, monoclines, whatever happened to exist. Later the flat sediments, having served as a sort of template, would be eroded off, leaving a geological puzzle.

This idea also had its problems, and for several decades geologists argued for one or the other theory — antecedence versus superposition — or tried to piece together something plausible from parts of both.

Meanwhile, new evidence came to light, beginning in the 1930s. Geologists searched the deserts west of the canyon, expecting to find deposits from the ancient, antecedent river; but they found none. On the contrary, they found the Muddy Creek Formation (described above), which seemed to point at the astonishing idea that as recently as six million years ago, there was no Colorado River flowing through the Grand Canyon.

Could the river be that young? It seemed impossible. Evidence in the upper stretches of the Colorado showed it to be 37 million years old, or older. How could this be?

Maybe it drained in a different direction.

It was this idea that Edwin D. McKee, one of the founders of Grand Canyon geology, suggested with a group of his colleagues at a 1964 symposium on the Colorado River. McKee proposed that the ancestral Colorado might have avoided the Kaibab Plateau entirely by turning not west as it does today but southeast along the valley of the modern Little Colorado River, but in the reverse direction — either to an inland sea or to the Rio Grande and eventually the Gulf of Mexico.

It could have done that for millions of years until a second river, a young stream emptying into the newly opened Gulf of California, worked its way headward and captured the waters of the Colorado. Stream capture is a natural process of watercourses. As a river erodes the highlands at its source, it grows longer, building an ever-larger drainage system. Eventually, it can breach the divide that separates it from a neighboring river and divert the waters of the second stream into its own channel. By this procedure, also called stream piracy, the more vigorous river wins by cutting faster than its eventual victim.

If the canyon was created in this way, it means that its shape was determined by headward erosion of a young drainage system that chewed its way upstream into and through the Kaibab Plateau, until it met the old Colorado. In the vicinity of the modern Desert View, the two rivers became one, headed off together toward California, and finished carving the canyon.

Well... not quite. It's worth pointing out here that geology is an evolving science, in which theories function as starting points, as seeds for further research. To say that Edwin McKee and other geologists proposed a theory is not to say that they believed in it with some kind of religious fervor. Rather, they sketched a scenario based on known evidence — a possibility subject to change as contradictions and conflicting evidence arose.

Arise they did. With more fieldwork, it became clear that the ancestral Colorado could not have flowed toward the Rio Grande. At the same time, evidence accumulated to support the idea that no ancient river flowed out of the Grand Canyon into the Basin and Range country of Nevada. Evidence included the following:

On the south side of the canyon, there is a deposit of alluvial gravel eroded from highlands to the southwest. The highlands are no longer high, having foundered during the great rifting that built the Basin and Range topography of Nevada. Nonetheless, they were there up until about 20 million years ago, and they represent the only possible source of the granite and gneiss that make up the alluvial gravel.

How long has the gravel been there? Fortunately, the deposit in question was covered by a volcanic flow called the Peach Springs Tuff, which can be dated by radiometric means at 17 million to 20 million years of age. Obviously, the gravel was there when the tuff arrived.

Farther to the northeast, on the other side of the Grand Canyon, the same gravels are found. They came from the same southwestern highlands, and clearly, they could not have gotten there if the canyon had existed. Gravel does not do well when it comes to crossing deep canyons. The conclusion? As of 17 million to 20 million years ago, there was a continuous surface between the two deposits, and therefore no Grand Canyon.

Better than that, these northern gravels are also overlain by datable volcanic rocks — in this case a basalt flow dated at six million years of age. The basalt, like the gravel, came from the southwest. Neither it nor the gravel could have gotten there if the canyon had existed six million years ago.

There is another location on the Shivwits Plateau where a long, narrow promontory is topped by a basalt flow seven million years old. The promontory is miles long, yet the basalt lies on top of it. How could molten rock flow so neatly along a narrow finger of land without dropping off the edge? In places, the cliff edge actually transects volcanic vent cones. Had the canyon existed when they erupted, the basalt would certainly have flowed into it. But it did not. Clearly it was there before the canyon, and the promontory is explained by the protective cap of lava.

The conclusion was clear. Six million years ago, there was no through-flowing Colorado River at the western end of the Grand Canyon. In fact, there wasn't even a canyon. Nor did the old Colorado River, which was

at least 37 million years old, flow southeast to the Rio Grande. It left only one direction for the river to go: north or northwest.

But then, how the hell did it get across the Kaibab Plateau?

The Sinking Ship, seen here from Grandview Point, reveals the tilted layers of the Grandview Monocline, the structure that caused the Colorado River to cut downward at this point and create the Grand Canyon.

The Latest Theory

Theories come and go, but the process is not as disorganized as it might seem if you follow the scientific literature. Although theories are not cumulative, evidence is, and if interpreted correctly, the evidence always moves science forward. In other words, there is progress. The latest theory for the formation of the Grand Canyon is undoubtedly not the final word, but it is almost certainly closer than previous ones.

It goes like this. By studying a map, you'll notice that the river runs more or less straight through Marble Canyon until it hits the Kaibab Plateau, where it describes a broad curve and then meanders the rest of

Grand Canyon National Park

Red Butte, south of Tusayan, is a remnant of soft mudstone formations that once covered the Grand Canyon region. The same layers are still present to the east and north. Red Butte has survived thanks to a hard protective cap of volcanic rock.

the way. Rivers meander naturally. They take other courses when constrained.

What would constrain the river along this broad curve? Perhaps a formation called a racetrack valley. To picture how this formation came to be, we need to imagine another 5,000 feet of layered rock on top of the rocks we see today at the canyon. These were softer rocks, much softer than the current surface of Kaibab Limestone.

Then came the Laramide Orogeny. Far beneath the canyon, uplift formed a dome, a sort of blister rising beneath all those layers. Erosion soon began its work, and naturally the top of the dome eroded first because it was higher. As layers were worn down, a pattern of concentric rings became evident, the rings outlining the shape of the dome the way growth rings in wood outline a knot.

Some of the rings, or layers, were made of harder rock than others. The harder ones eroded more slowly, so that they stood up, forming a pattern of circular cliff bands rising above circular valleys — what geologists call racetrack valleys because of their curving shape. Current evidence points to the idea that the ancestral Colorado flowed around the Kaibab in a racetrack valley, continuing on to the northwest.

Where did it go from there? This is the subject of much searching, and so far, only partial evidence has turned up. Ancestral Colorado River gravels have been found scattered on the Shivwits Plateau, which shows that the river probably did not drain north along the fault zone on the west side of the Kaibab Plateau.

Still, no one has yet mapped the old channel. Chances are it's gone, removed by erosion and not to be found. Similarly, the original racetrack valleys are long gone from the Kaibab Plateau, but the same rock units can still be seen to the north, where they make up what is called the "Grand Staircase" stepping up toward the highlands of Zion National Park.

As time went by, the racetracks grew ever outward, receding from the rounded and very resistant dome of Kaibab Limestone that until this day forms the surface of the landscape for miles around. The river might have continued that way. Indeed, it would certainly have done so, in effect slipping off the shoulder of the plateau until it found its way around the southern tip. But in the end, the very limestone that had resisted penetration by the river forced it to begin cutting vertically downward.

Back in Laramide times when the Kaibab Plateau was uplifted, a small but significant fold had been made on the edge of the East Kaibab Monocline. If you drive east from Grandview Point, you go down a short, steep hill — this is the Grandview Monocline, and it doesn't seem like a significant feature. But it is.

For ages, the Colorado River had been avoiding the Kaibab Plateau, eroding in the soft Moenkopi Formation, when suddenly it ran into the Grandview Monocline, which tilted up the other way. There was now Kaibab Limestone on both sides. The river was trapped between two hard rocks with no easy way out. At this point, the southward migration of the river stopped, and from here on, its cutting had to be downward, instead of following the slope as it had previously.

Well, that's fine, but then what? How did the Colorado River end up in the Gulf of California?

The answer has to do with continental movements. The underlying shape of the land changed, and drainage patterns with it. Around 20 million years ago, tectonic forces switched from lifting and compressing to stretching and pulling apart. The Pacific Plate began moving more to the north. As pressure was released, there was massive subsidence of previously uplifted land.

Highlands to the south and southwest of Grand Canyon (the ones that had given rise to our telltale gravels) foundered and sank. A large region to the west broke into a pattern of basins slung between mountain ranges — the classic topography of Nevada. There was confusion among established drainages. River courses that had existed before were broken up. Water flowed into basins with no outlets.

The rifting continued, and among its results was a new sea, the Gulf of California. As the gulf opened, a river began flowing into it, building a delta and an estuary, depositing layers of sand and mud. As the layers piled up, the delta extended southward; that is, the newer materials were deposited farther downstream. This is a handy thing for geologists. Materials eroded from the river's headwaters appear neatly layered in the delta, and by analyzing the deposits, much can be learned about where the river was flowing, and when.

A prime example is the appearance in that delta of fossils that could only have come from Mancos Shale on the Colorado Plateau, an area drained by the ancestral Colorado River. In older parts of the delta, these fossils are lacking. Suddenly they are present, and the meaning is clear: 5.3 million years ago, the lower river, eroding headward, breached a critical divide between its drainage and that of the ancestral Colorado. It happened somewhere west of the Kaibab Plateau. By doing so, it captured the upper river and diverted its flow southward. The two rivers were joined. That moment marks the birth of the modern Colorado River.

This theory contains elements of older ideas, including superposition and stream piracy. It demonstrates that ideas and rivers can both evolve.

The rest happened fast. Incredibly fast. Some two million years later, the Grand Canyon was within 500 feet of its current depth. In the past 1.2 million years, as dated by lava flows (see below), the river has cut less than 50 feet deeper.

Unless the consensus of science has gotten it far wrong, the oft-cited idea that the canyon reflects the passage of time, that by pondering it we can somehow get in touch with the flow of eons, is erroneous. In a geologic sense, the only thing old about the canyon is the rock in which it has been cut. The canyon itself — the gorge, the gully, the air-filled, reverberating space — is a recent creation.

The Next Outdated Theory?

The canyon humbles geologists and laymen alike. In studying the latest ideas on the evolution of the Colorado River, it is tempting to believe that the truth is now revealed, that this is the way it happened. But it's good to look back just a few years, for the sake of perspective, to the "latest word" of the early '70s. Then, the prevailing idea called for the ancestral Colorado to drain into Lake Bidahochi in northeast Arizona, a terminal pond with no outlet. Granted, this was the idea thrown out as a starting point for further investigation. But for a while it was cited as the best explanation of the problem.

Meanwhile, support for an ancient stream of some kind seemed to come from the dating of lava flows deep in the canyon. The date of 1.2 million years, mentioned above, demonstrated that the river had eroded only 50 feet since the eruption of that lava. Fifty feet in a million years? Well then, that should give us an idea of how old the canyon is. At that rate, it would take 10 million years to carve 500 feet, and 100 million to go a mile. Although no one suggested a constant rate of erosion over all that time, one geologist wrote: "The deepening of the canyon has progressed at a rate of only about an inch every two thousand years since the lavas reached the canyon bottom. This is a very slow rate indeed, and signifies the importance of vast intervals of geologic time in the formation of the features we see today."

Not long after that, it became clear that the canyon could not be more than 5.5 million years old. That bit of information seems reliable now. But it makes you wonder what other ideas will be discarded in the coming years. And much of what we think we know about the canyon must be taken with a grain of sand — hopefully one sharp enough to remind us of how much there is still to learn.

The Biggest Dams

There is no better example of the speed of change in the canyon than the big lava dams that have periodically stopped the Colorado River. At least 12 of them occurred over the past million years, all of them in the western end of the canyon. Every one of them disappeared as the water chewed them to bits. Their story can be read in patches of volcanic rock plastered to the canyon walls. Also in dikes and extrusions and lava cascades, and in occasional remnants of sediments that collected in reservoirs behind the dams.

The dams illustrate one of the great canyon stories — clear evidence that this is anything but an eternal landscape. On the contrary, it's a radical landscape, changing fast, undergoing major remodeling in a blink of the geologic eye.

The construction of a lava dam would have been a marvelous spectator event. John Wesley Powell thought so. Drifting through the eroded remnants of the old lava, he wrote: "What a conflict of water and fire there must have been here! Just imagine a river of molten rock running down a river of melted snow. What a seething and boiling of waters; what clouds of steam rolled into the heavens!"

Powell had the basic image right, but recent research reveals more specifics. The lava for some of the dams originated from vents in upper levels in the canyon, far above the river (all of this in the western third of the canyon). The lava flowed across the flat Esplanade, then spilled over the rim, cascading 3,000 feet down steep canyon walls to the river. In most cases, the lava flowed quickly, building dams faster than the river could fill the new lakes. The effect was to block the river in a matter of hours, and then keep it from overflowing for days or even years while the impounded waters rose. At the upstream contact point, where water and lava did battle, a steep lava front would be built. Meanwhile, the bulk of the molten material would be streaming down the suddenly dry canyon bottom, flowing for miles in a strange volcanic imitation of the real river, but piling up to depths measuring hundreds of feet. To call them dams is a bit misleading, if it calls to mind graceful tapered structures like the Glen Canyon or Hoover dams. The lava dams were more like elongated blobs that ran for miles. The longest one occupied 84 miles of the canyon bottom.

Some dams were built all at once, in single massive flows that lasted a few weeks. Others grew in stages, with enough time between deposition periods for the river to overflow and erode channels before the next installment of lava arrived.

Of them all, the Prospect Dam was the most impressive. It formed 1.2 million years ago. Its top was 2,300 feet above the canyon bottom, at an

Michael Collier

In the western half of the canyon are numerous lava flows from eruptions that spilled over the rims and temporarily dammed the river.

elevation of 4,000 feet. The resulting reservoir, calculated by tracing the 4,000-foot contour upstream, backed up beyond the head of modern Lake Powell. Delta deposits from the Colorado River flowing into that giant lake can be found in the Bullfrog Basin area near Hite Crossing. If the same lake existed today, the top of the Glen Canyon Dam would be about 300 feet underwater.

In the heart of Grand Canyon, the lake overflowed the inner gorge, inundating the Tonto Platform almost to the base of the Redwall Limestone. The lake waters reached into tributary canyons, far up Kanab Creek, Havasu Creek, and the Little Colorado.

The lake behind Prospect Dam was far larger than Lake Powell. It took an estimated 22 years to fill — 22 years before the river finally overtopped the lava dam and began grinding it to bits. Much of this is speculation based on current river levels, and educated guesses about what it must have been like. For example, what were the conditions of the riverbed below the dam during those years while the lake was filling? No water was flowing over the dam, and it might have been as dry as an old bone.

Diagrams showing how lava dams might have been eroded by the river. First a lake would have formed behind the dam. Once full, the lake would overtop the dam (top) and a small waterfall would form at its lower end. Aided by the undercutting of loose river sediments beneath the lava (middle), the waterfall erodes the dam in a headward direction, until the weakened dam collapses (bottom) and the lake empties.

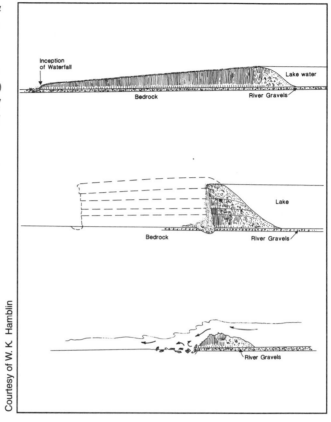

Courtesy of W. K. Hamblin

On the other hand, the lava dam settled on a riverbed of gravel and sand that would have been porous. If not sealed off somehow, the loose materials might have washed out and allowed at least some of the water to leak out beneath the dam. In any case, it must have been quite an event when the lake filled and the river began pouring over the top.

In his article describing these dams, W. K. Hamblin draws a compelling picture of their destruction by the river. He points out that Niagara Falls is continually destroying the ledge that causes it. The ledge, and the falls, are retreating at the astonishing rate of three feet per year. The pounding water creates turbulence at the base of the falls, undermining the limestone, causing it to collapse.

In a similar way, water falling over a lava dam in the canyon would scour the riverbed gravels from beneath the dam and cause it to collapse and migrate upstream as a vertical cliff face. Eventually, considering that the Prospect Dam began as a 2,300-foot-high obstruction, the falls could have been enormous. No river of comparable flow on Earth today drops over a fall anywhere near that height.

Other dams were nearly as big. They included the Toroweap Dam, 1,443 feet high; the Ponderosa Dam, 1,130 feet high; the Esplanade Dam, 960 feet high; the Whitmore Dam, 900 feet high; the Buried Canyon Dam, 850 feet high; and so on, down to a midget of only 226 feet high. The currently biggest drop on the river is called Lava Falls (it is not caused by a ledge of lava but by huge basalt boulders carried to the river from adjacent Prospect Creek). With a drop of only 37 feet over a distance of 600 feet, it is a fearsome rapid.

Each dam was cleared away by the river. According to estimates, the whole process might have taken no more than 20,000 years from the time a dam was formed until it was gone. What remain are very thin patches of volcanic rock plastered on the canyon walls. But this raises an interesting question: Why stop there? If erosion could clear out the lava all the way to the canyon walls, why not keep right on going and erode the walls themselves? The lava seems to be telling us that the canyon is not getting much wider. For some reason, in some places, the walls of Grand Canyon appear to be at equilibrium.

The thought of lava dams makes me think we live in quiet times. Millions of people in southern Arizona and southern California rely on the Colorado River for water. How would they cope with a complete stoppage of the river by lava? It would take only a small eruption, something much smaller than the explosion of Mt. Saint Helens. Just half a cubic mile of lava would be more than enough to inflict a natural disaster with enormous consequences.

Deeper Yet?

Most of the dates regarding erosion of the canyon come to us courtesy of lava, which can be dated by the potassium/argon method. When lava cools, the radioactive clock starts ticking.

From volcanic material in the Muddy Creek Formation, we know that six million years ago, there was no Grand Canyon. From a basalt flow in Iceberg Canyon, we also know that 3.8 million years ago the river was within 500 feet of its current depth. Similarly, because the Prospect Dam lava flow is 1.2 million years old and remnants of it are found within 50 feet of the modern canyon bottom, we know that the river has cut less than 50 feet since the dam was created. The river has carried a huge volume of material (the subject of the next chapter) but it hasn't sliced much deeper.

This is a slow rate of erosion compared to what the river did in the canyon's younger stage: in the previous three million years or so, it cut the whole blasted thing. It appears that when confronted by the lava, the river carved back to the canyon floor, regained its former position, and stopped. For the last 1 million to 1.5 million years, the river has been in equilibrium of sorts.

From a hydrologic point of view, this makes sense. Every river seeks the path of least resistance. By laws of hydrology, rivers overcome obstacles. If a slope is too steep (as in a waterfall or rapid) the river seeks to smooth it out. If a channel is too straight, the river creates bends of a certain radius. Likewise, if bends are too tight, the river will try to straighten them. So it's natural that the Colorado would eventually stop wearing downward and, in effect, take a break. Its current average gradient of about 10 feet per mile does not compel it to dig deeper. Yet it still finds considerable work to do.

Along its course through the Grand Canyon alone, the Colorado claims hundreds of tributaries. They range in size from the Little Colorado River to tiny creeks and dry ravines. Being desert drainages, these tributaries might go for many years without contributing much to the main river, yet when they do, they do it in a big way. A summer thunderstorm or a good hard winter rain can turn a dry wash into a thundering conduit for flood debris. Rocks, gravel, even huge boulders come tumbling out of side canyons into the river, continually adding to the work it must do.

The rapids thus caused are treated like mini lava dams, irritations to be removed by a river that knows where it wants to be. Debris gets in its way. It chews up the debris in an attempt to regain equilibrium. It's not chewing on the bottom of the canyon; it chews on the canyon wreckage that gets thrown into it. How that junk gets there is another story.

3
The Power of Erosion

In the early days of geology, the Grand Canyon was considered a prime example of the great erosional feats that could be accomplished if just given enough time. Time and the river flowing, as one book title put it.

It's only natural for us to think so. Seen from the perspective of our short lives, landscapes do seem to last forever. The only thing that changes their shapes in any regular fashion is erosion. But we don't see it. Erosion is considered to be a subtle process, so subtle that it has become a symbol for eternity, as in the fable of the marble monolith. According to the fable, there is a block of marble that measures exactly one cubic mile. It floats in some mythical dimension where nothing can touch it or affect it in any way, except for once every thousand years, when a sparrow flies to it, lands lightly upon its perfect surface, and flies away. Eternity, says the fable, is the time it will take for that sparrow's feet to wear the block down to nothing.

Implicit in the fable is a reverse lesson — that a sparrow's feet can wear away solid rock. That if allied with the irresistible force of time, even a tiny bird can do mighty things. So too with erosion, we think. Most of the time it works in small units like raindrops, or molecules of air, which by themselves have no real strength. They move other small units like flecks of clay and grains of sand. For the most part we take it on faith that in their cumulative billions, working over vast periods of time, they can achieve great results.

Still, when you look at the size of a sand grain, and hold that up against the Grand Canyon, this business of its being a recent feature can be a bit hard to swallow. No more than 5.5 million years old? Most of the work done in perhaps three million years? That's not enough time.

The very thought seems somehow impudent.

Yet for me, this is the chief mystery of the Grand Canyon: its continual juxtaposition of what seem to be opposites. The near with the far. Vertical cliff and horizontal plateau. Short-lived human beings and ancient rocks. Shadow and light. The strong and the weak. The hard and the soft.

Lao Tzu, the Chinese author of the Dao, enjoyed these apparent paradoxes, but understood that opposites can produce a more unified whole. He might have been speaking of the canyon and thinking about erosion when he wrote:

"The softest stuff in the world penetrates quickly the hardest;
Insubstantial, it enters where no room is."

The Little Canyon

Lao Tzu might have noticed another apparent contradiction: that the Grand Canyon is remarkable not for its bigness but for its smallness. The Grand Wash trough just below the Grand Canyon is much bigger in terms of sheer volume removed by erosion, but it is nowhere near as impressive to look at because it's too big. And for real size, consider what the Mississippi River has done. It has eroded a volume of material that would fill the Grand Canyon many times over. Yet no one stands in Denver and looks out to the east thinking what an amazing erosional feat has been performed between the Rockies and the Appalachians. Instead, they think about Denver's air pollution.

Canyons, as opposed to valleys or larger landforms, are created by a tension between erosion and the lack of erosion. They are features of arid regions, where a river or stream works at the bottom, but there isn't

Grand Canyon National Park

enough erosion to widen the sides. This is best illustrated by slot canyons, where walls actually overhang and in places block one's view of the sky. Slot canyons occur in homogeneous rock of the type common around Lake Powell. They aren't much more than enlarged cracks, often beautifully sculpted by moving water. Water flows through in narrow ribbons, slicing deep but not widening.

The Bright Angel Trail descending from the South Rim takes advantage of a break in the cliffs caused by the Bright Angel Fault. Movement along the fault has caused a difference of 186 vertical feet between rock layers on the west (right side of the picture) and the lower east side.

On a grand scale, consider Marble Canyon below Navajo Bridge near Lees Ferry. Here the canyon walls are high and vertical, cut through the limestone and eolian sandstone of the Kaibab, Toroweap, and Coconino formations. There are no overhangs to speak of (as in slot canyons), and no broad ledges or steps of the sort that characterize the canyon profile farther downstream.

This is an important bit of information, for rock type influences the shape of the Grand Canyon. Softer rock forms slopes. Harder forms cliffs. The hardest of all, the Vishnu, forms a steep-walled V. In combination, the varying hardness of rocks account for the canyon's distinctive stairstep profile. Were the rock of all one hardness, the walls would have a far different form. The canyons of central Idaho are good examples of this. Although Hell's Canyon of the Snake River is deeper than the Grand Canyon, it has an entirely different feel. The rock is essentially the same from top to bottom. There are no distinct horizontal layers or long lines of vertical cliffs, and for some reason, probably a visual trick based on shapes and colors, it seems less grand.

Hard Rock, Soft Rock

At its bottom lies the canyon's hardest rock, a beautiful substance called Vishnu Schist — black, smooth-grained, polished by the river to a sheen like that of fine marble sculpture. You want to stroke it, sit on it, feel it against your cheek as you lie on the shore of the river looking into the roiling water. Almost two billion years old, this could be the rock that symbolizes eternity.

It's a different story if you climb up about a thousand feet, out of the inner gorge across the Tonto Platform to the Bright Angel Shale. This stuff is so soft you can kick it apart with your boot. Pour water on it and it seems to melt. If the entire canyon were cut in shale, you might easily picture it happening in a short time.

What makes rock harder or softer? Sedimentary rocks found in the canyon are of three types: mudstones (which include siltstone and shale), sandstone, and limestone.

Mudstones are made of little platelike particles. In deposition, they fall every which way, but tend to settle in a horizontal position, where they get bonded together by recrystallization and by minerals — mostly calcium carbonate — that act as cement. The trouble is, the plates fit so tightly that there is little room for cement, resulting in soft rock that breaks easily between layers. Even a boot sole can break them. When eroded, it forms slopes of varying steepness, depending on its consistency.

Sandstone is made of round sand grains that stack poorly, leaving plenty of interstitial room for cement. Sandstone, therefore, can be strong and very hard, as long as there is enough cement to fill the spaces. When undercut, if shears to form cliffs.

Limestone is made essentially of pure cement with few or no grains of anything else. Because the cement is soluble in water, limestone's durability is related to the surrounding climate. Limestone in a dry climate is very hard. In a wet climate, where water keeps it constantly soaked, it is soft and easily eroded. In the canyon, limestone usually forms vertical cliffs; the Kaibab and Redwall limestones are good examples.

You might say that it's the job of erosion to make hard rock into soft rock, a process helped by earth movements that break rock along fault lines, thereby creating zones of weakness. Broken rock is more easily eroded because water can work its way through the cracks and affect more surface area. This explains why streams and side canyons, notably the long, straight Bright Angel Canyon, often follow fault lines.

The shape of the surrounding landscape also has an impact on how erosion has shaped the canyon. Because the Kaibab Plateau slopes gently toward the south, water falling on the South Rim drains away from it. The small amounts that do make it into the canyon must work against the dip, or angle, of the rock strata. The result, easily seen on a map, is unsymmetrical erosion. There are fewer side canyons on the south side of the river, and they are shorter.

The opposite is true on the North Rim, where water drains with the dip, into the canyon. In doing so, it feeds permanent streams, lengthens side canyons, and gnaws the rim farther back from the river. Individual cliff bands on the North Rim are the same thickness as corresponding bands on the South Rim (being of the same geological structure) but steps and slopes between the cliffs are longer in the horizontal direction, resulting in a more gradual average rise. With only a few exceptions, the canyon's permanent streams all pour in from the north side. The notable exceptions are Havasu Creek and the Little Colorado River, neither of which draws its water from the Kaibab Plateau. Havasu Creek's headwaters are many miles south near the town of Williams. The Little Colorado rises on Mt. Baldy in northeastern Arizona's White Mountains.

The connection between water and erosion is not a direct one. That is, a little more water doesn't cause a little more erosion. The equation is complicated by many factors. For one, ample moisture encourages vegetation, which in turn can protect rock from erosion. In the desert Southwest, vegetation is sparse and so is rain. But when it does come, raindrops hit exposed ground at speeds of about 30 miles per hour. If you look closely during a desert storm, you can see sand grains bounce. Also, naked desert ground absorbs water slowly. A hard rain, of the sort that

Grand Canyon National Park

The hardness of rock layers influences how they erode. Here, the smooth, wind-deposited Coconino Sandstone forms a monolithic cliff.

comes in summer thunderstorms, does not soak in. Instead, it runs off in sheets, collecting in ravines that in turn pour into creeks and produce flash floods.

Of course climates change, and what we see today is not necessarily indicative of conditions that existed here a million years ago, or even ten thousand years ago during the most recent ice age. Northern Arizona was wetter and cooler then — wet enough that Douglas-fir trees grew on the Tonto Platform, some 3,000 feet lower than their current limit. However, conditions during the Pleistocene were unusual. The climate here has been predominantly arid for a long time.

During winter, snow falls gently and has little erosive power. Yet as it melts, it penetrates crevices in the rock, and there, through the action of freezing and expanding, it has a powerful impact. In lab tests, water exerts a force of 20,000 pounds per square inch when it freezes; although in nature the force is less than in the ideal conditions of a laboratory, this process, called frost wedging, is one of erosion's strongest tools.

It goes without saying that frost action is limited to the rims where freezing temperatures during winter are common. On the North Rim, which is about 1,000 feet higher than the South Rim and gets large amounts of snow, winters are more severe, and there is more frost action. On every clear winter morning, the south-facing cliffs thaw in the warm sun, and every night they freeze again. On the South Rim, temperatures are warmer in general, less snow falls, and when cold weather does strike, the shaded north-facing cliffs can stay frozen for days at a time.

So far, we've been talking about the cumulative effects of many small actions. But sometimes erosion moves in bigger ways. It happened one morning a few years ago on Isis Temple, a butte on the north side of the river across from Grand Canyon Village. It was a calm day, the sky beautifully clear, when suddenly there came a roar and a cloud of dust, and tons of rock headed for lower ground. The collapse appeared to have been a spontaneous event, but actually, the slab of rock had probably been tilting for years, maybe thousands of years. Again, the period of our observation is too short to see the processes that lead to such rapid events.

A study in Chaco Culture National Historic Park described how part of Pueblo Bonito was buried beneath a big rockfall in January of 1941. The Anasazi people who built the pueblo and lived there some 800 years ago had recognized the danger. They had tried to stop it by building a retaining wall under that chunk of rock, and whether the wall had any effect or not, the huge rock was still there when archeologists began studying the abandoned pueblo. They called it Threatening Rock, for obvious reasons.

After the national monument was established, park service employees, wondering just how threatening Threatening Rock really was, started measuring, and found the rock was slowly moving — tilting outward and accelerating. Eventually it fell. By extrapolating their figures, they determined that Threatening Rock had begun to fall some 2,000 years earlier.

This sort of major rockfall happens with surprising frequency in the canyon and is categorized as either slab failure or rock avalanche. The first type happens when huge plates of stone separate from vertical or overhanging cliffs. Some, resulting from differences in compressive stress, leave behind curving, conchoidal fracture lines. Deep within the rock there is enormous pressure from its own weight and that of overlying layers. Where the rock face meets air there is only atmospheric pressure, and eventually something has to give. Before the fall, there might have been no cracks in the rock, and no sign of impending collapse.

Rock avalanches, on the other hand, occur where numerous fractures, or micro-joints, have already weakened the rock. Moisture in the fractures might precipitate failure. So also might the undermining of soft layers beneath the cliff-forming strata; when shale washes out from beneath a cliff, the cliff falls.

It doesn't always fall forward. There is another type of slope failure called rotational landsliding, in which the cliff loses its footing and slides (rather than toppling) to a lower position. This seems to be a major factor in the widening of the canyon. It occurs most commonly where the river has cut to the base of the Bright Angel Shale, exposing a soft, unstable slope that is too weak to provide a firm base for the overlying load of Redwall Limestone and Supai Group. As the shale base weakens, a concave fault line forms in the overlying layers, releasing a catastrophic landslide. It's a bit like leaning against a wall, standing on a pile of blocks. If someone begins pulling out the blocks at the base of the pile, eventually the blocks under your feet will give way, and you'll slide to a sitting position.

Peter Huntoon, in his 1975 paper, proposed that this is one mechanism by which the canyon establishes a stable profile. When the river cuts through the Bright Angel Shale, the higher layers slide, and the remaining canyon wall finds itself with a broader and therefore more stable base. One clearly visible example of this is found along the river between Deer Creek and Tapeats canyons, where millions of years ago a rotational landslide blocked the river, filling the channel. The river then cut a new channel to the side. The blocked section of the old channel remains buried by slide debris, visible in cross section.

These are no small events. One large rotational slide whose remnants are found in the lower canyon was 1.2 miles in length.

The River as Conveyor

One way or another, whatever goes down ends up in the Colorado River. Wind might carry some dust away from the canyon, but essentially every cubic yard cut loose by erosion goes out by river, and ends up somewhere downstream. Currently, it all piles up in the vast settling pond of Lake Mead. Before Boulder Dam was built, the river took it to a magnificent delta on the Gulf of California. It will, some day, again.

It has been calculated that the canyon's volume is roughly 5.45 trillion cubic yards — 1,000 cubic miles swept away by the unceasing transport device that is the Colorado River.

The river does its work with the help of the grit and sediments it carries, which serve as abrasive agents. The faster the water, the more sediment it carries, and the more erosive it becomes. But even without sediment, the raw speed of moving water causes erosion, sometimes on a large scale, by means of a phenomenon called cavitation.

Cavitation is the formation of partial vacuum bubbles in water as it moves across a slightly irregular surface. Cavitation happens where water moves fast, as it does behind a poorly designed ship's propeller, or in whitewater rapids where cells of water have been observed attaining speeds of 30 miles per hour. The movement causes a lessening of pressure that allows pockets of air to appear. In

After a rotational landslide filled its former channel, perhaps in the Pliocene, the Colorado River cut a new path to the south. The old channel, filled here with a V of lighter-colored rock, is 500 feet above the current river level.

Courtesy of Richard Hereford

effect, the water boils; the popping sound that comes from a tea kettle as it approaches a full boil is due to an action very similar to cavitation. Bubbles explode into existence for a moment, but they lack the energy to sustain themselves against the water pressure and collapse. In a river, cavitation occurs on the downstream sides of rocks, where the water moves the fastest. The effect is like a powerful air hammer capable of shattering solid rock.

A spectacular example occurred during the 1983 flood, when the fast-rising waters of Lake Powell threatened to overtop the Glen Canyon Dam. With all turbines running and the river outlet tubes fully open, the lake still rose until finally, to shed the excess flow, engineers opened the two spillway tunnels that had been bored through the bedrock on either side of the dam. They were meant to handle just such an unusual circumstance, but they had never been adequately tested, and when the need came, they nearly failed. Dropping hundreds of vertical feet at a steep angle, the overflow began to cavitate inside the tunnels, tearing off bits of rock at first, then huge chunks of rock as the situation worsened. The shock waves caused by the enormous air hammers of cavitation could be felt through the floor of the visitor center on the solid rock above the dam.

Worried that cavitation might destroy the tunnels, engineers were forced to release less water, but that meant allowing the lake to rise. Before it was over, the lake actually rose above the top of the spillways and would have flooded them except for hurriedly erected walls of plywood above the spillway gates.

When the crisis subsided, engineers went into the tunnels and found cavities measuring 30 by 150 feet. It took some 2,500 cubic yards of concrete to repair the damage. Since then, air channels have been cut into the tunnels to prevent a repeat situation.

How much material can a river transport? Water increases its carrying capacity to the sixth power of its speed. That is, a stream moving two miles per hour will carry 64 times as much material (two to the sixth power) as a slow stream moving at one mile per hour. At 10 miles per hour, the carrying capacity is a million times as great as that slow stream. This means that the river flowing quietly accomplishes little; it's during floods that real work is done. Also, it would have less to do without tributaries hauling down loads of rock to be pulverized and carried away.

David Edwards

The process even sounds impressive. You can stand beside almost any of the canyon's big rapids and listen to rocks rolling on the river bed. Putting your ear near the water — or better, under the water — you can hear the clicks and thumps and thunderous crashes of a river bed in constant turmoil. Rocks roll and skip like billiard balls. Sand blizzards are raging in the flumes.

With the river flowing at 85,000 cubic feet per second during the flood of 1983, Crystal Rapid developed an enormous, boat-eating "hole," caused by a boulder carried into the river on a debris flow.

As you ponder all that motion and power, a paradox comes to mind. It has to do with the largest boulders in the river. The best example is at Crystal Rapid, which boasts the biggest hole in the river. A "hole" is what river runners call the maelstrom that develops on the downstream side of a large boulder or a rock ledge. The water pours over the drop with tremendous force and collides with slower-moving water; in a manner of speaking, it blasts a depression, or hole, in the surface of the river. The surrounding water tries to flow back into the hole but is kept out by the force of the falling water. The result is a wall of froth like a continual wave breaking upstream. The most impressive holes have walls of whitewater crashing in from three sides. The roar is deafening. Unlucky boats can disappear inside such holes and become trapped, recirculated between the down-pouring flume and the breaking waves.

The big hole in Crystal Rapid, which at high water once flipped and recirculated a 33-foot pontoon boat, was created by two events. The first was a heavy winter storm in 1966 that dropped 14 inches of rain on the North Rim, touching off a series of flash floods in side canyons. One of these roared down the Crystal Creek drainage and hurled a huge volume of rock, gravel, and sand into the river. The debris formed a fan extending about 200 feet farther into the river than the previous shoreline, pinching the river to a width of about 100 feet. Before the flood, Crystal Rapid was little more than a riffle. Afterward it became a serious boating challenge, thanks in part to the constriction of the river (constrictions cause standing waves) but also to several large boulders dumped there by the flood.

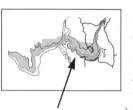

Crystal Rapid

The second event was another flood that happened in 1983. Caused by fast snowmelt and warm rains in the headwaters of the Colorado River, this was the same flood that damaged the spillway tunnels at Glen Canyon Dam. At the peak of flooding, the dam was releasing 92,200 cubic feet per second, some three times the usual maximum flow rate.

It was a big flood, the highest flow of water through Grand Canyon since the gates of the Glen Canyon Dam were closed in 1963. Its impact reverberated throughout the canyon, an impact that is still being measured. At Crystal Rapid, one change came quickly. The river shifted the big boulders a few yards downstream, rearranging things just enough to create Crystal's famous hole.

This is the paradox: At its highest level in decades, the Colorado River failed to move the boulders in Crystal Rapid more than a few feet; yet Crystal Creek, an intermittent tributary that experienced a flash flood of some 10,000 cubic feet per second, carried those same boulders a long distance. How could it do that?

The story begins with the storm in 1966. It lasted four days, from December 3 through December 7, and caused widespread flooding across four states. Just how much rain fell over the canyon was hard to measure because there were only two precipitation gauges in the area most affected by the storm. One was at the North Rim Entrance Station, and the other was at the actual canyon rim about 10 miles south. A month earlier, both had been converted to storage gauges, designed to collect moisture from the entire winter. The one on the rim was not read until the following May. The one at the entrance station, however, was checked right after the storm and was found to have collected 17 inches of water. Allowing for what might have fallen in November when the gauge was set up, rangers estimated that 14 inches of rain had fallen in the December storm.

They wouldn't have known without that one rain gauge. Weather in northern Arizona is about as variable as it can be. On the South Rim, 4.65 inches fell. At Jacob Lake, 6.6 inches. At Phantom Ranch, 2 inches. At Lees Ferry, .76 inches. In general, the numbers increased with elevation, which is to be expected. The North Rim Entrance Station stands at 8,780 feet. The South Rim rain gauge is at 6,965 feet, while Phantom Ranch is at 2,570 feet. There are mountains in Utah about 100 miles north and in Arizona 70 miles south that are much higher than the North Rim, but those areas received less rain. It appears that the storm aimed is maximum punch straight at the Kaibab Plateau, as if it wanted to provide a perfect demonstration of patterns in Grand Canyon erosion.

The following summer, a team of scientists led by Maurice Cooley surveyed the damage from what they called the "catastrophic flood." They found plenty — although words like *damage* and *catastrophic* are the wrong terms for erosion at the Grand Canyon. Erosion built this place. *Improvements* might be a better word.

Major improvements. Water had poured off the plateau and down numerous side canyons leading to the Colorado River. Streambeds were scoured to bedrock. In places, all loose material including shrubs and trees was carried off. Channels were deepened and new channels cut. The Park Service had just finished building a new water pipeline from Roaring Springs in Bright Angel Canyon to the South Rim. When Bright Angel Creek flashed, it destroyed the pipeline and the powerhouse. In some streams, flow rates were judged to be the highest in several hundred years. Judging from archeological sites affected by the flooding in Crystal Creek Basin, it appeared that there had been no equivalent flooding for at least 800 or 900 years. The scientists' report stated: "The prehistoric Indians must have experienced flash floods, but the flood of December 1966 probably was greater than any since the general abandonment of eastern Grand Canyon by the Pueblo Indians about A.D. 1150."

While these floods were clawing at the North Rim, the impact on South Rim drainages was minor, a fact that fits well with the overall pattern of Grand Canyon erosion. The north side has eroded much faster than the south, and this storm demonstrated part of the reason why.

The scientists made special note of one spectacular result of the floods — phenomena they called mudflows. No one had ever reported acually seeing such a thing in action, but the evidence they left behind showed that they were not mere flash floods. In their wake they left a sort of plaster smeared on rocks, trees, stream banks, and canyon walls. Flash floods are mostly water. These mudflows were more solid. On flat surfaces near the mouth of Crystal Creek, the edge of the hardened mud flow stood about an inch above the ground, suggesting that the mud had been the consistency of cake dough. By moistening some of the mud in the laboratory, the scientists achieved the same consistency with 40 percent water by volume. More than a dozen similar mudflows had occurred in other North Rim tributary canyons, although only in the Crystal Creek and Lava Creek drainages were they strong enough to flow all the way to the river.

The scientists also noticed that flash floods had come in advance of the mudflows and then followed after them. Also, where the mudflows had encountered gravel bars, terraces, and other features, they obliterated them. In places, the mud marks were at different elevations on opposite banks of the creeks; along one creek, the mud marks were 12 feet higher on one side than on the other. These mudflows were the first of their kind to be studied in Grand Canyon, and although the scientists found evidence of one much earlier flow, they had no way of knowing that what they were describing is actually a common occurrence. Since that 1966 flood, many debris flows, as they are now called, have been recorded in the canyon, and a few have been witnessed.

If you were camped in the right place at the right time, you might see something like this:

You have set up your tent in the bottom of a side canyon not far from the river. As evening falls, thunderstorms are brewing over the high country. Lightning flickers against the cliffs and a troubled wind stirs the warm desert air. Seeing the dark clouds when you arrived, you wisely considered the possibility of a flash flood and pitched your tent on a terrace 50 feet above the dry creek bed. Good thing, too. The sky opens.

There isn't much rain here at your camp, just a sprinkle and a few gusts of cold air from the belly of the storm. But you can see that higher up, the rain is falling in torrents. The canyon rim disappears behind a smear of gray hung with bolts of lightening. For 10, 15 minutes you watch the show. And then comes the flood. It's like someone tipped over a giant tub of dirty water, and it's all coming at once. Carrying all sorts of junk, mostly vegetation picked up from the floor of the canyon. Brown and frothy, it moves with a hiss as the advancing front meets parched sand.

Surprisingly, it moves slower than you might have expected. You could jog ahead of it easily. If you had camped in the creek bed, you'd have no trouble getting out of its way — assuming you were awake, not zipped securely in a tent, asleep in the dark. Terrible thought.

Once the debris-laden front passes, the flow turns more liquid. It fills the canyon bottom several feet deep, a small brown river where an hour earlier the only things moving were lizards. Standing waves form in the center of the channel. Turbulence boils in the wake of boulders. Willow bushes are laid flat, only their tips waving above the surface.

Granite Rapid, photographed in 1938, occurs where the river squeezes past debris dumped out of Monument Canyon (foreground).

Grand Canyon National Park

The result of the 1966 debris flow in the Crystal Creek drainage is shown in these two photos. Above, the mouth of the creek and Crystal Rapid as they appeared in March, 1963; opposite, three months after the debris flow in March of 1967 the river is constricted and the rapid has become wilder.

Minutes later, the flood subsides. The river begins to shrink, leaving behind a sheen of fresh mud on everything that was in its path. You think, "That was impressive."

But then comes something right out of a science fiction movie, the sort of geological event you might associate with other planets. Coming down the canyon is a river of rocks. Rocks of all sizes, from pebbles to boulders. The noise is terrific. The speed is astonishing, faster than you could run. Whole trees are borne along in the flow. It begins to ebb, then rises. It ebbs again, and rises again, flowing in a series of pulses. A few minutes later, it is over.

This is a debris flow, which turns out to be a major means by which sediment reaches the Colorado River. In some drainages, debris flows run all the way to the river several times in a century.

Described in detail by Robert Webb, Patrick Pringle, and Glenn Rink in a 1989 paper, a debris flow is not a flash flood, although it behaves somewhat the same and might be triggered by one. The defining difference is that flash floods are mostly water (above 80 percent by volume)

Bureau of Reclamation, Mel Davis

while debris flows contain between 15 and 40 percent water. Debris flows are slurries of mixed clay, sand, pebbles, and rocks up to the size of large boulders — the whole mix lubricated by water but not carried by it.

If you've ever mixed concrete, you know that when you add water to the dry material you reach a point when the mix suddenly acquires a loose, jellylike consistency. It wobbles when shaken. It pours easily into forms. Its ingredients — cement powder, sand, and chunks of gravel — are evenly distributed throughout. Then if you add just a little more water, everything changes. The solids settle to the bottom of the mixing trough and water collects on the surface. If it contains too much water, concrete is very difficult to pour.

Debris flows behave in ways you wouldn't expect. The center of the flow can scour a canyon to bedrock and shear off large cottonwood trees, while on the margins, brittle plants like cacti survive undamaged. They move fast, on the order of 10 to 15 feet per second, with a maximum speed of 25 feet per second. (The speed of flash floods is variable, with a maximum of 22 feet per second.) On the outside of sharp bends, centrifugal force shoves the slurry up against the wall; this is why mud marks can be so much higher on one side of a canyon than the other.

So much about debris flows remains a mystery, probably because they happen so fast and few have ever been witnessed. Although he has studied their effects for years, Webb believes that to actually see one in action would be incredibly good luck. Among the more intriguing puzzles is the question of the pulsing flow. Webb suggests it might be the result of several debris flows moving down various side canyons and combining sequentially in the major drainage. As each debris flow joins the main one, it contributes a fresh load of sediment and causes a pulse. Even more dramatic is the theory of rolling boulder dams. Webb's idea is that clusters of large boulders, pounding along in close ranks, might temporarily hold back the flow and then release it. Each release would create another surge.

Because they are triggered by a combination of rainfall and slope failure, debris flows often occur at the same time as flash floods. However, these phenomena are not connected. Either can happen without the other, and in fact they usually do.

Small debris flows stop after moving a short distance. Their sediments pile up in the bottoms of side canyons for years before a major debris flow cuts everything loose and carries it all the way to the river. One well-documented flow occurred in 1984 in Monument Creek. Triggered by one inch of rain from a single intense thunderstorm, a slope avalanched and set off a debris flow that ran 2.8 miles, carrying an estimated 300,000 cubic feet of sediment to the head of Granite Rapid, pinching it further against the opposite wall. Among its cargo were a number of large boulders, one weighing 37 tons. However, unlike at Crystal Creek, the river-choking boulders did not make it into the channel, which is probably a good thing considering that Granite is already one of the canyon's most challenging runs.

Anyone would be interested, but a river runner especially, in the capacity of debris flows to transport large boulders. The 1984 Monument Creek flow carried one measuring nine feet in diameter. The 1966 Crystal Creek flow moved one measuring 14 by 7 by 6 feet, weighing an estimated 47 tons, to within a mile of the river. The largest of all boulders known to have been carried to the river by a debris flow stands in the river at mile 62.5. It weighs 280 tons.

For millions of years, the Colorado River has been accepting rock and other debris hauled down from side canyons. It has come in the form of hot lava, rotational landslides, silt from flash floods, rocks falling from the cliffs, and debris flows. All of it, throughout the river's history, has been chewed up and carried away. No doubt the process will continue. Nothing stops erosion for long.

But in the short term, the Glen Canyon Dam has changed the way the river works. By controlling floods, it has lessened the river's ability to move large rocks that arrive by debris flow. This is of some concern to river runners, as rocks pile up and rapids become more difficult. So far, no rapid has become too difficult for skilled boaters to navigate with good equipment. But it would take only one big debris flow — perhaps only one big boulder — to create an impassable rapid.

When it happened in 1984, the Monument Creek debris flow dumped its 300,000 cubic feet of cargo in the space of one to three minutes. Who said erosion is a slow process?

On the South Kaibab Trail near Cedar Ridge.

Where to See Geology

At the Grand Canyon, geology is everywhere. But to see it up close, the best way is to walk down (and up!) one of the trails that leads to the river. There is simply no better way to experience the canyon than to hike across it on a trail like the Kaibab, from one rim to the other. Better even than a river trip, a cross-canyon hiking trip puts you in contact with the rock and provides an essential understanding of the canyon's scale.

But long hikes are not for everyone, and there are shorter, highly rewarding options. My favorite is the South Kaibab Trail to Cedar Ridge. The trailhead is near Yaki Point, east of Grand Canyon Village. From the rim to Cedar Ridge it is 1.5 miles, which takes about one hour (twice that coming back); the vertical drop is about 1,000 feet. In that distance, you pass through the canyon's top strata: Kaibab Limestone, Toroweap Formation, Coconino Sandstone, and Hermit Shale. Interpretive signs along the way point out the intersections of layers, which are not always easy to recognize; the Kaibab and Toroweap seem to blend together. As you walk, you can feel the texture of the rock changing beneath your feet, becoming quite soft when you reach the red Hermit Shale that covers Cedar Ridge. Among things to look at here is a display of fossilized fern leaves, in situ, protected by a glass case.

Below Cedar Ridge, the trail drops through Supai Group cliffs on its way to the river at Phantom Ranch — a trip that requires more preparation (more water, food, time, and energy). Please note that even walking to Cedar Ridge can be more demanding than it looks.

There is no way of getting deep into the canyon except by walking, riding a mule, or floating the river. You can drive to Lees Ferry, but although it is at river level, it is no deeper into the rock layers than at Grand Canyon Village. On the contrary, Lees Ferry stands on the Moenkopi Formation, which is above the Kaibab Limestone. It is one of the peculiarities of the Grand Canyon that almost anywhere you can drive around its rims, whether to Point Imperial at 8,800 feet elevation or Marble Canyon at 3,200 feet, the road runs over the familiar old Kaibab Limestone.

The reason for the differences in elevation is the East Kaibab Monocline, the great fold that created the Kaibab Plateau. The monocline is clearly visible from viewpoints in the area of Desert View on the South Rim, and from Point Imperial on the North Rim. Paved roads traverse the monocline at two points, both of which provide spectacular views. Along Highway 64 between Cameron and the South Rim, huge uptilted slabs eroded in the shape of andirons attest to the steepness of the fold. From Highway 89A between Lees Ferry and Jacob Lake, there is a view across the Marble Platform that includes the startling gash of Marble Canyon.

South Rim Viewpoints

On the South Rim, two roads run along the edge of the canyon: the East Rim Drive and the West Rim Drive. (In summer, the latter is closed to general traffic; shuttle buses provide access.) A good place to begin is Yavapai Point, where the museum offers a geologic overview and shelter from stormy weather. From its windows, the expansive vista takes in most of the central canyon. Panoramic drawings identify landmarks and rock layers. Other exhibits explain important geologic themes.

At Pima Point, several stretches of the river are visible, along with one of the canyon's rapids, Granite. Like all the others in the canyon, it is caused by boulders and other material dumped into the river from side canyons — in this case, Monument Canyon. In 1984, a debris flow carried an estimated 300,000 cubic feet of sediment to the head of the rapid. The debris included a number of large boulders, including one weighing 37 tons.

Visible from either Moran or Grandview point (between the two points) is a formation called the Sinking Ship. Superstructure and all, it seems to be going down beneath surrounding horizontal strata. The "ship" marks the

Grandview Monocline, a small but significant fold that forced the Colorado River to cut downward rather than continue migrating toward the south.

From Lipan Point there is a revealing view of the Grand Canyon Supergroup. Its soft red and white layers at the bottom of the canyon have eroded to a broad, relatively open valley. The difference between soft and hard rock is dramatically shown just downstream, where the Vishnu Schist forms the dark, steep-walled inner gorge.

Lees Ferry

Lees Ferry occupies a sheltered pocket in the shadow of the Echo Cliffs and Vermilion Cliffs. Here you can see the rock layers that once covered the Grand Canyon rims before they were stripped clean by erosion. The soft red layer so prominent along the Lees Ferry road is Moenkopi Formation (sandstone and siltstone), which lies directly above the Kaibab Limestone. (Tiny traces of Moenkopi can still be found along the South Rim and in such remnants as Red Butte, south of Tusayan.) Continuing upward from the Moenkopi, the layers at Lees Ferry are as follows: Shinarump Conglomerate, relatively thin and resistant; Chinle Shale, soft and multi-colored; and the Glen Canyon Group, comprising Wingate Sandstone, Moenave mud- and siltstone, Kayenta Formation, and the beautiful, pale, massive Navajo Sandstone, the same

rock that makes up the cliffs of Zion National Park.

North Rim Viewpoints

The North Rim feels quite different from the South Rim, but the geologic lessons are similar. The rock layers are the same (again, the Kaibab Limestone forms the rim). Perhaps the most interesting thing about Bright Angel Point, the usual starting place for a North Rim visit, is its distance from the canyon proper. From here it is eight miles down Bright Angel Canyon to the Colorado River. The view that most people think of as the Grand Canyon is in fact only a side canyon. This is typical of North Rim tributary canyons, which have been eroded farther back from the river than the South Rim — the result of drainage patterns and the natural dip, or angle, of strata. Bright Angel Canyon has been carved along the noticeably straight Bright Angel Fault, a line of weakness that continues on the far side of the river; it is easily visible as a 186-foot displacement of strata on the distant South Rim (the western block being higher than the eastern block).

On the horizon are the gentle summits of the San Francisco volcanic field, the highest of which is Mt. Humphreys, 12,643 feet high. It last erupted 400,000 to 600,000 years ago, although the field has been active as recently as the 11th century.

The Cape Royal Road leads to vistas

U.S. Air Force

High-altitude (U2) photograph of the western end of the canyon, the Grand Wash Cliffs, and Lake Mead. The picture was taken looking north.

on the eastern edge of the plateau, looking down at Marble Canyon. From Point Imperial the East Kaibab Monocline is again prominent. Cape Royal, at the end of the road, is surrounded by temples and buttes, erosional remnants that anywhere but the canyon would be called mountains. There is no better place than this to get a sense of the enormous amount of

material carried off by erosion to make the Grand Canyon.

The West

Toroweap Point is a long, bumpy drive from the nearest pavement. The trip begins west of Fredonia, Arizona, on BLM Road 109, and the route is usually signposted from there; maps are indispensable in the case of missing

signs. The reward is an isolated view of
the western canyon, including the
volcanic Uinkaret Mountains and the
remnants of the great lava dams that
occurred about a million years ago.
Other rough roads lead over the
Uinkarets to yet more remote sections of
the canyon. This is no place for delicate,
lightweight vehicles or unprepared
travelers.

It is also a long drive — but a paved
one, most of the way — to Pearce Ferry
(take the turnoff to Dolan Springs, 27
miles north of Kingman on U.S. 93). At
Meadview, there are spectacular views of
the Grand Wash Cliffs, marking the end
of the Grand Canyon. One particularly
grand perspective can be had from the
airstrip north of Meadview (caution: the
airstrip is not abandoned; planes land
periodically). Here, you can look out
over a wonderful contrast of horizontal
strata (the Colorado Plateau) lying
peacefully beside the shattered geologic
wreckage of the Basin and Range
Province.

4
The Distribution of Living Things

Walking up a side canyon one afternoon near the river, I find a rattlesnake. He lies beside a rock in the middle of the trail. I stand a few paces away, but I nearly stepped on him before seeing him. That would have gotten the attention of us both.

In the movies, rattlesnakes are killers that attack little children until Dad comes up with a big stick and heroically turns the snake into pulp. In other rattler scenes, horses rear, riders fall into cactus, guns blaze, women shriek, and bitten victims die with inspiring last words. Movie snakes are always enormous.

This one must have missed the movies. He's less than two feet long, curled up in a brownish pink pile among the rocks in the shade of a bush. His color matches the ground. Lucky for me I stepped over him. I didn't see him until my foot was coming down. My weight was committed to the rock just above him. I could have walked into a rapidly developing situation. Instead, his eyes are still closed and he hasn't moved. I think he's sleeping. From the pulse of his breathing, I can tell that he is very much alive. I could get a stick, wake him up, test his reaction. I could make him behave the way a rattlesnake is supposed to behave, a quivering bundle of menace. But if I did that I'd be doing what guys in the movies do: if a critter isn't paying attention, poke it until it does something entertaining, like attack or run for its life.

I personally think this is a dishonorable way to treat animals and a worse way to learn any truth about them. So I move to a boulder a safe distance away, just in case he wakes up and panics, and open my book on reptiles. Down here, I learn, he can be only a Grand Canyon rattlesnake, known by the formal name *Crotalus viridis abyssus.*

He is the right color, this pale shade of dusty pink, and he has the markings described by the book. Judging from his characteristic flat head, he is clearly a rattler. Yet more telling than anything else is his very presence at this point in the Canyon: about a half mile from the river, at 2,500 feet elevation. His close relatives, *C. v. lutosus* and *C. v. nuntius* (other subspecies of *Crotalus viridis*) don't live down here. They don't generally visit here. They live on the rims, the latter on the North Rim, the former on the South Rim. One glance at the distribution map, and I know that if this is *Crotalus*, this deep in the canyon, it is most likely *abyssus.*

Most likely — but not absolutely, taxonomically for sure. Subspecies by definition are capable of interbreeding if given the opportunity. Rattlesnakes are not great travelers but they do move, and a large Grand Canyon rattlesnake was once found on the South Rim at Cape Solitude. Those who study them admit that the boundaries between *lutosus* and *abyssus*, and between *abyssus* and *nuntius*, are fuzzy lines that individuals might occasionally cross.

However, I'm a good distance from the rim at this point, and I accept this fellow as a sleeping *abyssus*. Of course he never consulted a map. He just lives here because conditions meet his needs.

It seems a simple question: Why is the rattler here? The answer could be that the food supply is generous, the climate is right, or that no predator has yet gotten hold of this snake. All those factors apply, but they aren't the first answer. The first answer is rock, the underlying structure of the landscape, upon which all natural history stories must begin.

Why is this snake here? Because this planet is the right distance from the sun. Because the continent we call North America drifted to its current latitude, placing the Grand Canyon at about 36 degrees north. Because the land was uplifted and eroded to this particular shape, and

David Edwards

A Grand Canyon rattlesnake lies coiled and unalarmed in thick vegetation near the Colorado River.

because to the west, the Sierra Nevada Mountains have created a rain shadow that keeps this region arid. The rain shadow is the result of prevailing weather patterns, which are in turn dependent to a large extent on global position. If the continent were to drift far enough either to the north or south, the prevailing winds would be different. There could be a lot more rain here, or it might be colder, and then *Crotalus viridis abyssus* would not find the bottom of the Grand Canyon to its liking.

Of course the snake isn't the only one affected by these conditions. It is part of a community of plants and animals, all of them adapted to living here. They include rodents on which the snake feeds, shrubs under which it takes shelter from the sun, predators that hunt the snake, and numerous others, each one connected by its own lines of dependency to the system as a whole. Each one has its own story.

But for the moment, let's stay with the snake, because there's another thing to consider about his being here: Without the canyon, he might not exist at all. In addition to shaping the local environment, the landscape has shaped the development of a species.

In simplified form, the idea is as follows. The Kaibab Plateau was once a continuous habitat upon which lived a single species of rattlesnake. When the canyon sliced through the plateau, the rattlers were separated into distinct populations — separated as much by climatic differences as by the physical barrier of sheer cliffs. Eventually the canyon cut deep enough to create a whole new habitat, lower and warmer than either rim. At some point, snakes within the canyon stopped regular genetic mixing with snakes on the rims, and the three subspecies began to develop.

Another often-cited example of the same process is the famous white-tailed Kaibab squirrel, a creature that lives only in the ponderosa pine forest of the North Rim. It is closely related to the Abert squirrel, which is common on the South Rim and in areas of ponderosa forest throughout Arizona, New Mexico, and Colorado. At some time in the recent past, when vast forests covered most of northern Arizona, Kaibab and Abert squirrels were genetically the same. But when the climate changed for the warmer, forests shrank. Some plants disappeared from the area altogether. Ponderosa pines retreated upslope, finding suitable conditions on plateaus and mountains that often stood isolated from each other like islands in a sea of inhospitable climate. As the forests became isolated, so did some of the animals that lived in them, including the Kaibab squirrels. Genetic mixing ceased, and although the squirrels live similar lives and (except for coloring) resemble each other physically, they are now classed as separate subspecies. They would be capable of interbreeding if given the chance, but isolation prevents that from happening; with time, they are likely to become two distinct species, no longer able to interbreed.

The key to this concept is that the canyon presents a barrier to the movement of plants and animals, and to the intermingling of their genes.

Of course, for some species, the canyon is no barrier at all. A raven can make the crossing in a few minutes on outstretched wings. Spiders float across on the ends of silky filaments, driven by the wind. Even plants can fly across, as seeds carried on the air or in the digestive tracts of birds.

For other species, the barrier is less a matter of physical ability than behavior or inclination. Kaibab squirrels could easily scramble across to the South Rim, but without continuous forest to lead them on, such a migration is very unlikely. Strictly speaking, I suppose even this Grand Canyon rattlesnake could make the journey to either rim, especially if it stayed on the well-graded Kaibab Trail. It could follow the switchbacks, slither over the Phantom Ranch suspension bridge (or swim, for that matter) and dive for cover when mule trains came by. An adventurous, ambitious snake could do it, but snakes don't behave that way. They do not migrate the way birds do, setting out with specific destinations in mind. If snakes move across country they do it in search of food, or as a result of population pressure. A snake doesn't look across the Colorado River and think, "Hmm, I wonder if the kangaroo rats are fatter over there; think I'll check it out." For that matter, a snake can't see clearly enough to form such a long-range view of its surroundings. Even if it were capable of thinking such thoughts, no vision of far horizons would stir its dreams. So here it stays, only a few hundred feet above the river, with no reason to go anywhere else, and I leave it in undisturbed slumber — by all appearances content to be a snake at the bottom of the Grand Canyon.

Sky Islands, Dinosaurs, and Lost Valleys

By all rights, a fabulous landscape should have a few fabulous creatures. The Grand Canyon has no Loch Ness monster, no rumors of Sasquatch, and although it seems a perfect place for them, no reputation as a hot spot for UFOs. On the other hand, what could be better than dinosaurs living on islands in the sky? Or Lilliputian horses hiding in lost valleys?

Ever since Charles Darwin first studied the finches of the Galápagos archipelago, islands have been a favorite subject for biologists interested in evolution. Far from the genetic mainstream, and often limited in the number of species, island populations follow their own paths of development with occasionally surprising results.

In Grand Canyon, there are islands of a different sort — the tops of buttes that stand separated from the rim. If you could fill the canyon with enough water, they would become real islands; instead, they are surrounded by a sea of air and ringed by formidable cliffs. In the 1930s, Harold E. Anthony, curator of mammals at the American Museum of Natural History, took an interest in these isolated, virtually impregnable

Grand Canyon National Park

Park Naturalist Edwin McKee measures a small horse caught in the Canyon of Little Horses during the 1938 expedition to investigate rumors of desert-stunted animals.

patches of land. What might be found up there, marooned and isolated for God knows how long? In those years the canyon was thought to be immensely old; if so, the buttes might have been cut off from the genetic mainstream for a very long time. Perhaps millions of years.

In 1937, at the suggestion of Grand Canyon officials, Anthony announced an expedition to investigate the summit plateaus of Shiva Temple and Wotan's Throne and compare the creatures found there with those on the neighboring North Rim. The expedition would begin with Shiva Temple, whose tree-covered summit was about one square mile in extent. Getting there would require traversing a narrow ridge from the North Rim to a saddle, and then climbing 1,300 vertical feet to the plateau summit. As far as they knew, no one had ever done it.

Publicity, which the expedition initially encouraged, soon got out of control. An eager press heard that Anthony was looking for variant or relic forms of life, and this led to wild speculation. Relics of vanished species? What species? Perhaps dinosaurs? This was big news. There might be live dinosaurs on the Grand Canyon's Lost Plateaus — surrounded by sheer cliffs, standing high above the waves of time! The press had great fun playing up the possibilities.

Anthony had never suggested dinosaurs. His hopes were far more modest. But his actions did little to dampen the drama. He and his party, which included Grand Canyon National Park superintendent Minor Tillotson, made a big deal of the proceedings. They set up a base camp on the North Rim, spoke of first ascents, and radioed back reports like astronauts on the moon. Compared to the buildup, the results were anticlimactic and demonstrated that the summit was neither as isolated nor so difficult to achieve as they had hoped. Along with the rodents that they collected for later analysis, they found deer antlers and Anasazi artifacts. There were no unique species.

There was, however, an interesting sidelight to the expedition, one that reflects how seriously — you might say humorlessly — it was taken by its participants. Official reports never mentioned the discovery on Shiva Temple of five recently deposited soup cans and a package of film. As it happened, Emery Kolb (who along with his brother Ellsworth operated a well-known photo studio on the South Rim) had hatched a plan to climb Shiva Temple in advance of the vaunted expedition. He went with his friend Gordon Berger and found it easy enough that three weeks later he returned with his daughter Edith and two others.

When he learned of this, Tillotson was furious. Robbed of his first ascent, he took Kolb's action as an insult. Kolb, fearful of official retaliation, apologized profusely, kept silent, and let the superintendent bask in all his undeserved glory.

As for the little horses, there had been rumors for some years of a band of horses trapped by a landslide in a remote canyon and reduced by hard desert conditions to the size of dogs. These miniature creatures had become somewhat famous in carnival sideshows and magazine articles. In 1938, a group of park officials that did not include the superintendent went to investigate. What they found were smallish animals belonging to the Havasupai Indians, and a few wild horses, which although smaller than normal were nowhere near the size of dogs. The carnival animals were most likely Shetland ponies in the hands of enthusiastic promoters. If, in all its remoteness, the Grand Canyon has produced evolutionary wonders, they remain to be found.

Topography and Climate

The pioneer in the study of how living things are distributed over a landscape was Clinton Hart Merriam. As director of the U.S. Biological Survey, he led a small expedition to the Grand Canyon region in 1889. He had come to observe plants and animals of what for him was new terrain. In addition to that work, he left with the seeds of a concept for which he was to become famous — that communities of plants and animals change with altitude as they do with latitude. He was the first person to express in scientific language the observation that if you climb a mountain, you pass through zones of vegetation similar to those you would find on a journey from south to north.

And nowhere better to see this progression than in the area of the Grand Canyon. From Phantom Ranch on the Colorado River to the summit of the nearby San Francisco Mountains, a distance of about 80 miles, there is a vertical difference of over 10,000 feet. Conditions in the bottom of the canyon approximate those of southern Arizona, while the climate on the top of Mount Humphreys (at 12,643 feet) resembles that of northern Canada.

On the peaks, Merriam described several highly visible bands of vegetation. Ponderosa pines ring the mountain at its base and extend outward for some distance before yielding to a forest of pinyon pines and juniper. In the other direction, going uphill, the pines give way to aspen and fir, which in turn surrender the mountain heights to a dark, cool forest of spruce and mixed fir. Merriam hadn't spent much time in the mountains; perhaps this is why he was so struck by the distinct vertical zonation. As he traveled to the canyon bottom and climbed the peaks, he was also struck by the wide temperature differences caused by changes in altitude. Putting the two together, he reckoned that temperature was the determining factor. After further study, he recognized that other influences were at work and that the situation was a good bit more complicated than it had first appeared to be. It certainly was. More than a hundred years later, biologists are still trying to untangle the complex web of influences on the distribution of plants and animals.

Some of these complicating factors are well known and hardly need mentioning. For example, slopes that face south are warmer and drier than north-facing slopes, because the sun shines on them more directly.

The wind blows harder on exposed ridges than in sheltered valleys, regardless of altitude. Cold air sinks, forming invisible rivers that flow down the slopes of mountains and along the floors of canyons; to these places, it brings unexpectedly cool conditions. By the same token, hot air rises, creating unusually warm conditions on the edges of south-facing cliffs. Beyond atmospheric effects, there are differences in soil and precipitation to consider. And so on. Taken together, these effects create what are called microclimates — small pockets of variation in coolness, warmth, shade, moisture, and other factors.

Although microclimates occur anywhere on Earth, they are particularly noticeable in desert environments, where broad fluctuations are the rule. The explanation lies almost entirely with aridity, the skin-parching dryness of desert air. Without rain, there is not enough moisture in the air to moderate temperatures. Without clouds, there is nothing to shade the earth from intense sunshine, and nothing to prevent heat from escaping during the night. Moisture in the ground would keep it cool by evaporation, but the soil of deserts is often dry, and during the day it gets very hot.

A hot day in a humid setting is hot everywhere because humidity carries heat to every nook and cranny of the landscape. A hot day in the desert needs qualifying: What part of the desert are you interested in, and at what time? There is a big difference between shade and sunshine. With nothing to block its power, the desert sun speaks with authority and turns some expectations upside down. For example, mountain slopes are often hotter than valley floors because cool night air sinks, and because the sun angle is more direct on exposed slopes than it is on flat ground. This varies with seasonal solar movements, to the point that when the sun moves north in summer, slopes that face *northwest* can be the warmest of all, because they receive the full blast of the afternoon sun. It is better to face the sun early in the day; better yet, as many desert creatures do, avoid it altogether. The fluctuating temperatures go surprisingly deep. If you put a thermometer six feet underground in a humid climate such as western Europe, you will find that the temperature is essentially constant — through winter and summer, despite rain and snow. But do the same in Arizona's Sonoran desert (which includes the lower reaches of Grand Canyon) and you will record annual fluctuations of around 19 degrees Fahrenheit. As deep as 12 feet below the desert surface there is a significant annual temperature cycle. Of course the biggest temperature swings occur on the surface, where dark rock can get hot enough to actually fry an egg. Some plants and animals are capable of coping with such conditions. Most are not.

Moisture can fluctuate as much as temperature, and annual rainfall figures are misleading at best. The figures reflect the broadest of averages taken over a number of years. Any particular location in any one year might see entirely different amounts. One heavy rainstorm can easily increase the annual precipitation to double the average. Other years, there will be far less than average. Also, the distribution is spotty, particularly during thunderstorm season, which happens in July and August over the canyon. A storm might dump several inches of rain at one location, while a few miles away another place remains dry. During the famous storm of December 1966, 14 inches of rain fell at the North Rim Entrance Station. At Phantom Ranch, about 12 miles south at the bottom of the canyon, only two inches fell, while at Cedar Ridge Trading Post, less than 50 miles due east, there was a light rain of .37 inches.

Besides total rainfall, the important thing to watch with desert precipitation is how it comes down. Heavy rainfall, which is common in summer thunderstorms, is practically useless. It runs off stony desert ground in a hurry. It creates flash floods and triggers debris flows. It creates canyons. But except in streamways and low areas where water collects and has a chance to saturate the ground, heavy rain does little for growing things. On the other hand, very light rainfall barely wets the surface and evaporates rapidly. Good rain, really useful rain, must come slowly and in enough volume to soak deep into the ground. Typically in the Grand Canyon area, winter storms are of this sort.

Competition is yet another factor affecting what plants grow in a given location. Cacti, for example, possess efficient water-collecting root systems. By wringing the soil of moisture, a cactus can prevent the seedlings of competing species from surviving. But this is true only if moisture conditions are marginal; a surplus of water would remove the advantage enjoyed by cacti.

Even a flat desert experiences wide fluctuations. Add to those the effects of the Grand Canyon's dramatic topography, and you get microclimates like crazy. For example, to understand the way plants and animals are distributed in any small portion of the canyon, you need to

Douglas-fir trees grow in the relatively cool and wet micro-climate immediately below the South Rim. The same species does not survive on the rim itself, which is warmer and drier.

Grand Canyon National Park

observe where water collects and where it runs off. You need to know where the sun shines most intensely and where it never shines at all. Then consider seasonal differences. As the sun shifts its position, days grow long or short, average temperatures change, and weather patterns shift. And elevation — it is nearly 8,000 vertical feet from the highest point in Grand Canyon National Park to the lowest. Cold air drains from the highlands at night, pouring in frigid streams along canyon bottoms that were piping hot during the day. At the same time, heated air rises from sun-baked cliffs, creating a narrow zone of warmth along the south-facing rims.

When all these and other factors are weighed, it becomes clear why the canyon has such an enormous variety of climates, conditions, and creatures — and why the picture is so easily muddled. Everywhere you look, you find exceptions to the rules.

Chaparral grows thickly where White Creek cuts a steep canyon through the Redwall Limestone on the North Rim.

For one, take Douglas-fir. A common tree on the higher areas of the Kaibab Plateau, it is usually found at elevations over 8,200 feet where winter snows lie deep and the soil is moist throughout the year. As you move south from the summit of the plateau (toward the North Rim) the elevation decreases, the climate gets warmer and drier, and Douglas-fir essentially disappears, to be replaced by other species. This is the normal pattern, and you'll look long and hard for a Douglas-fir tree among the pinyons, junipers, and ponderosa pine on the South Rim. Conditions are too warm and too dry, and having looked at the neat altitudinal diagrams of plant distribution, you'd be inclined to think, "Of course. This is too low for Doug fir."

But wait. If you walk to the rim itself, and look down at the trees growing in the first few hundred feet below the cliff edge, you'll see Douglas-fir doing very well indeed. The reason is that the shaded pockets just below the rim face north. They receive relatively little direct sun. Their soil has more moisture. Conditions are cooler. The climate resembles that more commonly found 1,000 feet higher.

The reverse situation occurs on the North Rim. Here the cliffs face south. They collect winter sun and generate warm updrafts that in turn support, along the very rim, a thin strip of pinyon-juniper woodland complete with yucca plants growing well above their usual upper limit.

As if to confuse matters further, the deep canyons that slice into the North Rim act as conduits for frigid air that drains off the high plateau. Along these canyon bottoms, montane forest types grow as if they were up on the plateau. Here, the expected pattern is turned on its head — a warm zone of pinyon and juniper lies *above* a cool zone.

Clearly, the distribution of living things in Grand Canyon is not purely a matter of altitude. Both animals and plants will overlap their assigned territories. Some species do well in more than one zone, or for that matter, in all of them. Ravens, for example. To them, the whole world is a merry playground. No borders, no rules. Nonetheless, we can describe in broad outline several climatic zones (often referred to as life zones) in the Grand Canyon. The next few chapters describe these in greater detail. Elevation figures are general and subject to local revision. Also, keep in mind that the change from one zone to another is gradual. The distinctive species of the two zones mix, resulting in greater diversity than either zone would contain by itself.

However, the basic idea is a useful one. We don't have to understand every factor to have a good idea why Douglas-fir thrives on the North Rim, survives marginally on the South Rim and lives not at all on the Tonto Platform. For a Douglas-fir to grow on the Tonto Platform would be nearly as strange as for a trout to live in the canopy of a forest.

Life Zones at Grand Canyon

Beginning at the North Rim at the highest point in the canyon area, the Boreal Zone extends from over 9,100 feet to around 8,000 feet. This is a montane environment characterized by aspen, spruce, and fir trees and some ponderosa pine. Winter snows cover the ground throughout the Boreal Zone for months at a time, reaching considerable depths in the higher areas. The climate approximates that of a Canadian forest, where cold weather and snow begin in October and persist into June. To a northerner, however, the winters here are mild. Twenty below zero is about as cold as it ever gets, and even in January the southern sun has a power that is rarely felt in British Columbia. Annual snowfall is upward of 150 inches; when this is added to summer rains, the total annual precipitation averages 25 to 30 inches.

Between 8,000 and 7,000 feet, the Transition Zone is dominated by ponderosa pines. Also called western yellow pine, ponderosas are large, stately trees with long needles and huge columnar trunks. Growing in nearly pure stands, they form an open forest with lots of space between trees and deep cushions of pine needles on the ground. There is a distinct lack of undergrowth. The monotony is broken by occasional stands of Gambel oak and mountain-mahogany. In forest openings and along meadow margins, aspen trees might be found.

Pure stands of ponderosa pine are extensive on the Kaibab Plateau. On the South Rim, which is around 1,000 feet lower, ponderosas are frequently mixed with pinyon and juniper trees before fading out altogether a few miles south of the rim. There is one pure stand surrounding Grandview Point; as you might predict, this is the highest area on the South Rim.

Among the canyon's strange effects is the way the transition zone gets pinched out along the edge of the North Rim. Where conditions are right, spruce and fir (Boreal Zone plants) march right to the edge of the cliffs. Here they meet not ponderosa but pinyon and juniper. The part of the Kaibab Plateau that would support extensive ponderosa pine forests has been

Plant Communities of Grand Canyon

In a general sense, Grand Canyon plants and the animals associated with them occur at specific elevations. A rough summary is as follows. Elevations are in feet.

9,100 to 8,000: Boreal Zone. Forest of spruce, fir, and aspen; also mountain grassland.

8,000 to 7,000: Transition Zone. Ponderosa pine, often in pure stands; in shaded or cooler areas, extending to about 6,500 feet. Associated plants include Gambel Oak, aspen, and white fir.

7,500 to 4,000: Upper Sonoran Zone. Further divided into pinyon-juniper woodland; mountain scrub and chaparral (Gambel oak, shrub live oak, serviceberry, mountain snowberry); sagebrush; and blackbrush desertscrub.

4,000 to 1,200: Lower Sonoran Zone. Found mostly in the western end of the canyon; hot-desert shrubs, trees including catclaw acacia, honey mesquite, creosotebush, ocotillo, brittlebush, and Joshuatree; also cacti such as barrel removed by erosion. It has become the Grand Canyon. The transition zone is essentially gone. It can still be found on remnants of the plateau surface — for example, on the Walhalla Plateau, a long peninsula stretching south from what you might call the mainland.

In a practical sense, the juxtaposition of pinyon and juniper with spruce and fir represents an aberration, a sort of biologic unconformity. These species normally don't mix, and it can be confusing to see them together. Ruby-crowned kinglets in the same area as pinyon jays? Yuccas growing near wintergreen? The canyon can seem a mighty peculiar place.

From around 7,500 feet extending down to about 4,000 feet is the Upper Sonoran Zone. It begins with pinyon-juniper woodland (which travelers will recognize as the classic woodland community of the high desert) and changes in its lower range to blackbrush scrub, yucca, agave, Mormon tea and various cacti. To help make sense of its diversity, the Upper Sonoran can be subdivided into five distinct associations, or subcategories. Pinyon-juniper woodland occurs between 4,000 and 7,500 feet. Mountain scrub and chaparral occupies the same elevational range. Desert grassland is found between 3,800 and 5,200 feet. Blackbrush scrub ranges from 3,000 to 5,500 feet. And lastly, the sagebrush association occurs from 4,000 to 7,000 feet. Depending on where you find them, these plant groups mix with each other or stand separate. Their occurrence has to do with various factors such as soil type, moisture availability, and temperature range and is discussed in more detail in the next chapter.

Finally we come to the Lower Sonoran Zone, below 4,000 feet and continuing to the lowest point in the park at 1,200 feet. Summer temperatures in this zone commonly rise above 100 degrees, and there is very little rain — less than 10 inches a year on average, and most of it from brief summer thunderstorms. It does freeze in winter, but never for long, and never very hard. The zone is roughly defined by the Inner Gorge, that part of the canyon below the broad shelves of the Tonto Platform and the Esplanade. Especially toward the canyon's western end, Mohave species mix with creatures from the Sonoran (southern Arizona) and the Great Basin (Nevada) deserts. The gorge provides a corridor from lower, warmer areas through which plants and animals are able to penetrate deep into the plateaus — some species get to within 40 river miles of Lees Ferry.

There are two habitats where water plays the major role regardless of the life zones in which they occur. One is the riparian habitat along the Colorado River and its many tributary streams. Water-loving plants such as cottonwoods and willows grow along the banks providing habitat for raccoons, skunks, ringtails, toads, treefrogs, and others. Because permanent streams flow through most important side canyons (and quite a few small ones also), there is extensive riparian habitat available. These moist areas are among the most densely vegetated and diverse locations in the canyon. There is also the Colorado River itself, a complex world of fish, insects, and aquatic plants where water, not aridity, is the central fact of life.

World in a Jar

Carrying the idea of life zones further, scientists are now attempting to develop computer analysis techniques that combine information on all the factors affecting distribution. The three main ones are aspect, elevation, and slope. They also include soil type, drainage patterns, precipitation, topography, behavior of plants and animals, weather patterns, human influences, and anything else that can be measured and might have a bearing on the subject.

Believers in the power of computers say that ecology is not just more complex than we think; it is more complex than we *can* think. According to theory, computers working with complicated mathematical instructions can deal with the vast, interconnected web of relationships and reduce the results to a comprehensible level.

To model the ecology of the Grand Canyon on a computer, we must construct a body of information built in layers and then tell the computer to correlate elements from the various layers. Layers could include all the factors mentioned above, in addition to roads, boundaries, buildings, trails, archeological sites, and anything else that seems pertinent. Special layers can be devoted to items of particular interest, like habitat for endangered species, or known falcon nesting sites, or places unusually susceptible to erosion. What you end up with is a supermap, which the computer can analyze for any number of variables and use in making predictions. For example, what happens if the river level rises a foot?

The computer will draw a new map showing the wider and deeper stream. A more complicated question: How high would the river rise during a flood of 200,000 cubic feet per second? This is a lot more difficult. To accomplish this, the computer must account for the way water flows — where it would pile up, how fast it would run through narrows, how much it would slow down in wide places, and more. Combining that hydrological information with calculations of the canyon's cross-sectional volume, and taking into account the potential for rapid erosional changes in the river bed, the computer could describe the behavior of the flooding river and its eventual impact on the canyon. Given more data, coupled with a vegetational map, it could predict the effects of the flood on streamside plants and animals.

At least, that's the theory. Obviously, the computer needs an enormous amount of information to work with if it is to produce complex models. And the models must be checked repeatedly against real situations or they risk becoming little more than exercises in theory. Still, the potential is great. The National Park Service's Michael Kunzmann and several colleagues have developed a sophisticated model for the effects of fire based on data collected during a prescribed burn on Point Sublime. Among other data, they measured vegetation before the fire, noted all atmospheric conditions, and measured the fire's strength using aerial infrared cameras, pyrometers on towers, and thermocouples in the soil. After the fire, they analyzed the effects on various species, asking such questions as, "How much fire does it take to kill half the mature ponderosa pine trees?"

The benefit of this for the park, assuming the model is accurate, lies in management of prescribed burns. A national park is less interested in controlling fires than in understanding them as a natural force and using them as management tools. Ideally, naturally caused fires at Grand Canyon are viewed in the same way as flash floods — forces of nature that have helped create the landscape we see today. In practice, the situation is more complicated. Nearly a century of fire suppression on the North Rim has dramatically changed the forest. Understory growth has become more dense. White fir have encroached into once-pure stands of ponderosa pine. Before suppression became the rule, natural fires would periodically clear out the fir trees without seriously damaging the mature, fire-resistant pines. A little fire can be good for a forest. But a big fire could be disastrous, and paradoxically, suppression has made a big fire more likely by allowing a heavy fuel load to accumulate. A fire in the wrong conditions (a drought, for example) could now sweep through large areas and burn so hot that all the trees would be killed.

The solution might be for the park to intentionally start small fires that would remove the white fir and other understory plants but leave most of the ponderosa pine alive. To do this successfully requires a thorough understanding of how fires behave. It requires, according to Kunzmann, a computer model. The world in an electronic test tube.

I understand why these ideas are appealing. But in the end, I suspect the natural world is likely to confound us, as it has always done in the past.

5
The Kaibab Plateau

For the Paiutes, it was an important summer hunting ground. They called it *kaiuw a-vwi,* or "Mountain Lying Down," perhaps because instead of a distinct craggy summit, its recumbent heights roll through a gentle landscape of meadow and forest. White settlers, when they arrived on the scene, called it Buckskin Mountain because its abundant deer provided them with meat and hides. The official name today is the Kaibab Plateau. The very opposite of a canyon, it lies 8,000 to 9,000 feet high, covered with snow in the winter and fragrant with the smell of mountain wildflowers in summer. While the adjacent desert shimmers beneath a hot sun, and lizards in the Inner Gorge go underground to escape the heat, cool breezes sigh through the forests of the plateau.

So do summer visitors. After driving up from the baked flats that surround the plateau, the shade of tall trees brings grateful expressions of relief. You want to turn off the air conditioning, open the windows, and let in the perfumed alpine air.

The big trees standing like columns in a cathedral are ponderosa pines. Zane Grey, in his book *Last of the Plainsmen,* described the climb from the Marble Platform up the east slope of the Kaibab:

The trail rolled over the ridges of pinyon and scrubby pine. . . . From one of these ridges I took my last long look back at the desert, and engraved on my mind a picture of the red wall, and the many-hued ocean of sand. The trail, narrow and indistinct, mounted the last slow-rising slope; the pinyons failed, and the scrubby pines became abundant. At length we reached the top, and entered the great arched aisles of Buckskin Forest. The ground was flat as a table. Magnificent pine trees, far apart, with branches high and spreading, gave the eye glad welcome. Some of these monarchs were eight feet thick at the base and two hundred feet high. Here and there one lay, gaunt and prostrate, a victim of the wind. The smell of pitch pine was sweetly overpowering.

It's still like that. The road from Lees Ferry to Jacob Lake follows roughly the same route Grey took in 1907. Even in a car, moving fast, the sun-pounded trip across House Rock Valley can be a hot test of patience.

Kaibab Plateau

Once you begin climbing, the view from halfway up the plateau is still one of the most dramatic in the region. The Marble Platform stretches away like a polished floor, bounded by the Echo Cliffs and the Vermilion Cliffs and marked by the dark angular slash of Marble Canyon. As Grey put it, "The irregular ragged crack in the plain, apparently only a thread of broken ground, was the Grand Canon. How unutterably remote, wild, grand, was that world of red and brown, of purple pall, of vague outline!"

After that come the trees. Arriving in the shaded openness of the forest, you feel a strong urge to stop the car, walk away from it on the springy mat of pine needles, and inhale deeply. It's a sweet place, this island of conifers and aspens, where plants tend not to be spiny and animals more often have fur than scales. The plateau is home to mule deer, mountain lions, coyotes, badgers, bobcats, wild turkeys, and what is arguably the world's handsomest squirrel.

It's hard to imagine better country for deer. Trees and associated plants range from pinyon and juniper woodland to ponderosa pine, to a dense moist forest of spruce and fir. Through these forest habitats, the deer move with the seasons, finding good summer range on the heights and easy retreat from winter snows on the lower and drier edges of the plateau. More on them later.

A few numbers: The Kaibab Plateau covers 1,152 square miles above 6,000 feet elevation, with an additional 120 square miles slightly below 6,000 feet. Its highest point is 9,200 feet elevation. It receives an annual precipitation average of 25 to 30 inches, most of which falls in winter as snow. Summers are temperate, with a climate similar to that of alpine areas in the northern Rockies. Winters, however, are warmer than you'd find farther north; nights rarely get colder than minus 20 and sunny days rise to freezing or above.

Ringed by escarpments, the plateau is defined on one side by the great upward fold of the East Kaibab Monocline (the slope Zane Grey climbed on horseback). Its west and north sides are marked by Kanab Canyon and the Kaibab Fault respectively, while on the south it is cut off by the Grand Canyon. Geologically speaking, the plateau continues on the other side of the canyon, but under a different name, the Coconino Plateau.

At its widest, the Kaibab measures about 30 miles. All around its perimeter are deep canyons and rugged cliffs. It is, all told, a spectacular and exciting piece of geography, and although only its southern end is contained within the national park, it makes sense to consider it as a whole unit.

Life on the Plateau

On all sides, but especially where it meets the Grand Canyon, the plateau is sliced to ribbons by ravines and tributary canyons. For something that's supposed to be flat on top, it's an ornery, ill-tempered sort of place to find your way around on. For all those broad aisles beneath the ponderosa pine, those churchlike spaces where you could drive a truck for miles without a road, there are other places where you can spend all day going a couple of miles on foot. The plateau appears flat only in comparison to the erosive monstrosity of its partner, the Grand Canyon.

Despite its often rugged surface, the Kaibab is built along horizontal lines. Where the two worlds of plateau and canyon come together, they stand in high contrast. Beside the plunging depths, sylvan meadows

The Kaibab Plateau was called Buckskin Mountain by white settlers because of its abundant mule deer. The deer move with the seasons, wintering among the pinyon-juniper woodland, giving birth in the ponderosa forest, and summering in the cool highlands.

Arizona Game and Fish Dept, Steven W. Smith

stretch luxuriantly. Cool green shadows dwell beside red rocks glaring at the sun. There's an old saying: An icicle falling from the North Rim becomes rain before it hits the ground.

The underlying rock is Kaibab Limestone, a porous material easily dissolved by water and riddled with caverns and subterranean passages. Although about 30 inches of precipitation fall each year on the plateau (including an average winter snowfall of around 12 feet), there are no permanent streams on the plateau and little standing water. It mostly drains off through the limestone. A few reservoirs occur where sinkholes (depressions caused by collapse of underground chambers) fill with soil and other debris, allowing them to retain water. These are tiny but important sources of water. Without a hint of sarcasm, local folks call them lakes.

Because the plateau is shaped like a rough dome, and because forest types are determined to a large extent by elevation, the various vegetative belts are arrayed in a roughly circular pattern. The highest areas are covered with a mixed coniferous forest of Engelmann spruce, white fir, ponderosa pine, Douglas-fir and alpine fir. Below 8,800 feet, alpine fir drops out of the mix and spruce becomes less common. Eventually, ponderosa pine becomes the dominant species, to the point that from around 8,000 feet to the canyon rim, it grows in nearly pure stands with very little undergrowth. Breaking up the solid coniferous patterns, aspen trees are found throughout all these forest communities. In areas where snowmelt collects and saturates the ground, mountain meadows provide open spaces. Finally, below all these vegetative communities, along the fringe of the plateau, is a belt of pinyon-juniper woodland, which is considered in the next chapter.

These "belts" of vegetation are by no means symmetrical on all sides of the plateau. For example, pinyon-juniper woodland forms a broad band on the north and west slopes of the plateau, but only a narrow strip on the south along the dissected rim of the canyon. Although narrow, this strip is long, snaking its way for some 100 miles, following the bays and peninsulas of the canyon rim.

Similarly, the ponderosa forest is most extensive on the north and west. Like the pinyon-juniper, it gets pinched out along the canyon rim and is found scarcely at all on the southeast corner. This is the doing of topography, of course; it is that southeast corner where the canyon has its greatest rim-to-river relief, from Point Imperial (8,803 feet) to the Colorado at 2,800 feet. Whatever part of the plateau might have supported ponderosa pine at that point has been swept away.

Grasslands occur beneath the plateau on the north, west, and east sides. Strictly speaking there is no grassland on the south side because of the canyon's interruption. However, if we picture the plateau without the canyon — that is, continuing over to the South Rim and down its long gradual slope — the pinyon-juniper does indeed grade gently into grasslands around the crossroads community of Valle. If the canyon had never sliced it in two pieces, we would see the plateau as a single highland.

The deer herds move through all of these zones except the grasslands, which provide poor cover and not much food. In summer mule deer prefer the high forest, both ponderosa pine and spruce-fir. When winter arrives in late October or early November, the deepening snow drives them down to the pinyon-juniper woodland. In spring, the deer move slowly back to higher elevations, moving upward with the snowline. Females choose the ponderosa forest to give birth, perhaps because it provides the right mix of openness and cover.

For unknown reasons, deer aren't very enterprising about where they look for food. They will return in great numbers to areas of poor forage, virtually ignoring nearby areas where the vegetation is nearly untouched. Wherever the country is broken into ravines and cliffs, they meet their major natural predator, the mountain lion. Lions generally stay near the rim country, and although they prey on hares, rabbits, small rodents, and other animals, deer are by far their major food. No one seems to know how many deer a lion kills, but estimates are on the order of one per week. At the same time, estimates of lion numbers are uncertain. One three-year study concluded that there were 40 lions on the Kaibab Plateau in 1977, and fewer than half that many in 1980. As of 1990, there were thought to be around 60 pairs of lions on the whole north side of the canyon. In any event, it seems unlikely that lions exert enough pressure on the deer population to keep it from increasing.

There are two other deer predators on the plateau. They are bobcats and coyotes. Both are said to be capable of taking deer, but it's hard to measure their impact. The major foods for bobcats are rodents and birds. Coyotes are the classic omnivores, eating anything with nutritive value and some things with none at all. They can hunt cooperatively, in packs, running relays until they have exhausted an adult deer.

A hundred years ago, there were timber wolves here, but they fell victim to a policy of killing predators in favor of the "nice" animals. Mountain lions, although hunted with fierce determination (Zane Grey's book is about a lion hunt) managed to survive, and their population is healthy once again. Coyotes, as they do everywhere, flourished despite all efforts to remove them. In fact, they might be doing better than ever. It is said that coyote numbers increased dramatically after wolves were extirpated.

On the subject of predators, it should be mentioned that black bears were historically present on the Kaibab but were never common, and they haven't been seen for a long time. Several unverified historical reports speak of grizzlies on the North Rim. One was said to have been killed in South Canyon around 1860; another was seen in 1880. Considering their documented presence in the nearby Pine Valley

Mountains of southwest Utah, it seems entirely possible that grizzlies once roamed the canyon area. But no more.

The Ponderosa Forest

The dominant tree of the Kaibab is ponderosa pine, also called western yellow pine and, affectionately by locals, P-pine. It occurs between 7,000 and 8,000 feet, extending down to around 6,500 feet where local conditions make it possible — on shaded north-facing slopes and where cool air drains from the plateau into the canyon.

In pure stands, the ponderosa forest is open enough to walk for miles without scrambling over deadfall or having to find your way through tangles of undergrowth. It forms a beautiful cathedral forest, with trees 60 feet tall and up to four feet in diameter (Zane Grey's enthusiastic estimates notwithstanding). The wind whistles through the treetops, while below the forest floor is still. Occasional stands of Gambel oak and thorny locust

A ponderosa pine forest in winter. Where it occurs in pure stands, P-pine creates an open, cathedral-like atmosphere.

Grand Canyon National Park

provide a thin understory. Oregon grape and Arizona fescue, a bluish grass, grow close to the ground. For the most part, the ground is covered with pine needles.

The deer use the ponderosa forest during most of the year, staying out of it only when snows are deep. They feed on Gambel oak, both browsing the twigs and eating the acorns. Other mammals common to this forest include striped skunks, Uinta chipmunks, Mexican voles, porcupines, mountain cottontail rabbits, and golden-mantled squirrels. Among reptiles are Great Basin gopher snakes and Great Basin rattlesnakes, both uncommon; and short-horned lizards, which prefer places where the forest is thin enough to let in generous sunlight. Important birds in this forest include nuthatches (white-breasted, red-breasted, and pygmy), Cassin's finches, common flickers, mountain chickadees, dark-eyed juncos, red-tailed hawks, goshawks, and Steller's jays.

Of all these animals, the one most closely associated with ponderosa pine is the Kaibab squirrel. A dashing creature, the Kaibab is a big, dark gray squirrel with a white tail and long ear tufts. It is related to the Abert squirrel, the common tree squirrel of the southwest, but has become distinct by virtue of isolation.

The Kaibab squirrel is totally reliant on ponderosa pine. It is found only where there are P-pines, either in pure stands or mixed with spruce and fir. In spring, it eats the male flowers, which look like bunches of miniature cones on the ends of branches. The flowers are rich in pollen and highly nutritive. All summer, as cones develop, the squirrels gnaw them apart and remove the growing seeds. Their most important food in warm season is fungi from the forest floor, particularly "truffles," which they dig up from beneath the pine duff.

Winter brings hard times. Unlike red squirrels, Kaibab squirrels do not build food caches. They store nothing for the winter. When snow covers the ground and no other food is available, the squirrel resorts to the only thing left: the inner bark of pine twigs. He clips off a twig with a neat bite of his front teeth, discards the terminal clump of needles, and peels the twig down to the inner bark — the xylem and phloem. Although plentiful, it is not good food. Studies show that if limited to inner bark for more than 60 days, the squirrels lose weight and suffer from nutritive deficiencies that can result in death. Thus, snow cover is the most important factor in mortality. One study showed that between

Grand Canyon National Park

The Kaibab squirrel, native to the Kaibab Plateau and nowhere else, is recognized by its flamboyant white tail. It lives only in ponderosa pine forest. Kaibab squirrels and Abert squirrels (which live on the South Rim and in ponderosa forests throughout the Southwest) are subspecies of Sciurus aberti.

22 percent and 66 percent of the total population died during the winter — a rate closely connected to the number of days when more than four inches of snow covered the ground.

In some ways, the Kaibab and Abert squirrels have backed themselves into an evolutionary corner. Without P-pine, they cannot survive. More adaptable species can move to different areas, find different food, or store enough to get themselves through times of scarcity. Not Kaibab and Abert squirrels — although they will eat other foods, including the seeds and bark of different conifers, dwarf mistletoe berries, acorns, various green plants, and even insects, they remain limited to Ponderosa pine forests and, at least during snowy winters, a diet of pine twigs.

On top of that, they need a mixed forest. They can't be like the eastern gray squirrels, which live happily in cities, and learn to feed on just about anything, and still outwit cats, dogs, and the efforts of home owners to keep them out of bird feeders. The tassel-eared squirrels are more specific in their needs. They want interlocking branches. They want big trees. They aren't particularly fast climbers.

In this respect, the squirrel is like the giant panda, which eats only bamboo. Actually there is an advantage in this. The panda stays awake all winter. Its food is widespread and plentiful. Black bears that live in the same area must go into hibernation for the winter because, lacking the panda's physiologic adaptations, they cannot survive on bamboo alone.

The squirrel and the panda both rely on a food that is among the most common and dominant plants in their habitats. Given the natural conditions for which they evolved, they do just fine. The biggest threat to both bamboo and P-pine (and therefore pandas and Kaibab squirrels) is human intervention.

Fortunately, Kaibab squirrels have another thing going for them: a lack of pine martens, which are efficient squirrel predators. Pine martens are not present at the Grand Canyon. But there are goshawks and red-tailed hawks, both of which take squirrels. Nests offer some protection. Squirrels build them high in the trees using pine branches and other materials, and prefer to build in a cluster of trees with interlocking crowns, thus providing alternate access and escape routes. When all the trees around a nest tree are cut down, the squirrels have been observed to abandon the nest. Nests are used all year, with winter nests being more substantial in construction—all the better for warmth.

The Spruce-Fir Forest

The highest forest in the Grand Canyon area is also the wettest and most dense. It is an alliance of Engelmann spruce, Douglas-fir, white fir, alpine fir, ponderosa pine, and aspen in varying proportions. There is enough moisture to support moss, lichens, liverworts, sedges, bracken, wild currants and strawberries, deer vetch, monkeyflower, and more. The very opposite of the open desert, it is a fierce tangle of standing and downed trees. You could stroll pleasantly through the ponderosa pine forest, but here you feel more like a very clumsy rabbit burrowing through the brier patch. There is an area on the northeastern edge of the North Rim called the Iron Triangle. The name reflects its impenetrable nature—but only to humans and other large animals. Red squirrels, also called pine squirrels and

Pine squirrels, also called red squirrels or chickarees, are smaller than Kaibab squirrels but more conspicuous. Their high, chattering call echoes through the spruce and fir forest that is their preferred habitat.

chickarees, live happily in the densest thickets. They are conspicuous animals on account of the noise they make — at each other, at intruders, sometimes seemingly at nothing in particular. If they were people, their doctors would advise them to relax, lower the stress levels of their lives, chill out before their hearts fail. To call these guys active is an understatement.

Summer rain, more than five inches of it in July and August, brings out the mushrooms — morels, puffballs, coral mushrooms and others. Deer feed on all kinds, even the deadly amanita. So do red squirrels, which eat the mushrooms fresh and also dry them for the winter by hanging them out on branches like laundry. This caching of food is a characteristic of the *Tamiasciurus* genus. If they aren't squawking, you can often locate them by the thudding sound of fresh pine cones falling. From midsummer through fall, these squirrels are busy in the treetops, nipping off cones of pine, spruce, and fir. They cut a few dozen, then

Blue grouse inhabit the dense spruce-fir forests that cover the highest elevations of the Kaibab Plateau.

climb down and gather them up, carrying them to a storage place that is also the eating site.

The eating site is indicated by a midden of cone scales that pile up over the years. Generations of squirrels might use the same location — always one squirrel at a time. Red squirrels are not communal. They fiercely defend their stores of cones, which represent survival in the winter. The midden might be two or three feet deep and 15 feet in diameter. Near its center, there is usually a solid perch — a fallen log or a tree branch — where the squirrel sits and husks the cones. The unopened ones are buried in the midden and dug out as needed. When eating, the squirrel sits up on its haunches, holding the cone with its paws like a big cob of corn. In seconds, a cone is reduced to a spindly core, the seeds eaten and the scales added to the growing midden.

When you see how fast they destroy a pine cone as big to them as a watermelon is to us, it's amazing that they can store enough food to last the winter. Of course pine seeds aren't their only food. They also store mushrooms and other vegetation. They will rob nests to eat baby birds and have an appetite for insects and carrion.

Red squirrels seem to live happily in a wide range of conditions, but not all forests are equal in their eyes. They prefer mature forests with both young and old trees and plenty of downed timber. They avoid clear-cuts and the stands of same-aged trees that grow up after replanting. Although they live in the ponderosa pine forest, they are never very far from spruce and fir. One reason might be that they need cool, moist ground in which to cache their cones; in the dry ground of the ponderosa forest, the cones will open, and the seeds will be lost.

Other animals found in this forest include porcupines, coyotes, deer mice, western harvest mice, bushy-tailed woodrats, Uinta chipmunks, least chipmunks, long-tailed weasels, and others. Wild turkeys, nothing like their pale domestic cousins, are fairly common. In the fall, the males form squads containing dozens of birds and patrol the forest in a restless fashion. Other birds include blue grouse, ruby-crowned kinglets, red-breasted nuthatches, Audubon's warblers, and mountain chickadees in the most dense parts of the forest. In meadows, meadow edges, and open aspen groves live Williamson's sapsuckers, broad-tailed hummingbirds, mountain bluebirds, and warbling vireos. In the evening near canyon rims you might well hear the booming voice of a great horned owl or the less common call of a flammulated owl. There are Mexican spotted owls in the forest, but they are rarely seen. A few western garter snakes live here despite the short summers. Among reptiles and amphibians are Great Basin spadefoot toads, horned lizards "horny toads," and Utah tiger salamanders. The salamanders present an interesting problem. They live in pools and marshes throughout the high areas of the plateau but are rarely found in their adult forms. However, if removed to the laboratory, they mature into small adults. An explanation might be that the summers are too short for larvae to become adults. But then how do they breed? Probably at least some of them are neotenic, meaning they can live and breed in their larval form.

Mountain Grasslands

An early summer evening, on the edge of a Kaibab meadow; it's a nice place to be walking, along the line between forest and open space. Such clearings are rare on the plateau, which is dominated so thoroughly by forest. Called mountain grassland parks, they occur in level basins and shallow valley bottoms. The highway from Jacob Lake to the North Rim follows a series of them, giving a false impression of their frequency. They include Pleasant Valley, DeMotte Park, Little Park, and others.

This afternoon it rained. Now the sky is clear, and I can feel that the temperature is a bit warmer under the trees than in the open. In the meadow, a low mist has begun to gather, as the warm exhalations of the turf meet the rapidly cooling evening air. A hermit thrush is calling from the top of a fir tree, filling the dusk with its lovely, spiraling, flutelike song. Against the sky I can see bats flying.

It's hard to know which of the park's bats these are. I see them only as silhouettes. They could be any of several myotis species — long-eared myotis, fringed myotis, long-legged myotis, or California myotis, all of which are found along the North Rim. Field marks, as described by their names, are not easily seen on the wing, or even in the hand, without a chance to make direct comparisons. If it were June, when the young are born, I might look for single babies clinging to their flying mothers. Bats don't make nests. They can't leave the babies behind while they forage.

I'm fairly sure they are not the most common bats in the Grand Canyon. That honor goes to western pipistrels. (This is a good but strange name for a bat. I approve. These admirable creatures deserve better-sounding titles than they are usually given.) Pipistrels are more readily identified than some other bats because they emerge early in the evening, often before sunset and often in large numbers cruising along the canyon rims. From the right vantage point, you can look down at them and pick out their gray bodies between black wings.

On the edge of this meadow several miles from the North Rim, I doubt that these "flittermice" are pipistrels, but I'd like a closer look, so I toss pebbles in the air, one at a time, almost straight above me. The bats sense them instantly and converge like baseball players to a pop fly. None is fooled for more than an instant. They quickly distinguish stone from insect and veer off in search of the real thing.

Even in the meadows, which look so regular in appearance, there are zones of vegetation. The lower ground is wetter and supports a large variety of herbaceous plants including clover, mountain dandelions, wild daisies, and buttercups. The grasslike plants in these wetter places are mostly sedge, but these make up less than 10 percent of the vegetation.

Grand Canyon National Park

A North Rim mountain grassland, or park. This mix of aspens, conifers, and meadow plants provides habitat for a larger variety of animals than any one vegetation type can by itself.

Where the meadows are better drained, grasses predominate, mixed with wildflowers including buckwheat, pussytoes, cinquefoil, saxifrage, wild daisy, phlox, mountain parsley, and clover, the last of which is a preferred food of deer.

There is some question about why these meadows are here in the first place. Surrounded by dense forest, they occur in level basins or shallow valley bottoms, and they appear to be self-maintaining, not the temporary result of forest fire or some other passing event. Some local influence discourages the growth of trees.

In places, the meadows are ringed by small conifers that seem to be encroaching, as the forest would be expected to do, but growth rings show that although they are only five feet tall, these trees are as much as 30 years old. Trees of the same age in the adjacent forest are around 30 feet tall. Something on the edges of the meadows stunts the growth of these trees.

What keeps these meadows open? There are several theories. Because melted snow and rain collect here, perhaps the ground is too wet at

Some Animals of the Boreal Zone

Spruce-Fir-Aspen Community
Ruby-crowned Kinglet
Red-breasted Nuthatch
Yellow-rumped Warbler
Mountain Bluebird
Williamson's Sapsucker
Broad-tailed Hummingbird
Dark-eyed Junco
Blue Grouse
Three-toed Woodpecker
Red Squirrel
Northern Pocket Gopher
Longtail Vole
Uinta Chipmunk

Ponderosa Pine Community
Pygmy Nuthatch
White-breasted Nuthatch
Hairy Woodpecker
Downy Woodpecker
Northern Flicker
Brown Creeper
Wild Turkey
Mountain Chickadee
Steller's Jay
Cooper's Hawk
Abert (Tassel-eared) Squirrel (South Rim)
Kaibab Squirrel (North Rim)
Mule Deer
Mountain Lion
Porcupine
Striped Skunk
Nuttall's Cottontail
Uinta Chipmunk
Deer Mouse
Mountain Short-horned Lizard (Horny Toad)

critical times, preventing seedlings from getting started and slowing the growth of established trees. If seedlings do get started, they might die in the heat of summer sun. It's also been suggested that soil bacteria emit toxins that affect woody plants but not grasses and herbaceous plants.

The meadows and the meadow edges are busy places, although much of the activity is hidden. D. Irvin Rasmussen, who in the 1930s wrote a lengthy monograph on the ecology of the Kaibab Plateau, gives brief mention to what he calls the "cantankerous meadow mouse." He gives no scientific identification for this creature (although meadow mouse is an outdated term for a vole), and I wonder what the story is behind such an unusual common name.

I know that if I lived its life, I might be cantankerous too. It's an exciting, fast-paced world down there beneath the waving grasses, a world inhabited by large numbers of pocket gophers, deer mice, and longtail voles. Although under ideal conditions a vole can live about two years, the average life expectancy of a vole in wild conditions is something like two months. It must be about the same for a mouse. To survive as a species, mice reproduce at an astonishing rate; females are almost constantly pregnant, and the young go off to meet their fate within weeks of their birth. The little rodents fall prey so easily to coyotes, owls, hawks, snakes, weasels, badgers, and other predators that I have trouble thinking of them as individual animals. They become almost a commodity — berries, as it were, on the mammalian bush, ready for the picking.

On summer evenings shortly before sunset, small bands of deer move into the meadows from the forest margins. Interestingly, it is not grass that they seek. Above all, they prefer clover but eat a variety of other herbaceous plants. Back in the 1920s, when the deer population hit its peak, they had less choice. Hundreds of deer could be seen daily. They were a tourist attraction, and for a while it was fashionable to believe the big herds were a sign of good management. A man named T. G. Pearson reported that on the evening of August 21, 1924, he counted 1,028 deer in meadows between DeMotte Park and the North Rim.

Rasmussen pointed out the irony of deer in the meadows, saying that they prefer to feed on mushrooms and browse in the surrounding forest. Large numbers in the meadows, he maintained, were a sign of poor conditions elsewhere on the range. And in the 1930s, the condition of the Kaibab deer range was receiving great attention.

The Kaibab Deer Herd

Ask biologists, or attentive biology students, about the Kaibab Plateau, and it's likely they will say "Oh yes, the deer." The Kaibab deer are famous for an incident that happened during the winter of 1924–25. For decades afterwards, the story of that incident was taught to high school and college biology students. It was a taken as a classic lesson of natural management, a warning against the danger of human manipulations not based on science, and positive proof that predators are necessary to the health of their prey. In recent years, it has also become a lesson in how history becomes muddied and how nature refuses to fit simple concepts.

It goes like this: In 1906, President Theodore Roosevelt established the Grand Canyon Game Reserve, encompassing essentially all of the Kaibab Plateau. Roosevelt had made his first visit to the canyon in 1903. On that trip he made a famous speech, saying, "Leave it as it is. You cannot improve on it. The ages have been at work on it, and man can only mar it. What you can do is to keep it for your children, your children's children, and for all who come after you, as the one great sight which every American . . . should see."

In the succeeding years, he signed three pieces of legislation that had significance for the canyon. The first created the game reserve. The second,

Grand Canyon National Park

Deer have browsed these aspen trees as high as they can reach. The photo was made in 1953.

in 1907, changed the nation's existing system of forest reserves to national forests, and in doing so, clarified their mandate. The third item was Roosevelt's personal accomplishment. He thought the canyon should be a national park, but Congress wasn't ready for that idea and refused to pass the necessary legislation. So Roosevelt took advantage of a new law, the 1906 Act for the Preservation of American Antiquities, to achieve his goal by executive declaration. The law gave the president the power to set aside national monuments (which differ from national parks primarily in the way they are established, not the way they are managed) regardless of what Congress or other forces thought about it. On January 11, 1908, Roosevelt's signature created Grand Canyon National Monument.

The idea of natural preservation for the good of the nation was a visionary concept, but it was as yet undeveloped and in many ways unsophisticated. Roosevelt had said, "Leave it as it is." But in practical terms, this translated to, "Manage it like a garden." That is, tend it and weed it and encourage it to grow the things we like to see. For its time, it was advanced thinking — the recognition that nature in its wild state was a thing of beauty, capable of lifting the human spirit and worthy of preservation.

What it failed to recognize was that in appreciating wild nature, we cannot afford to be selective. The game reserve was primarily intended to protect the Kaibab Plateau's mule deer. The monument (and later the park) had a broader mission. But neither had any room, in the eyes of early managers, for the bad influence of predators. Accordingly, wolves, mountain lions, coyotes, and bobcats were deemed undesirable. Government hunters set about trying to eliminate them with the idea that deer and other approved species would flourish. At the same time, hunting was prohibited, and large herds of sheep and cattle were ordered out of the game reserve.

As the story goes, the deer did indeed flourish, increasing in numbers until they became a major tourist attraction. "Show herds," they were called by promoters. Sometimes hundreds of deer could be seen in the meadows just north of the park boundary, and with a few exceptions, most observers thought that was just fine. How nice it was to see so many deer!

Until 1924. It was dry that summer. The range looked pretty bad. The deer looked terrible. People got worried. A committee of experts was sent to assess the range and make recommendations. What they saw that summer left them appalled. They described conditions as "deplorable, in fact they were the worst that any member of the Committee had ever seen." The committee recommended that the deer herd be reduced by as much as half, although they did not put a number either to current or desirable population levels.

There were other bleak assessments of the deer herd's health that summer, but no action was taken before winter set in. It was to be a famous winter. Many deer died, and they continued to die over succeeding years, in what was regarded as a big natural catastrophe.

How big? According to the old story, the one taught to two generations of biology students, the Kaibab deer herd went from around 3,000 or 4,000 animals in 1906 to a high of 100,000 in 1924; whereupon it crashed to below 10,000 by the mid-1930s.

Why? Simple, says the old version. After the game reserve was established, managers committed a compound error. Predators were killed, hunting was banned, and other grazing animals — as many as 200,000

sheep and 20,000 cattle — were removed from the range. With no natural enemies and reduced competition for food, the deer bred like bunnies,
ate themselves out of house and home, and met the inevitable, tragic end.
Had the population been controlled at a reasonable level (30,000 animals
was suggested), the die-off would have been avoided, a larger, stable population of deer could have been maintained, and the range would not have
suffered the long-term damage of severe overgrazing.

The Kaibab incident was cited as a clear example of the relationship
between predators and prey. Predators, it was believed, controlled the
population of their victims. It was a dynamic relationship in which the
increase of prey resulted in easy hunting, which in turn led to an increase
of predators. Soon there would be enough predators to cut the prey population back, after which the predator population would also decrease,
and the whole thing would begin again. The result was a balance whose
fine-tuned mechanisms had developed over thousands of generations. It
was a balance that, if not interrupted, would maintain all affected populations — everything from grass and trees to mountain lions — at stable,
sustainable levels.

Like so many other simple concepts, this one proved inadequate to
explain the complex workings of the natural world. As it happens, predators do not by themselves control the populations of their prey, and
there is no better example of this than the one provided a few decades
later — once again — by the Kaibab deer.

The years in question were 1946 through 1955. By this time, wildlife
management professionals agreed that predators were essential —
whether wolves, lions, coyotes, or hunters. Wolves were gone, and still
are, and many wildlife managers thought that was just fine. On the other
hand, coyotes had never been exterminated, nor had lions. Both species
could recover and do their part of the job. But of all solutions, hunting
seemed to be the best. Not only would the deer herd be kept at a sustainable level, but people would benefit from the harvest, and that would
bring political support for good game management and wild lands in
general.

With varying regulations and varying levels of public support, hunting had been permitted on the Kaibab since the fall of 1924. Our story
picks up in 1945, when 1,000 permits were issued. That year, hunters
complained about a lack of deer and insisted that something be done to

Skyrocket (Gilia aggregata) *blooms abundantly in open meadows and ponderosa pine forest on the Kaibab Plateau where it occurs in two colors, a bright showy red and a more subdued pink. It is among many herbaceous plants eaten by deer.*

Grand Canyon National Park

make their chances better. Accordingly, in the 1946 season, no doe permits were allowed, and buck permits were limited to 500. But this reduction of permits was apparently a political decision, and a temporary one at that. Hunters were dissatisfied with the number of deer, but field managers weren't convinced that populations were low at all. They estimated the deer herd at 21,000 animals, and they worried about another serious increase. They wanted more permits, not fewer, and over the next few years the Arizona Game and Fish Department doubled the number of permits each season. Despite this, the deer population rose to 57,000 in 1949. Hunting was obviously not doing the trick.

In 1950, limited doe hunting was reinstated. Also, a second, late hunt was initiated. But the population stayed high. In 1953, 10,000 permits were allowed. In 1954, 12,000 permits. Then it happened again. Despite all the increasing pressure by hunters (and despite some recovery on the

David Edwards

Rock squirrels, as their name implies, prefer areas of broken cliffs and rock outcrops throughout the canyon; on the North Rim, they are found commonly in the pinyon-juniper woodland. They grow up to 20 inches in length, including their bushy tails, and like other ground squirrels carry loads of seeds in cheek pouches.

part of lions and coyotes), there was another die-off during the winter of 1954–55. A careful survey that spring counted about 18,000 dead deer. A population boom and crash had happened even in the face of intensive predatory pressure by hunters; when something like that happens, it's nature trying to tell us that we don't understand something important.

On top of that, investigators began looking back at the long-accepted figures for the 1924 Kaibab incident and found some interesting things about the estimated population size. It turns out that at the time of the event there were few observers, few data, and large disparities among population estimates — depending on whose opinion was believed, there were 30,000, 50,000, 60,000, 70,000 or 100,000 deer on the plateau that year.

The famous graph, the one reproduced in dozens of textbooks, was based on four points, none of which was backed up by any consistent scientific counting method. Why did Rasmussen, a respected ecologist and the maker of the earliest published version of the graph (1941) give credence to those four points above all others? And why did he choose to connect them in a symmetrical curve showing an exponential rise to 1924, followed by an identical exponential fall? There is no explanation. The curve, and the choice of points on which it was based, were arbitrary.

It seems that he might have had equal justification for accepting the forest supervisor's annual estimates, which showed a more gradual rise peaking at 30,000 animals and staying essentially flat from 1923 to 1929. Yet Rasmussen put his money on the more dramatic scenario.

Two years later, Aldo Leopold took the same graph and redrew the curve to an asymmetrical sigmoid, rather like a very steep cresting wave. Again, it was an arbitrary decision not based on hard evidence. This is the curve that became bible for two generations of game managers. It was never based on anything more solid than speculation about the rise and fall of the deer population. In fact, there is some question about whether the whole event happened at all.

It was Graeme Caughley, a New Zealand biologist, who first raised objections to the accepted numbers. In a 1969 paper, he wrote, "Little can be gleaned from the original records beyond the suggestion that the population began a decline sometime in the period 1924–1930, and that this decline was probably preceded by a period of increase. Any further conclusion is speculative."

Who knows what happened on the Kaibab in 1924? There is ample evidence that the deer hammered the range. Any number of observers commented loudly about what they saw as terrible and deteriorating conditions. There were skinny deer, and they were eating everything in sight. Years later, locals referred to the time when DeMotte Park, the big meadow just north of the park entrance, was a dust bowl. But what does this mean?

Even the definitions of overgrazing are subject to question. A given patch of ground looks different through the eyes of a cattle rancher, a sheep rancher, an elk, and a deer. It is a common assumption that animal populations in an ideal world remain generally stable from one year to the next. By this assumption, big or sudden changes are the sign of a tipped balance, of something gone wrong. But what if instead of years, we looked at centuries? Then we might see a different pattern. Perhaps fluctuations in animal populations occur as episodic events. They look like catastrophes, but they are not the result of any particular management failure, nor what could be called a malfunction in a natural system. Quite the contrary; seen from a different perspective, catastrophes can look pretty good. Forest fires are a prime example of this. Their destruction is not exactly pretty to look at, but the ecological implications can be beautiful to contemplate (the recycling of nutrients back to the soil, the creation of new meadows, and further examples of the profound circle of nature.). At the very least, we have to be careful about declaring their impact harmful to the natural system.

So what are we to make of the Kaibab deer story? What really happened in 1924? What caused it? No one knows for sure, and it seems likely to endure as a puzzle and a good story.

6

Blackbrush and Rattlesnakes

The Upper Sonoran

It's a steep climb out of the Inner Gorge near Sockdolager Rapids. Up over the Vishnu Schist, through a slot in the Tapeats Sandstone, and suddenly there is open space. I am on the rim of the Inner Gorge, looking down at the river 1,000 feet below. Behind me, a flat surface stretches away for a mile or so to the next band of cliffs, then up and up 3,000 more feet to the distant South Rim. On the other side of the river, across the dark gorge, there is a corresponding flat surface. It, too, leads to vertical cliffs that soar upward some 4,000 feet to the North Rim.

This is the Tonto Platform, a sort of shelf deep within the canyon. Standing on it, I have a feeling of sudden release into a world of sky and light. It feels more like a mountain valley than a canyon.

Seen from the rim, which is the way most people see it, the Tonto looks almost flat, but like most things in the natural world, its initial appearance is deceptive. There are scattered rocky ledges. Dozens of side canyons, some only 40 or 50 feet deep, force long detours. It can take a hiker all day to go a few miles. If you haven't planned ahead, you can get into trouble. People who haven't done much canyon hiking do it all the time, looking at a map and thinking 10 or 15 miles looks like a

Some Animals of the Upper Sonoran Zone

Pinyon-Juniper Woodland
Gray Vireo
Gray Flycatcher
Bushtit
Plain Titmouse
Pinyon Jay
Black-throated Gray Warbler
Mountain Lion
Gray Fox
Mule Deer
Badger
Desert Cottontail
Stephens Woodrat
Rock Squirrel
Piñon Mouse
Fence Lizard
Sonoran Gopher Snake (S.Rim)
Great Basin Gopher Snake (N.Rim)
Western Collared Lizard

Chaparral, Mountain Scrub, and Tonto Platform
Rufous-sided Towhee
Scrub Jay
Mourning Dove
Loggerhead Shrike
Red-tailed Hawk
Black-throated Sparrow
Bighorn Sheep
Ringtail
Canyon Mouse
Cactus Mouse
Whitethroat Woodrat
Desert Woodrat
Whitetail Antelope Squirrel
Grand Canyon Rattlesnake
Western Collared Lizard
Desert Collared Lizard

reasonable distance for a day. They are wrong. In summer, temperatures easily go over 100 degrees, pushing 120 on really hot days. It would be not only uncomfortable but unwise to walk this trail then. There isn't much shade to rescue a foolhardy hiker on the Tonto in summer.

But this is early May, a nice time for strolling through the blackbrush on a narrow dirt path. Back in the gorge before I came over the edge, I could hear the Colorado's distant thunder echoing off the rock walls. It filled the space and would not let me forget the river's presence. Now, a short distance back from the rim, the sound of the river vanishes. There's no sign of water here. It feels and looks like the heart of the desert, a dry, bony world slung between the rims and the river.

A hundred feet away, apparently feeling for updrafts along the Tapeats Sandstone cliff, a vulture wobbles by on its strange, seemingly unstable wings — looking, always looking. But also smelling. Vultures, I've heard, find carrion by its odor. My nose detects only the heady mix of yucca perfume, cliffrose, desert dust, and hot rock.

There were good rains last winter, and everything is growing vigorously. Globemallow, mariposa lilies, evening primrose, desert phlox, and yucca are flowering, along with most of the cacti. Black-throated sparrows perch on the bushes and, defying the spines, on cacti also; they nest in the salt bush. One flies out as I come near, and looking in, I find squeaking young sparrows.

Two hours later, I arrive at my intended camping place, a dry wash lined with catclaw acacia trees. There is no water here, but I planned ahead and brought two gallons in my pack. Finding a flat gravel surface amid the blackbrush, I lay out my bag under the open sky. Already a few stars are winking through as the atmosphere goes transparent. Bats circle in the shadows on the edge of my night vision, themselves wisps of shadow, moving patches of darkness. There is no wind, just the astonishing, pervasive quiet of the desert. For a few minutes, my noisy cookstove pushes back the silence, but when I shut off the gas, it falls back in around me, enveloping and comforting. Like the desert, my supper is simple. Instant soup, some bread and cheese, a cup of tea, and about a quart of water. It comes out of my bottle tepid and tinted with the iodine I use for purification, but I drink it eagerly. The elixir of life.

I could not be more content. This desert seems a gentle world for people like me sitting on foam pads with bellies full of dinner and plans for tomorrow.

"But aren't you worried about snakes?" some people would ask, remembering stories of rattlers crawling into the bedrolls of snoring cowboys. "Or scorpions — what would happen if you rolled over on one in your sleep?"

The thought could make me nervous; in fact it does now and then, and I wish for a tent with its zippered security. But I rely on experience. In hundreds of nights spent sleeping on the desert ground, I've never been attacked by anything more dangerous than a mosquito, although I once nearly lost a battle with a ringtail trying to get the loaf of bread I was using for a pillow.

The desert region of Grand Canyon is a far more hospitable place than stories would tell. I think of it as a kind of paradise, especially on evenings like this. The air is warm, there are no flies or mosquitoes to bother exposed skin. I lie here beneath the sheltering sky, threatened by no discomfort, thinking what a good and little-known place is the Tonto Platform.

The Tonto Platform

The "Tonto," as it is affectionately known to all who spend much time beneath the rims, is a sort of ledge suspended in the canyon, bisected by

Grand Canyon National Park

The Tonto Platform, seen here from the area of Indian Garden, is a broad, relatively flat valley suspended between the canyon rims and the river.

the river and interrupted by numerous side canyons. It is also called the Tonto Plateau, but it isn't really a plateau at all. Prominent throughout the central canyon, it is caused by the differences in two rock layers: soft Bright Angel Shale lying on top of hard Tapeats Sandstone. The Bright Angel erodes easily. The Tapeats does not. As the Bright Angel is removed, it undercuts the layers above it, helping to widen the upper walls of the canyon and exposing the flat surface of the Tapeats.

In the western reaches of the canyon, the Tonto pinches out and is replaced by a similar structure called the Esplanade — another platform exposed by the retreat of soft rock layers above a hard layer, in this case the Esplanade Sandstone, top layer of the Supai Group. The Esplanade is present at river mile 114 (below Bass Rapid) but becomes much wider and more evident beyond mile 143 near Kanab Creek. At the eastern end of the canyon, the Marble Platform takes the place of the Tonto. Lying at about the same elevation, the Marble Platform has a similar climate, but because the base rock is Kaibab Limestone, there are noticeable plant differences — particularly an absence of blackbrush and an abundance of saltbush.

Here, in the central canyon, it's all blackbrush.

Blackbrush is a true-grit sort of plant, a brittle, homely bush with small, leathery leaves, spiny twigs, and gray branches that turn black when wet. Although its maximum height is six feet, it rarely grows over 30 inches tall on the Tonto. The bushes are well-spaced, leaving what appears to be plenty of room for walking. Wrong. The spaces never line up in straight paths, and there are just enough cacti and other prickly things to demand continual vigilance. Each bush requires an adjustment of course. Each cactus or yucca has to be stepped over. Eventually the continual weaving and twisting brings fatigue.

Somewhat better is to follow watercourses, since on the Tonto they are dry for much of the year. Streams that flow generously through higher levels often fail to make it across the thirsty Tonto, which lies exposed to sun and wind. Nonetheless, dry creek beds make for relatively easy walking; although you slog through soft sand or step carefully over boulders and rounded cobbles, it's usually easier than trekking through the blackbrush.

Creek beds are good travel routes for another reason: they provide the best chance at this level in the canyon of finding water. It might appear at rock outcrops that force underground flow to the surface. Or a thunderstorm might temporarily fill the streambed, and for days afterward, pools of water will linger beneath trees and in the shade of rock ledges. The pools won't be clear, like spring water. They might be the homes of tadpoles and insect larvae and jillions of unseen protozoans. But water in the desert is a gift for all and is always shared by many.

Along these ephemeral watercourses grow plants associated with blackbrush but not quite as capable of thriving in the open. Here, they find just enough extra moisture to survive. Acacias provide thin shade for hikers and nesting sites for blue-gray gnatcatchers. Higher in the drainages, cliffrose, rabbitbrush, and mountain joint-fir are found. Juniper trees also extend their range downward along the dry creeks. Where they meet, junipers, pinyons, and blackbrush share the same ground.

Of the birds, only black-throated sparrows seem truly at home here. Formerly called the desert sparrow, it builds a small, cup-shaped nest deep within the protection of spiny shrubs and cacti. If you're walking

Blackbrush and joint fir (Mormon tea) grow in lines along cracks in smooth bedrock, their placement determined by their need for water and soil that is not otherwise available on this piece of ground.

through the blackbrush and startle a small feathered missile from the bush, it's likely to have been a black-throated sparrow. Mourning doves and loggerhead shrikes also frequent the blackbrush during summer.

The doves are interesting for their ability to deal with conditions as they find them. Doves nest on the ground, or in the fork of a tree branch, or in an old nest built by some other bird. They live happily in cities wherever there are trees or shrubs. They also do well in the desert, as long as there is water in the vicinity. At the canyon, they live everywhere except the highest spruce-fir forests. Both adults incubate eggs, but only the male makes the familiar mourning call, a sound I have always thought was more soothing than sad.

Throughout the canyon, mammals are more abundant than birds, and this is particularly true of the Tonto. Because of their nocturnal habits, however, you don't see many of them. Their presence is indicated by burrows in the shelter of shrubs and cacti — burrows everywhere, once you start looking for them. It's hard to know what animals made them. We can only peer down these little holes and think about the mice and chipmunks and shrews and kangaroo rats and skunks and squirrels who lie curled up, sleeping and cool in their subterranean nests. Also on the Tonto are woodrats, or packrats. They don't dig burrows. Instead, they build houses of sticks, leaves, chunks of bark, dry stems, prickly-pear lobes, and just about anything else they can haul. The houses are usually tangled around the base of a shrub or cactus and are virtually impregnable. A single woodrat might maintain several houses, living in one and using the others for temporary shelter.

Shelter from heat and cold? Yes, but also from predators. Like the other rodents and tasty morsels of the desert, woodrats need cover from coyotes, ringtails, gray foxes, spotted skunks, and bobcats. And, seemingly most appropriate in the spiny desert, snakes, including the Grand Canyon rattlesnake — our old acquaintance *C. v. abyssus.*

A place like the Tonto must be pretty good from a snake's point of view. The ground is flat and hard. There is cover beneath the shrubs and under numerous rock ledges. And there is a big variety of snake food, everything from small rodents and toads to the occasional bird. Snakes eat just about anything they can swallow: lizards, mice, woodrats, ground squirrels. Young snakes and some species in which the adults are small prefer lizards, maybe because they are thin and easier to swallow than plump mice.

Of all the snakes in Grand Canyon, rattlers hold the preeminent position, not because they are the boldest or strongest or most numerous, but because they are rattlers — poisonous, cold-blooded, and attention-grabbing. Much of what I know about rattlers I have learned from Laurence M. Klauber's superb book *Rattlesnakes.* Most of what anyone knows can be found in its pages, and if Klauber's enthusiasm does not warm our hearts toward snakes, the facts of their lives certainly inspire feelings of goose bumpy fascination.

I can only speculate about how this place must appear to a rattler. Whereas the canyon rims define my perception, and my thoughts are always drawn off to some distant butte, the rattler lives by a different set of parameters, a perspective never higher than a few inches above the ground. Its eyes are poor, but its sense of smell is keen, and it also possesses a heat-imaging ability through orifices, or pits, on either side of its head (hence "pit viper").

Rattlers hunt mostly by lying in wait beside animal trails at night and during the crepuscular times of day, those in-between times when reality blurs and creatures walk the line between darkness and light. Then the snake, with its multiple senses, has an advantage. Detecting prey, it strikes quickly, injects venom, and then backs off while the poison takes effect. With something small like a mouse the process can be a matter of seconds. Once the mouse stops moving, the snake approaches the motionless body with great care, as if cautious of defensive actions on the part of its victim. With flickering, chemically sensitive tongue, the rattler inquires into the condition of dinner. Finally, beginning with the nose, it begins swallowing.

Klauber says that when striking birds, reptiles, and amphibians, rattlers do not back off. Rather, they hold tight. He thinks this is because in the time it takes for the venom to act, birds could fly too far for the snake to find them; and in the case of reptiles or amphibians, venom is slower to act, giving them more escape time.

A Grand Canyon rattlesnake moves among the spiny pads of prickly-pear cactus. Generally shy and reclusive, rattlers are not seen by most visitors to the canyon.

Michael Collier

Although ambush is their most common hunting technique, rattlers can enter burrows and rock crevices, apparently tipped off by the smell of prey. Seeking shelter from the sun, rattlers also crawl into burrows during the heat of the day, and become in Klauber's words "advantageously located to make a meal of the owner." So much for the cozy protection of burrows.

In captivity, rattlers do an appalling thing. If it happens that two snakes seize the same mouse or rat and begin swallowing from opposite ends, one snake may wind up devouring the other. If the snakes are of equal size, it's a matter of which one first gets its jaws over the other one's face. After that, there is no rescue for the swallowed. This happens as if by accident; snakes are not usually cannibals.

Mealtime in general is hazardous for snakes. I once saw one that had been clawed open and killed from the inside by a rat it had swallowed too fast. The rat had eventually died (it was still in the snake) but in dying, it had managed a nasty sort of revenge. In another case, a specimen of Sonoran lyre snake now in the Grand Canyon National Park collection was found dead with a yellow-backed spiny lizard that was too big to swallow stuck in its jaws. The lizard's prominent spiny scales prevented the snake from regurgitating its poorly chosen meal, and both animals died. Mind you, the snake had not suffocated. Snakes' windpipes are not like ours. They end not at the back of the mouth but at the tip of the lower jaw and can be extended outside the mouth like a snorkel while swallowing.

The average meal for a rattler, according to Klauber, is about 40 percent of its body weight. I imagine how that would be for me. Weighing 140 pounds, I'd have to swallow a 52-pound fish in one bite. Even for snakes this can be problematic. In yet another instance of mealtime excess, a snake succeeded in swallowing its prey but was so weighted down that it couldn't move out of the sun and died — you might say from overheating as a result of overeating.

Other snakes that live on the Tonto include the California kingsnake, desert striped whipsnake (also called racer), Sonoran gopher snake (generally on the south side of the river), Great Basin gopher snake (generally on the north side), and the Mojave patch-nosed snake. None of these is venomous like a rattler. They finish off their prey by constriction, or by simply swallowing them alive. The way a desert striped whipsnake hauls a living frog or bird into its long gullet makes quick death by the venom of a rattler seem positively humane.

We don't think of snakes as having much in the way of emotion. Snakes seem the ultimate bloodless predators — cold and efficient — and this is probably not far from the truth. Whereas birds are obviously emotional creatures, the reptilian brain is often used as the perfect example of a pure biological machine. Be that as it may, snakes have a vulnerable side. In the canyon, snakes make meals for skunks, badgers, coyotes, ringtails, eagles, hawks, and other snakes, particularly kingsnakes and racers. Kingsnakes are known to have resistance to rattler venom, making them highly effective predators. Hawks yank snakes into the air and drop them repeatedly until dead. There are reports of ground squirrels, rats, wild turkeys, and even mice killing snakes. In places other than Grand Canyon, rattlers have fallen prey to rainbow trout, Latin American spiders, swarms of Mormon crickets, and at least one bullfrog. A collared lizard was found having caught a rattler; the observer approached, the lizard dropped the snake, which turned and bit the lizard, and the lizard died. Sad story; collared lizards are among the most colorful and interesting of the canyon's reptiles, always a pleasure to see. Finally, although I have found no confirmation of this, I can't imagine that ravens, who seem so talented in all other regards, leave themselves out of the action.

Among a rattlesnake's major enemies, surprisingly, are deer. Klauber again, quoting from a letter written to him: "I have seen buck deer kill rattlesnakes on three different occasions. They just back up and run and stomp them; then they turn and do it again. After a buck deer gets through, there isn't a piece of rattlesnake over one inch in length. A buck deer really makes sure that they're dead."

Lacking legs or wings, snakes run a certain risk from geography: they fall off cliffs. They get trapped in canyon potholes and starve or drown. They get stranded on sun-heated ground and can't find shelter; summer temperatures on the Tonto can kill a snake in about 10 or 12 minutes. Similarly, cold weather makes them incapable of moving. The cold might not kill them outright, but unless they've made it to shelter, it leaves them exposed and helpless to warm-blooded predators.

A weathered juniper tree seems to have the story of its hard life written in its eccentric shape.

PJ Woodland

I'm not sure why I find the Tonto Platform so appealing. Perhaps it has something to do with openness. When it comes right down to it, other areas within the Upper Sonoran Zone are much more interesting in a biologic sense. Above the Tonto are found chaparral, mountain scrub, and pinyon-juniper woodland; these three often occur together or adjacent to one another and support a bigger variety of plants and animals, especially birds, than any place on the Tonto.

I once camped in an area of mixed chaparral, pinyon, and juniper beneath the North Rim. The night was quiet, and I slept like a stone, completely unaware of the mountain lion that came past in the dark. The next morning I found clear tracks just yards from where I'd been sleeping. I followed them for about a half mile until they disappeared on slickrock.

Utah agave lives for 15 to 25 years before sending up a flowering stem, after which it dies. Also called century plants, agave are distinguished from yucca by the toothed margins of its sharp-pointed leaves.

Through binoculars, from a high point, I spent an hour looking for that lion. I thought he'd be dozing somewhere, lying out on a sunny ledge. I never saw him, but knowing he was there made a big difference in the way I felt about the place. Lions are more appealing than the scorpions that capture my attention on the Tonto.

In speaking about chaparral and other shrub communities, it makes sense to broaden our focus and have a look at pinyon-juniper woodland, which so often occurs in conjunction with the canyon's various desert-scrub associations. The pinyon at Grand Canyon is *Pinus edulis,* or Colorado pinyon, recognized by its paired needles. Another species, single-leaf pinyon, predominates to the north and west of Grand Canyon throughout the Great Basin Desert. The junipers here are mostly Utah juniper, *Juniperus osteosperma.* Oneseed juniper *(J. monosperma)* also occurs in the park but is less common.

Pinyons and junipers grow together in such close association that you almost never think of one without the other, hence the popular name "PJ." This is the characteristic forest cover of the southwestern uplands, inhabiting large areas of Arizona, Utah, Colorado, Nevada, and New Mexico. Neither tree grows much taller than 20 or 30 feet, with a normal average of about half that. The individual trees grow a respectful distance from one another, almost never forming the sort of impenetrable thickets found in riparian areas or in the spruce and fir zone of the North Rim.

What this means to an eye accustomed to forests of larger trees is that the PJ can look somewhat paltry. Biologists use the term woodland as if apologizing for the lack of a high shady canopy. But everything is relative. On a hot day, no spruce tree offers better shade than a gnarly old juniper. On a cold winter morning, no eastern oak burns more warmly. And no tree anywhere can match the fragrance of juniper smoke, which with one whiff can conjure up vivid memories of campfires and desert nights long past.

The pinyon is loved for its nutlike seeds. With 2,800 calories per pound, pinyon nuts have long been an important food item for animals and people in the Southwest. You have to get to them quickly before the jays and rodents do. The ground beneath pinyons is universally littered with hollow, rounded nutshells, each one exhibiting a neat hole where some creature nibbled into it. If you find an apparently overlooked nutshell, one without a hole, it is almost certainly empty and not worth opening.

Both trees, but especially junipers, take on eccentric, twisted shapes when battered by wind and age. Hardly a painting or a photograph of the canyon fails to include at least one weather-beaten juniper perched on a spectacular, exposed crag. It seems the perfect symbol for the hardiness and beauty of life standing against the faceless unknown.

Pinyon-juniper woodland occurs on both rims and for some distance below the rims, at elevations between 4,000 and 7,500 feet, but like all the elevation ranges for plants in the canyon this one is subject to local revision. PJ crowds the high edge of the North Rim, where warm air welling up from the canyon creates a limited zone of favorable climate — for instance, at Cape Royal, which is 7,865 feet high. There are large stands on the west, north, and east sides of the Kaibab Plateau, and all

Birds of the Rim

On both sides of the canyon, a few species of birds are prominent. Ravens, who never seem to take life too seriously, perch in juniper snags or play tag with each other far out over the abyss. Their solid black feathers can look white when glinting in the sun. Vultures are also common, recognized by their tippy, unstable soaring flight and wings held in a broad V (unlike eagles and falcons, who soar with wings held in a flat plane).

The small, fast-moving acrobats flying like buzzbombs past the scenic viewpoints are white-throated swifts and violet-green swallows. At one time, biologists grouped them as similar species. No wonder; they can be hard to tell apart and provide a good example of convergent evolution. Although swifts are related to hummingbirds, and swallows are songbirds, they both evolved to the same way of living—catching insects on the wing. The swallow has a solid white breast and a rounder body than the swift. The swift flies with an unusual twinkling motion of its wings that makes it appear as if the wings are alternating. Also, swifts usually fly faster than swallows.

across the South Rim. In addition, it spills down off the canyon rims onto terraces and mesas and rocky slopes.

As a rule, PJ grows where snowfall is light and winter temperatures are not severe—although it survives occasional extremes of minus 20 degrees Fahrenheit and lower. It prefers a precipitation range of 12 to 18 inches and tolerates anything from 8 to 20 inches. Of the two, juniper tolerates warmer and drier conditions; where pinyon fades out, juniper survives in pure stands. The reverse happens at high elevations, with pinyon climbing into colder regions than juniper can tolerate. Generally, juniper is the better pioneer. Where aridity or heat prevents pinyon seedlings from surviving on their own, junipers act as nursery trees, leading the way into new areas, providing shaded seedbeds for the pinyons. This explains why the trees are so often seen growing in close pairs.

It seems that the only reliable constants in PJ woodland are the pinyons and junipers themselves. Other vegetation varies widely, depending on numerous factors. The PJ seems to occur as an overlay on top of whatever else would naturally exist, be it sagebrush, blackbrush, manzanita, grama grass, yucca, scrub oak, or something else.

In the highest areas, sagebrush and a few other shrubs grow among the PJ, but the diversity and density is generally low. Being a cold-desert shrub, sagebrush finds the inner canyon too warm. It does best in places like Nevada's Great Basin, or the high, windswept, snowy plains of Wyoming. Only in limited parts of the Grand Canyon do favorable conditions exist—on higher but dry areas of the South Rim and on the western section of the North Rim.

Moving below the rims, we find among the PJ a richer understory, beginning with deciduous shrubs like Gambel oak, serviceberry, snowberry, and New Mexico locust. At lower elevations, those give way to evergreen chaparral species: scrub oak, manzanita, joint-fir, silktassel, Apache-plume, and others. Yet lower, we find blackbrush, snakeweed, rabbitbrush, mountain-mahogany, cliffrose, and barberry, and many other desert-scrub species. A unique situation occurs on slickrock terraces like the Esplanade. By its nature, the cracked and pocked surface collects far more water in some places than others, allowing an interesting mix of drought-tolerant species with plants that require more water.

The above description omits the many herbaceous plants and non-shrubby plants that occur in all these various associations. They include yuccas, agaves, and nolinas; prickly-pear, grizzly bear, cholla, and hedgehog cacti; buckwheat, penstemon, Indian paintbrush, Colorado four-o'clock, beeplant, larkspur, and more — far too many to list here. Among the PJ, the blooming season goes from late March to early June, and

A young mountain short-horned lizard, or horny toad. Horned lizards are born alive in "litters" of up to 30 thumbnail-sized replicas of adults.

Grand Canyon National Park

Perched on the South Rim, a juniper tree withstands the worst of canyon weather.

after a moist winter, the show is enough to send anyone digging for a guidebook to flowers.

How to characterize the animals that make their homes in this wonderfully diverse and widespread woodland? With the exception of the most dedicated riparian creatures (like treefrogs and water striders), you can find the bulk of Grand Canyon animals somewhere, at some time of the year, among the pinyons and junipers. Mule deer winter among the PJ. Mountain lions and bobcats live among the broken rimrocks. Bighorn sheep, who normally shun forest and thick scrub, can see far enough among the little trees to be comfortable — as long as there are cliffs nearby. Porcupines shuffle out of the higher forests to gnaw on pinyon bark. One June day, I found a wild turkey in the chaparral, far from its accustomed ponderosa pines. There are desert cottontails, black-tailed jackrabbits, rock squirrels, chipmunks, gray foxes, and more.

Some animals, however, are associated primarily with the PJ, and of these, none comes to mind more quickly than the pinyon jays who fly through the forest in raucous laughing gangs. Also the pinyon mice, who live exclusively on pinyon nuts and dwell where pinyons and cliffs are found together; of course vast areas of the canyon meet these conditions. Woodrats don't need the pinyon trees but are often found among them, especially where broken rock provides good nesting sites.

Collared lizards and fence lizards live in the PJ, as do the Sonoran mountain kingsnake and the Great Basin rattler. And lizardlike skinks: the Great Basin skink on the North Rim, the many-lined skink on the South. What a name. It makes you wonder what a skink says when it wants to insult another skink.

I prefer horny toads, more accurately but less poetically called short-horned lizards. They are very common, and this is a pleasing thing. Few lizards excite such affection from people — especially children, who delight in their minidinosaur appearance. They give live birth to as many as 20 babies that look just like adults but smaller. About the size of nickels, they waddle along the stony ground, charming anyone who comes across them.

I know about them because I lived for six years in a PJ forest south of Grand Canyon. There were horny toads all around my house, and every year I watched for the little ones. They pleased me as much as the broad-tailed hummingbirds that flashed like iridescent jewels among the wildflowers. By any conventional standard, the birds were beautiful and the horny toads were grotesque, but I found them both delightful. I suppose in that sense the lizards have something in common with the juniper. Both are prickly. Neither possesses what you would call grace. They have been shaped and sharpened by the hard conditions of the desert. Yet they both arouse the warm affections of those who know them.

Prickly-pear cactus in bloom.

Plant Communities Guide Section

South Rim

Most of the South Rim developed area is covered by a mix of pinyon-juniper woodland and ponderosa pine forest. This makes for a pleasant diversity. To see pure stands of pinyon-juniper, you can head south toward Valle, or east to Desert View. As the road drops in elevation, the ponderosa pines disappear, yielding the ground to pinyon, juniper, yucca, grama grass, and other plants of this association. As for ponderosa pine, a nearly pure stand can be seen in the area around Grandview Point, which is the highest ground on the South Rim.

Directly below the rim at Grand Canyon Village, local climatic conditions support stands of Douglas-fir. These are anomalous, the result of the protected northern exposure. More typical of the vegetation immediately below the rim is mountain scrub and chaparral mixed with pinyon-juniper woodland. The popular Rim Trail, which leads from Yavapai Point past Grand Canyon Village and all the way to Hermits Rest, provides excellent examples of these plants.

Any trail into the canyon will lead through a variety of plant communities. The Bright Angel Trail is a good choice because it drops quickly for the first 3,000 feet. Mountain scrub and chaparral prevail as far as Mile-and-a-half

House. At Indian Garden, several springs (and overflow from the pumping station) combine to make Garden Creek a permanent stream. There are cottonwood trees here, and other riparian plants. The stream soon cuts through the Tapeats Sandstone into a narrows, and although the cottonwoods disappear, riparian vegetation continues most of the way to the river. If you take the trail to Plateau Point instead of continuing on the Bright Angel to the river, you cross the Tonto Platform through blackbrush desert scrub.

You can make a similar journey by car on the road east of the park to Cameron, and beyond to Lees Ferry. The highway drops off the plateau (down the East Kaibab Monocline) and cruises through miles of desert scrub. It is not precisely the same as the Tonto Platform, because the substrate is limestone, not the shale and sandstone of the Tonto; nonetheless, many plants and animals are the same.

To visit the Lower Sonoran Zone you must hike to the canyon bottom or float the river. You can drive to the river at Lees Ferry, but the elevation there is just a bit too high for Lower Sonoran. The Diamond Creek road through the Hualapai Reservation is the single exception. It meets the river at Mile 227. The road begins at Peach Springs and is unpaved; the required permit can be obtained from tribal authorities in Peach Springs.

Although it is outside the Grand Canyon and the park, the road to Pearce Ferry is worth mentioning here. Interesting not only for its geological perspective (a fine view of the Grand Wash Cliffs and the mouth of the Grand Canyon) the road passes through some pristine samples of Mohave Desert, including what might be the country's finest Joshuatree forest. Vegetation in the western end of the canyon is a mix of Mohave, Sonoran, and Great Basin desert types, giving it an unusually rich floral diversity.

North Rim

The road from Jacob Lake to the North Rim passes through all the various forest types of the Kaibab Plateau, including pure stands of ponderosa pine, spruce-fir forest, and alpine grassland. Inside park boundaries, the Cape Royal Road traces the slope of the Walhalla Plateau, which extends like a long peninsula into the heart of the canyon. It begins at around 9,000 feet in elevation, where spruce and fir dominate, and descends gradually into ponderosa pine forest. At Cape Royal, there is pinyon-juniper woodland — not because the general elevation is that much lower but because warm air welling up from the canyon creates an appropriate microclimate.

Unknown to most visitors are several rough, unpaved roads that lead to isolated viewpoints, including Point

Sublime, Tiyo Point, and Swamp Point. Open only when conditions allow (ask at the Park Service information desk in the Grand Canyon Lodge), these roads give access to the old growth of the North Rim, quite a contrast to the logged Kaibab National Forest lands adjacent to the park. Yet the park forest is not exactly in its natural state. Nearly a century of fire control has permitted the invasion of ponderosa forest by white fir, and the growth of a dense understory. In the natural scheme, white fir and understory plants would be suppressed periodically by fire, while mature ponderosa trees, protected by thick bark and massive trunks, would survive. The Park Service feels the need for fire to play its natural role on the North Rim but is understandably cautious about the correct approach. A big fire fueled by the current congested understory could kill even the old ponderosas.

Below the North Rim, vegetation zones resemble those at similar elevations on the other side of the canyon. Only one trail gets heavy use here, the North Kaibab. For some distance below the rim, it is shaded by a mixed forest of fir and ponderosa pine, giving way to dense mountain scrub and chaparral. At Roaring Springs, and from there all the way to Phantom Ranch, the trail follows some of the canyon's best riparian habitat. It's a fairly strenuous trip, but there is simply no better way to experience the canyon's marvelous diversity than by walking (or riding a mule) from one rim to the other on the Kaibab Trail.

CHECKLIST TO SELECTED PLANTS

HERBACEOUS SPECIES

Venus Maidenhair Fern	*Adiantum capillus-veneris*
Slender Lipfern	*Cheilanthes feei*
Lipfern	*Notholaena parryi*
Woodsia Fern	*Woodsia mexicana*
Western Bracken Fern	*Pteridium aquilinum*
Smooth Horsetail	*Equisetum laevigatum*
Spikemoss	*Selaginella mutica*
Century Plant	*Agave utahensis*
Banana Yucca	*Yucca baccata*
Western Wheatgrass	*Agropyron smithii*
Arizona Three-awn	*Aristida arizonica*
Blue Grama	*Bouteloua gracilis*
Cheatgrass	*Bromus tectorum*
Sheep Fescue	*Festuca ovina*
Mountain Muhly	*Muhlenbergia montana*
Indian Ricegrass	*Oryzopsis hymenoides*
Giant Common Reed	*Phragmites australis*
Mutton Grass	*Poa fendleriana*
Squirreltail	*Sitanion hystrix*
Needle and Thread	*Sipa comata*
Rocky Mountain Iris	*Iris missouriensis*
Palmer's Onion	*Allium palmeri*
Weakstem Mariposa (Winding Mariposa Tulip)	*Calochortus flexuous*
Sego Lily	*Calochortus nuttallii*
Blue Dicks	*Dichelostemma pulchellum*
Mountain Bells	*Fritillaria atropurpurea*
Death Camas (Elegant Camas)	*Zigadenus elegans*
Calypso Orchid	*Calypso bulbosa*
Spotted Coralroot	*Corallorhiza maculata*
Stream Orchid	*Epipactis gigantea*
Broadleaf Cattail	*Typha latifolia*
Spreading Dogbane	*Apocynum androsaemifolium*
Whorled Milkweed	*Asclepias subverticallata*
Orange Milkweed	*Asclepias tuberosa*
Fringed Milkvine	*Sarcostemma cynanchoides*
James' Popcorn	*Cryptantha jamesii*
Purple Gromwell	*Lithospermum multiflorum*

Franciscan Lungwort	*Mertensia franciscana*
MacDougall's Lungwort	*Mertensia macdougalii*
Parry Bellflower	*Companula parryi*
Cardinal Flower	*Lobelia cardinalis*
Fendler Sandwort	*Arenaria Fendleri*
Mojave Sandwort	*Arenaria macradenia*
Common Chickweed	*Stellaria media*
Rocky Mountain Bee Plant	*Cleome serrulata*
Common Yarrow	*Achillea millefolium*
Mountain Dandelion (Orange Agoseris)	*Agoseris aurantiaca*
False Dandelion	*Agoseris glauca*
Pigmy Pussytoes	*Antennaria arida*
Mountain Pussytoes	*Antennaria parvifolia*
Meadow Arnica	*Arnica chamissonis*
Ragleaf Bahia	*Bahia dissecta*
Yellow Tackstem	*Calycoseris parryi*
Arizona Thistle	*Cirsium arizonicum*
Wheeler's Thistle	*Cirsium wheeleri*
Elegant Daisy	*Erigeron concinnus*
Princely Daisy	*Erigeron formosissimus*
Reddome Blanketflower	*Gaillardia pinnatifida*
Mountain Gumplant	*Grindelia aphanactis*
Broom Snakeweed (Matchbrush)	*Gutierrezia sarothrae*
Spiny Goldenweed	*Haplopappus spinulosus*
Kansas Sunflower	*Helianthus annuus*
Hairy Golden Aster	*Heterotheca villosa*
Fineleaf Wollywhite	*Hymenopappus filifolius*
Stemless Goldflower	*Hymenoxys acaulis*
Sand Aster	*Leucelene ericoides*
Hoary Aster	*Machaeranthera canescens*
Desert Dandelion	*Malacothrix glabrata*
Pore-leaf	*Porophyllum gracile*
Greenstem Paperflower	*Psilostrophe sparsiflora*
Redspike Mexican Hat	*Ratibida columnaris*
Axhead Butterweed	*Senecio multilobatus*
Tall Goldenrod	*Solidago altissima*
Wire Lettuce	*Stephanomeria tenuifolia*
Easter Daisy	*Townsendia exscapa*
Yellow Salsify	*Tragopogon dubius*
Golden Crownbeard	*Verbesina encelioides*
Goldeneye	*Viguiera multiflora*

Desert Aster	*Xylorhiza tortifolia*
Field Bindweed	*Convolvulus arvensis*
Stiffarm Rock Cress	*Arabis perennans*
Rough Wallflower	*Erysimum asperum*
Peppergrass	*Lepidium montanum*
Arizona Bladderpod	*Lesquerella arizonica*
Purple Bladderpod	*Lesquerella purpurea*
Watercress	*Nasturtium officinale*
Golden Prince's Plume	*Stanleya pinnata*
Hedgemustard	*Thelypodiopsis linearifolia*
Wild Candytuft	*Thlaspi montanum*
Stinking Gourd	*Cucurbita foetidissima*
Fendler Spurge	*Euphorbia fendleri*
Golden Smoke	*Corydalis aurea*
Green Gentian	*Frasera speciosa*
Storksbill	*Erodium cicutarium*
Purple Geranium	*Geranium caespitosum*
Scalloped Phacelia	*Phacelia crenulata*
Grand Canyon Phacelia	*Phacelia glechomaefolia*
Drummond's Pennyroyal	*Hedeoma drummondii*
Horehound	*Marrubium vulgare*
Field Mint	*Mentha arvensis*
African Sage	*Salvia aethiopis*
Desert Purple Sage	*Salvia dorrii*
King's Locoweed	*Astragalus calycosus*
Mottled Locoweed	*Astragalus lentiginosus*
White Prairie Clover	*Dalea candida*
Grassleaf Peavine	*Lathyrus graminifolius*
Utah Lotus	*Lotus utahensis*
Wright's Lotus	*Lotus wrightii*
Hill's Lupine	*Lupinus hillii*
Yellow Sweet Clover	*Melilotus indica*
Golden Pea	*Thermopsis rhombifolia*
Pine Clover	*Trifolium pinetorum*
American Vetch	*Vicia americana*
Blueflax	*Linum lewisii*
Adonis Blazing Star	*Mentzelia multiflora*
Globemallow	*Sphaeralcea grossulariaefolia*
Running Sand Verbena	*Abronia elliptica*
Trailing Windmills	*Allionia incarnata*
Menodora	*Menodora scabra*
Red Fireweed	*Epilobium angustifolium*
Scarlet Beeblossom	*Gaura coccinea*

Tufted Evening Primrose	*Oenothera caespitosa*
Hooker's Evening Primrose	*Oenothera hookeri*
Tall Yellow Primrose	*Oenothera longissima*
Clustered Broomrape	*Orobanche fasciculata*
Flatbud Prickle Poppy	*Argemone munita*
Skyrocket	*Ipomopsis aggregata*
Ipomopsis	*Ipomopsis multiflora*
Desert Mountain Phlox	*Phlox austromontana*
Longleaf Plox	*Phlox longifolia*
Desert Trumpet	*Eriogonum inflatum*
Redroot Eriogonum	*Eriogonum racemosum*
Western Bistort	*Polygonum bistortoides*
Miner's Lettuce	*Montia perfoliata*
Spring Beauty	*Claytonia rosea*
Dwarf Lewisia	*Lewisia pygmaea*
Umbrella Rock Jasmine	*Androsace septentrionalis*
Whitevein Wintergreen	*Pyrola picta*
Canary Columbine	*Aquilegia chrysantha*
Larkspur	*Delphinium nelsoni*
Naked Delphinium	*Delphinium scaposum*
Buttercup	*Ranunculus oreogenes*
Wild Strawberry	*Fragaria ovalis*
Cliff Cinquefoil	*Potentilla osterhoutii*
Bastard-Toadflax	*Comandera umbellata*
Coral Bells	*Heuchera sanguinea*
Wyoming Paintbrush	*Castilleja linariaefolia*
Maiden Blue-eyed Mary	*Collinsia parviflora*
Twining Snapdragon	*Antirrhinum filipes*
Scarlet Monkeyflower	*Mimulus cardinalis*
Yellow Monkeyflower	*Mimulus guttatus*
Twotone Owl's-clover	*Orthocarpus purpureo-albus*
Juniper Lousewort	*Pedicularis centranthera*
Southwestern Penstemon	*Penstemon barbatus*
Eaton's Firecracker	*Penstemon eatonii*
Thickleaf Penstemon	*Penstemon pachyphyllus*
Palmer's Penstemon	*Penstemon palmeri*
Utah Penstemon	*Penstemon utahensis*
Woolly Mullein	*Verbascum thapsus*
American Brooklime	*Veronica americana*
Desert Tobacco	*Nicotiana trigonophylla*
Mountain Parsley	*Pseudocymopterus montanus*
Wright Verbena	*Glandularia bipinnatifida*
New Mexican Vervain	*Berbena macdougalii*

Canada Violet	*Viola canadensis*
Kidneyleaf Violet	*Viola nephrophylla*
Pinyon Mistletoe	*Arceuthobium divaricatum*
Juniper Mistletoe	*Phoradendron juniperinum*
Canyon Grape	*Vitis arizonica*
Linarialeaf Penstemon	*Penstemon linarioides*
Sacred Datura (Jimsonweed)	*Datura meteloides*
Desert Four O' Clock	*Mirabilis multiflora*
Sulphur Eriogonum	*Erigonum umbellatum*

CACTI

Arizona Beehive Cactus	*Coryphantha vivipara*
Engelmann Hedgehog Cactus	*Echinocereus engelmannii*
Claretcup Cactus	*Echinocereus triglochidiatus*
California Barrel Cactus	*Ferocactus acanthodes*
Beavertail Cactus	*Opuntia basilaris*
Grizzly Bear Cactus	*Opuntia erinacea*
Desert Prickly Pear	*Opuntia phaeacantha*
Whipple Cholla	*Opuntia whipplei*

TREES AND SHRUBS

Oneseed Juniper	*Juniperus monosperma*
Utah Juniper	*Juniperus osteosperma*
Torrey Mormon Tea	*Ephedra torreyana*
Mormon Tea	*Ephedra viridis*
White Fir	*Abies concolor*
Two-needle Pinyon	*Pinus edulis*
Ponderosa Pine	*Pinus ponderosa*
Common Douglas-fir	*Pseudotsuga menziesii*
Western Mountain Maple	*Acer glabrum*
Ashleaf Maple (Box-elder)	*Acer negundo*
Squaw Bush	*Rhus trilobata*
Poison-ivy	*Toxicodendron radicans*
Desert Barberry	*Berberis fremontii*
Creeping Barberry	*Berberis repens*
Water Birch	*Betula occidentalis*
Knowlton Hornbeam	*Ostrya knowltonii*
Desert-willow	*Chilopsis linearis*
Arizona Honeysuckle	*Lonicera arizonica*
Blue Elderberry	*Sambucus cerulea*
Mountain Snowberry	*Symphoricarpos oreophilus*

Canotia	*Canotia holacantha*
Four-wing Saltbush	*Atriplex canescens*
Winter Fat	*Ceratoides lanata*
Big Sagebrush	*Artemisia tridentata*
Rabbitbrush	*Chrysothamnus nauseosus*
Brittlebush	*Encelia farinosa*
Groundsel	*Senecio douglassii*
Red-osier Dogwood	*Cornus stolonifera*
Greasebush	*Forsellesia nevadensis*
Roundleaf Buffaloberry	*Shepherdia rotundifolia*
Pointleaf Manzanita	*Arctostaphylos pungens*
Gambel Oak	*Quercus gambelii*
Shrub Live Oak	
(Turbinella Oak)	*Quercus turbinella*
Ocotillo	*Fouquieria splendens*
Catclaw Acacia	
(Gregg Catclaw)	*Acacia greggii*
California Redbud	*Cercis occidentalis*
Honey Mesquite	*Prosopis glandulosa*
New Mexican Locust	*Robinia neomexicana*
Fragrant Ash	*Fraxinus cuspidata*
Scrubby Wild Buckwheat	*Eriogonum corymbosum*
Wright Buckwheat	*Eriogonum wrightii*
Buckbrush	*Ceanothus fendleri*
Utah Juneberry	*Amelanchier utahensis*
Mountain-mahogany	*Cercocarpus ledifolius*
Fernbush	*Chamaebatiaria millifolium*
Blackbrush	*Coleogyne ramosissima*
Cliffrose	*Cowania mexicana*
Apache-plume	*Fallugia paradoxa*
Rock Mat	*Petrophytum caespitosum*
Desert Almond	*Prunus fasciculata*
Arizona Rose	*Rosa arizonica*
Common Hoptree	*Ptelea trifoliata*
Fremont Cottonwood	*Populus fremontii*
Quaking Aspen	*Populus tremuloides*
Coyote Willow	*Salix exigua*
Fendler Bush	*Fendlera rupicola*
Mock-orange	*Phildelphus microphyllus*
Wax Currant	*Ribes cereum*
Tamarisk	*Tamarix chinensis*
Netleaf Hackberry	*Celtis reticulata*
Creosotebush	*Larrea divaricata*

7
Wild West
The Lower Sonoran

From various points along the South Rim near Grand Canyon Village, you can see on the far western horizon a line of forested peaks. Their summits are gentle. They look a bit like the knuckles of a fist arrayed above the level plain of the canyon rim.

On hazy summer days they can disappear entirely, lost behind a scrim of bad air that oozes up from the Los Angeles basin. On good days, mostly in winter, the mountains pop into view with such clarity that the distance is hard to estimate; you could easily guess 30 miles or 130.

They are the Uinkaret Mountains, 65 air miles northeast of Grand Canyon Village. Volcanic in origin, they consist of cinder cones and lava flows aligned in a north-south direction. They are part of a volcanic field that contains hundreds of eruptive vents on both sides of the river, some on the very edge of the canyon. This is the area where lava dams blocked the canyon over a million years ago.

The highest of the Uinkarets is Mt. Trumbull (8,026 feet). The other knuckles are named Emma (7,700 feet), Logan (7,865 feet), and Petty Knoll. They preside over the western Grand Canyon, rising just outside the park boundary in a remote, little-visited region called the Arizona

Strip — a land of open spaces, broad grassy valleys, and long fault scarps that tip off into the most tangled and complicated and confusing geography in the Grand Canyon.

Uinkaret Mountains

The western canyon. Most visitors have no idea that it exists. A relative handful ever visit its distant corners. But consider this: the distance from Grand Canyon Village to the Uinkarets represents only about a third of the canyon's total length. The awesome panorama as seen from Yavapai Point, or any of the other popular overlooks on either rim, represents only a small portion of the whole. Phantom Ranch at Bright Angel Creek, visible from Yavapai Point and apparently at the very heart of the canyon, is only 87.5 river miles below Lees Ferry. Yet the canyon is 277 miles long. It's about a hundred miles to those distant Uinkaret summits, and another 90 miles beyond them before the Colorado River finally leaves the Grand Canyon. Big dang country.

What sort of place is it?

The geography out there defies easy characterization. Compared to the broad curving sweep of its central section — the part everyone sees — the western canyon's structure is more complicated, its splendidly remote rims less approachable, and its foot trails, where trails exist at all, more challenging. On the north side of the river, the western plateaus break into a confusion of peninsulas and side canyons. Getting to any of them is a long haul. After that, getting from one point of land to the next, although it lies just a few miles away as the raven flies, is a double long haul. It's no wonder that so few roads parallel any section of the canyon rim.

I like to think of how it would appear through the eyes of a California condor. Condors were once common here, judging from skeletal remains in caves and sightings from the last century. Although they are absent from the canyon now, there is talk of reintroducing them. The setting is ideal and this is a topic for later in the book, but meanwhile I have no trouble imagining a condor's flight over the western canyon.

Although birds obviously have the best equipment for moving over the canyon's wracked terrain, it would be a mistake to think that a pair of wings can smooth out all the irregularities, as if a soaring bird is separated from the land over which it flies. On the contrary, my condor is connected by a landscape of moving air that reflects the shape of things

Courtesy of W. K. Hamblin

Large terraces on both sides of the river are all that remain of Whitmore Dam, a natural obstruction built by lava flows that poured out of the Uinkaret Mountains and down Whitmore Wash.

below. Even on calm days there are rising thermals and plunging downdrafts that change as the sun moves. On a windy day, things get rough. Air currents tumble like rapids on the river, reversing, eddying, falling over cliff edges, roaring back upward, accelerating through tight places, expanding and slowing as they push out into open territory.

When the wind blows hard in the canyon, even such skilled fliers as peregrine falcons are grounded, unable to hunt or to bring food back to their nests. Wind is a significant factor in peregrine reproductive success.

So I imagine a calm day, and a relaxed condor riding on her great 10-foot wings, feeling her way over high plateaus and canyon depths, moving west from the familiar Kaibab Plateau. First, she crosses a broken zone of minor canyons in the plateau surface. (Not all of them are small; Snake Gulch is 2,000 feet deep in places.) Then comes the deep gorge of Kanab Creek, a significant canyon in its own right. Its junction with the Colorado River marks the approximate midpoint of the Grand

Canyon. I suppose the condor would descend a bit here, pulled down by the drainage of air in the canyon. On the other hand, if the day is hot, there might be updrafts from the sun-warmed stone. On these matters, I suffer from the ignorance of a ground-based creature.

Up again she rises, over the Kanab Plateau. A lower surface than the Kaibab, it averages around 5,500 feet elevation. Gone for the most part are the tall trees of the Kaibab, replaced now by pinyon and juniper forest. Two tributaries of Kanab Canyon — Hack and Grama canyons — reach deep into the plateau, but otherwise the surface is less cut up than the Kaibab Plateau. Open spaces covered by grass and sage alternate with the PJ. This is good condor country, and a good condor might linger in search of a meal. But ours is a tourist, so she cuts south to the edge of the plateau in order to follow the Grand Canyon rim. Here, she flies above the Esplanade, a broad terrace formed by the Esplanade Sandstone, forming a step between the higher layers (Hermit, Coconino, Toroweap, and Kaibab) and what lies below. In this section, the canyon has a different profile from its eastern reaches. There is no Tonto Platform. Instead, the walls plunge downward all the way from the Esplanade to the river, some 3,000 feet of vertical relief in a single, dramatic leap.

Nowhere is this better seen than on the western edge of the Kanab Plateau, where a long, grassy avenue called Toroweap Valley follows the line of Toroweap Fault to the canyon rim. This is a famous place, partly because a reasonably good road allows visitors to drive to the brink of the canyon and look down over that astonishing precipice. To a condor, such a drop is merely part of a day's cruising, and noting the dust from a truck on the dirt road, our bird swings over the valley and begins a spiraling ascent in order to top the Uinkaret Plateau and its mountains, the same peaks that were visible from way back at Grand Canyon Village. Uinkaret is a Paiute word meaning "Place of Pines," and here again we find ponderosa pines on the cinder-strewn heights. There are even some aspen trees on these mountains.

This is lonely country out here, lonely and big and rugged in the extreme. As our bird eases over the Uinkarets it passes another line of cliffs that mark yet another fault line and yet another plateau — this time the Hurricane Fault and the Shivwits Plateau. At this point, the Grand Canyon detours south in a great curving loop. Into the center of that curve marches the Shivwits, looking more like a tangle of narrow peninsulas than a coherent plateau.

The Esplanade is very wide around the nose of the Shivwits Plateau, but it's deeply incised by a number of long canyons, including Surprise, Burnt, Tineahebitts, and Separation canyons. It was at Separation that three members of Powell's first Grand Canyon expedition left their colleagues and tried walking out to safety. The rapids seemed to be worsening. They had very little food, and less hope. The dreaded Precambrian rocks of the inner canyon, the Vishnu Schist that marked the most difficult whitewater, had reappeared at river level, and no one knew how much farther they had to go. So three men set off on foot, only to be murdered somewhere up on the plateau. It was the granite that did it, the granite that shook what little confidence they had left. Ironically, the biggest rapids were behind them at that point, and the mouth of the Grand Canyon was only a few days ahead.

The condor can see it from here if he has drifted high enough. She can see the blue pooling glimmer of Lake

The lower end of Toroweap Valley is marked by Vulcan's Throne, a prominent volcanic cone perched on the rim of the canyon.

Grand Canyon National Park

Mead just beyond the Grand Wash Cliffs, a great rampart that marks the western edge of the Shivwits Plateau, the end of the Grand Canyon, and the beginning of the Basin and Range country.

All the way to the end, there is Kaibab Limestone on the highest points, the same stone that forms rimrocks throughout the canyon from Lees Ferry, up over the Kaibab Plateau and on westward. The underlying layers change somewhat, becoming thicker or thinner than in the eastern canyon, but they are basically all here, mostly visible, and usually familiar once you account for the differences. For example, the Hermit Formation thickens from as little as 100 feet below Desert View to about 900 feet at Grand Wash Cliffs. This results in a different profile, one that can be puzzling to a person familiar only with the eastern section of the canyon.

The South Rim is made up of the same plateaus as the north, but they are lumped together. The Kaibab, Kanab, and Uinkaret plateaus become the Coconino. The Shivwits is called the Hualapai.

On the Hualapai Plateau, the Redwall Limestone is the surface layer; everything above has been stripped off. As a result, the river is a relatively close 1,800 to 2,000 vertical feet below the rim. Seen from there, the water moves quietly past banks dense with greenery, creating a lush riparian scene. It's a pleasure to the eye at first glance, until you begin to notice something strange about the river here, something amiss. The banks are marked by parallel striations and their shapes seem wrong — oddly unnatural, not the way a river normally does things. And in fact, it's not a normal river here. This is the head of Lake Mead. These are deltaic deposits. The striations are caused by the water level dropping in stages. When Lake Mead is full, this is a lake. When Lake Mead falls, it looks superficially like a natural river. Its dual nature gives it an odd appearance. Not ugly, but rather like an accent you can't place.

Pearce Ferry and the Grand Wash Cliffs

On the far side of the Grand Wash Cliffs lies Pearce Ferry. It's not a town, but rather the historic location of a river ferry established by the Mormon church in 1876. The original ferry location is buried beneath upper Lake Mead, and the name now applies to a boat ramp. I drove there one summer day. The road was a surprise, not so much because it was paved most of the way, which is unusual for back roads in this region, but because it passed through what might be the finest Joshuatree forest in America — mile after mile of hills and valleys covered with the strange, cactuslike plants. Their paltry shade, along with the dubious shelter of creosote bush and an occasional catclaw acacia, provided the only relief in this otherwise wide open country. Baking in the untempered sun, the Grand Wash Cliffs shimmered and wavered uncertainly.

It seemed appropriate that they should appear unstable. I had just been reading about how these cliffs were created by movement along the Grand Wash Fault. There has been a total of 16,000 feet of displacement here, and it might not yet be finished moving. Because it is made of the same layers, the escarpment resembles walls exposed within the canyon; I could easily recognize the old familiar Kaibab Limestone way at the top of the cliffs.

Near the small community of Meadview, I caught glimpses of Lake Mead lying in its rocky basin to the west, surrounded by a wracked landscape of pinnacles and sharp ridges. The shape of the land made it seem that a rock sea, storm-tossed by the ages, was beating against the high walls of a relatively quiet continent. No tidy horizontal layering in that rock sea. Nothing flat out there except the water of Lake Mead, which seemed practically hallucinatory. If I had needed a signal that I was at a transition point in the geography, those sawtooth ranges would have done it. There's no land form like that on the Colorado Plateau, or in the Grand Canyon.

Soon the road turned to gravel and started down a long slope to the boat ramp. I was headed out to the point of a bend — what once was a bend in the river, now a curve in the sinuous lake. Ahead lay a bright, glowing blotch of green, incongruous in this desert of subdued greens. The green marked the new delta of the Colorado River, the Lake Mead Delta, where the river currently dumps all the sediment that comes out of the Grand Canyon. Of course, there's far less sediment coming down the river since they closed the gates on Glen Canyon Dam. During the time when it all was pouring into the head of Lake Mead (only about 25 years!), some 275 vertical feet of sediments collected at the head of the lake. Glen Canyon dam was intended, among other purposes, to slow the rate of siltation in Lake Mead.

The last miles of the Grand Canyon, as seen from the South Rim on the Hualapai Indian Reservation, show the effects of inundation beneath the waters of Lake Mead.

This trough at the base of the Grand Wash Cliffs is a popular place for sediments to collect. The last few miles of road are built on the Muddy Creek Formation, the material that provided the evidence that the Grand Canyon could not be more than about six million years old. Some year in the distant future, geology might record that for a brief period, a lake occupied the Lake Mead basin, backing up into the Grand Canyon for a distance of about 40 miles, leaving behind telltale sediments hundreds of feet above the river bed.

The elevation of Lake Mead, when full, is 1,225 feet, about 1,900 feet lower than Lees Ferry where the Canyon begins. As a result, the climate is warmer at this end of the canyon, and the plants are almost entirely different.

Three deserts — the Mohave, the Great Basin, and the lower Sonoran — mix their influence here and follow the river corridor upstream. You can picture the warm desert invading the trench of the Grand Canyon the way the rising waters of Lake Mead do. Migrating birds move this way, up the river. So do migrating plants, in the sense that through many generations, plants expand or shift their ranges. Distribution maps of Lower Sonoran species show a narrow salient, like a crooked, pointing finger reaching far into the Grand Canyon.

The plants found in this corridor are creosote bush, barrel cactus, ocotillo, yucca, agave, mesquite, catclaw acacia, saltbush, Krameria, cholla, and even a few Joshuatrees. Animals include spotted skunks, ringtails, desert bighorn sheep, cactus wrens, black-tailed gnatcatchers, greater roadrunners, black-throated sparrows, Costa's hummingbirds, Gambel's quail, and others. These are the plants and animals and conditions that most people think of when they picture the American desert — a place of cacti, scorpions, sand, and solpugids.

Solpugids?

The Gentle Desert and its Horrible Creatures

If you drive around the western end of the canyon on Interstate 15 through Las Vegas, or follow Highway 93 from Las Vegas to Kingman, stopping briefly only at scenic overlooks and camera vistas, you will see the desert as most travelers do. Especially in summer. The place is appalling. You see the heat, the glare, the emptiness, the scarcity of things, the power of that enormous baked and broken landscape. Bleak, forbidding, and poisonous. Weird to look at, yes, but what a place to have a breakdown.

It's true. The desert is like that. It will be always that way — eternally, forever intimidating, to hikers and motorists as well as to much hardier things. Buzzards, lizards, snakes and poisonous spiders, bats and cactus and yucca — none of them find it easy. It comes, then, as a sort of awakening to discover that this apparent wasteland also has softness, and delicacy; that some of the most fragile things on Earth abide here — the light of predawn, the air itself, the dry fragrance, the silence; and that the desert itself is fragile despite its power. Perhaps because of its power.

There is enough water in the desert. Exactly enough. For much of the year, although they fluctuate widely, temperatures are not extreme. Aggressive creatures, including people, are few. The desert imposes severe tests upon its inhabitants, but it also nurtures. It appears to hold everything, living and nonliving, in reverence, and it engenders the same feelings in visitors who take the time to see.

The desert has much to say, but it speaks quietly. It speaks through silence. Were it to shout, something of its essential nature would be lost. Some people don't want to hear this. They'd rather hear harrowing tales of danger. I have a theory to explain this: I think in order to treat our world as cruelly as we do, we need to think of it as a savage, unholy place where there occur events more terrible than anything in the human world. Such a view provides justification for our actions. We do this not only to other creatures but to other people by wrapping them in condemnatory myths.

The truth of the natural world is a rarely perceived treasure. It has more to do with indifference than with savage intent. There is nothing personal in the bite of an insect any more than we think violent thoughts when biting into an apple. The scorpion that stings a hiker bears no ill will toward the human race. The natural world is, as a whole, dispassionate; our relationship with it is a matter of the mind.

That said, stories can be told about life and death in the desert world that make the blood run cold, and most of them don't involve popular villains like rattlesnakes which, when they kill, at least do so quickly and swallow their prey without making a bloody mess of it. Thank God solpugids aren't bigger.

A solpugid (the name means "one that flees from the sun") is an arthropod with a slender, pale yellow body, large head, and prominent four-part pincerlike jaws for grabbing prey. Big ones are about three inches long. At first glance they resemble huge hairy spiders, but a closer look shows that they have only six legs rather than eight. Two appendages that look like front legs are actually long pedipalpi loaded with tactile sensors. Efficient predators, they hunt by speed and strength, pouncing on insects, spiders, and even scorpions. One observer reports seeing a solpugid catch and kill a night lizard by biting the lizard's neck, then rotating its awful jaws until the lizard died.

Spiders are more elegant, in a horrific way. They don't exactly swallow their victims. They vomit digestive chemicals into their prey and suck out the liquefied results. In Grand Canyon, the practitioners of this dining technique include the delightfully horrible black widows and tarantulas. Of the two, the black widow has far more potent venom, strong enough to be fatal to humans in about four percent of cases. Only the female is venomous. She is named for her occasional habit of eating the smaller male after mating, which as it turns out is a common behavior: solpugids do it, as do praying mantises.

Tarantulas, despite their fierce appearance, are not dangerous. Their venom produces less pain than a bee sting, and it takes some doing to get bitten by one. None of these creatures goes out of its way to attack humans. Their bites are purely defensive and happen only when they get stepped on, or grabbed.

Scorpions, of course, symbolize the worst that deserts have to offer, and this reputation is not unearned. Only one species found in Grand Canyon is dangerous, but it truly is something to watch out for. Between 1929 and 1948, the bark scorpion, *Centruroides sculpturatus* killed 64 people in Arizona (compared to 15 killed by rattlesnakes during the same period). On the other hand, because they are nocturnal, spend their days hidden underground or beneath logs, and do their best to avoid big dangerous animals like human beings, encounters are rare and avoidable.

The bark scorpion, Centruroides sculpturatus, *is about two inches long. Found behind the loose bark of cottonwood trees, it has a venom more toxic than that of a rattlesnake.*

Courtesy of the Arizona-Sonora Desert Museum

For me, the most alarming desert creature is the centipede, which here can grow up to nine inches long. I found one in a house one time, clinging to a wall, and captured it in a large glass jar. It was pinkish orange and translucent like the rubbery fake lizards and spiders that children enjoy so much. This one I didn't enjoy at all. As soon as it hit the jar, it came to life and began racing at high speed around its prison. I could hear the whirring of its many legs against the glass. My usual fascination for all living things vanished in a wave of involuntary repulsion. I ran outside with the jar and, unwilling even to risk taking the top off, I threw it against a rock some distance from the house. For some reason I wanted the centipede to escape, but I wanted nothing to do with it.

Since that first one, I've encountered others in the outdoors. I pick up a log or a rock and suddenly there it is, scurrying like a mad wind-up toy, and I skitter away in alarm. I know their venom is not dangerous. I know they are not hunting me. I suppose my reaction is innate.

Most creatures of the lower desert are abroad only at night, and this is one reason people think of deserts as being utterly barren. If they could see it in the dark, they would have a different impression, although maybe not a better one: in *Wildlife of the North American Deserts,* James Cornett tells how scorpions, since they are the color of the sand, can be hard to see in the light of an ordinary flashlight. However, under the UV rays of a "black light," they give off a pale green glow. On a field trip in southeastern California, he and a group of students walked out into the desert with flashlights. They stopped walking, turned off their flashlights, and stood together while "two of the students turned on portable UV lights. Walking around the perimeter of our group they located 46 scorpions within ten feet of where we stood!"

I think of these things sometimes, as I lie under the canyon stars. I always make sure my shoes are upside down for the night. In the morning, I shake them out before sliding my feet into them.

Coping with Aridity

By definition, a desert is dry. It's not always sandy, lonely, quiet, hot, thorny, barren, windy, empty, or scenic, but every desert is dry. The lack of water is what makes it a desert. More exactly, the rate of evaporation is the important factor. Never mind how much comes down — if the rate of evaporation is higher than the rate of replenishment, the result is a desert.

The dryness of the lower canyon is a bone-deep dryness you can feel in your skin and underfoot in the parched, sandy soil. You can see it in the clear blue sky. Jets sweep by without contrails, sunsets are amplified by airborne dust. Dryness is reflected in the design of plants that live there — thorny and waxy, succulent, leafless, and long-rooted. It's also evident by the absence of plants lacking those design features. No water lilies, no spring-beauties, no elm trees, no Kentucky bluegrass.

Dryness is what gives the desert its lizards and others that couldn't compete against wet-climate animals. Water would destroy the desert. Cacti would rot and die in the shade of the forest. Soil would form, and all sorts of things would grow up in thick profusion. Desert rocks would be buried in the accumulation of things. Canyons would begin to erode at the rims as fast as at the bottoms and soon become valleys. It would no longer be desert, and water would be cheap.

But here's the rub. The big paradox of the desert. Which is more important, water or the lack of it? Although dryness is the one essential fact of life in arid regions, it is water that makes deserts look the way they do. Water is the main erosive force. Its distribution determines what lives where. Its proportions define land forms. Water makes the clouds that float above the buttes and mesas and canyons, which water also made, carving them from sedimentary rocks that water laid down millions of years earlier. Water even colors the sky by refracting the sun's rays — blue at midday, red at sunrise and sunset.

Water carves the canyon; dryness keeps it from eroding to a mere valley. Water keeps the blackbrush alive; dryness keeps willow trees from crowding it out. Water fills the potholes it made, and runs in the creeks; dryness makes it precious. Water laid down the sandstones — in fact, water made the sand to begin with; dryness keeps it exposed where we can see it. Water makes it possible for us to walk through the desert wilderness; dryness keeps it wild.

As demonstrated by any of the inner canyon's creatures, there is exactly the right amount of water in the desert. Unless you are the wrong kind of organism. Do you remember the scene from *Lawrence of Arabia*, in which Lawrence tried to conserve water by drinking only as much as his

Bobcats prefer the broken rim country of the canyon, where they live among rock outcrops and cliffs.

desert-hardened Arab companion? The implication was that his soft English body demanded more water than it really needed, and that through discipline he could become more like an Arab and do with less.

How much water does a human body need to stay alive in the desert? The answer is well documented, thanks to a study conducted by a team of physiologists led by Dr. Edward Adolph in the early '40s during World War II. It was apparent that the U.S. Army would be fighting in deserts, notably the Sahara. Water, like all other supplies, was a strategic material. It was hard to transport, and expensive. There were military men who thought soldiers could be trained to live on less water than they might wish to drink. They thought sweating was a waste of water. Like Lawrence, they thought water conservation was a matter of toughness and discipline.

The Adolph group learned otherwise. Humans feel thirst after a one to two percent loss of body weight (less than a quart). If allowed to continue, things get serious after a five percent loss. At eight to ten percent, a person can no longer walk. Death comes soon after that — at about 12 percent in hot conditions and somewhere over 20 percent if overheating is not a factor. Of course, in the desert, heat is often a problem.

A human body in the hot desert takes on heat from almost everything around it. If the ambient temperature is over 92 degrees Fahrenheit, even the air in deep shade adds heat (because normal skin temperature is lower than that). Out in the sun, heat comes from all sides: from the air directly in contact with the skin, from the ground as radiant energy or through the shoes, from canyon walls or boulders, and directly from the sun's radiant energy. On a hot day, the desert is an oven. The ground temperature in Death Valley can reach 190 degrees Fahrenheit, not so far from boiling. You really can cook an egg on a dark rock in the canyon. You can also cook your goose.

The only way we soft-skinned humans have of staying cool in those conditions is by sweating. Over two million sweat glands pump moisture to the skin, where it evaporates, carrying off excess heat as it goes. The sweat glands operate as if attached to thermostats, increasing their flow when the body heats up.

The physiologists learned that sweating rates varied directly with heat gain, but not with water intake and not with desert experience. Put an Arab beside a young English adventurer named Lawrence on a desert sand dune at noon, and each man will sweat according to his personal metabolic requirements. (At rest, the average adult body produces 80 calories of heat per hour; dissipation of this heat through sweating requires about five ounces of water.) Letting one man drink all the water he wants and forcing the other one to go thirsty will not alter either one's rate of sweating. It's not the water that counts, it's the heat. Human bodies function in a very narrow temperature range. Maintaining a constant temperature is a necessity for survival. The greater the heat gain by a body, the more it sweats. When laws of physics are involved, there is no way to tinker with the equation and change the proportions.

Adolph and his fellow researchers measured sweating rates for various activities in a temperature of 100 degrees Fahrenheit. Walking in the sun with no clothing requires well over a liter per hour. In this case, heat gain to exposed skin is a significant factor. The difference between a clothed body and a naked one has nothing to do with the clothing somehow preventing the evaporation of sweat. By shading the skin, clothing shields it from direct contact with both sunlight and hot air. Remember, the amount of sweat is a result of heat gain. If clothing cuts down on sweating, it does that by reducing heat gain from the environment.

They also measured sweat in relation to temperature for three activities — walking in the sun, walking at night, and sitting in the shade or at night. They found that it takes more than twice as much sweat to walk in the sun as it does to sit in the shade.

The total amount of water consumed by a volunteer working in the desert, doing construction labor, when the high temperature reached 105 degrees Fahrenheit, was nearly three gallons in 24 hours. Three gallons! Yet 105 degrees Fahrenheit is not a particularly high temperature in the lower parts of Grand Canyon. Dr. Adolph points out that although he drank at will, the volunteer's urine output was not excessive — in fact it was a little below average, at .87 liters for the time involved — which means he lost virtually all that water through his skin. It also means that none was wasted.

By way of summary, walking naked through the desert in the middle of the day expends the most perspiration. With clothing — pants, shirt, and a hat, all made of breathable, light-colored fabric — the loss is cut by 20 percent. You save an additional 40 percent by sitting, not walking, and yet another 15 percent by sitting in the shade. All told, at 100 degrees Fahrenheit the difference in heat gain between walking naked in the sun and sitting in the shade is on the order of four to one. Other considerations are heat gain from the ground (it's better to sit up on something), the proximity of large radiating objects like rocks and vehicles, and wind. If it's a hot wind, it actually adds heat to the body, requiring more sweat than calm air of the same temperature.

None of this would be news to the creatures of the inner canyon, who are all susceptible to the same heat problems and make use of every conceivable water conservation and heat avoidance method. Those that can do so flee from the midday sun. Solpugids, spiders, Jerusalem crickets, snakes, rodents, lizards, and others go underground — into burrows, under flat rocks, into crevices, where underground temperatures can be 50 degrees Fahrenheit cooler than on the surface and humidity can be as high as 100 percent.

These animals come out in the cool of the night or make brief forays during the day. Their ability to handle the heat varies. For example, the whitetail antelope squirrel can tolerate a body temperature of 108 degrees

Fahrenheit before diving back underground to cool off. Scorpions can survive over an hour at 113 degrees.

Black-tailed jackrabbits do not burrow at all. Instead, they seek shade beneath bushes and overhanging cliffs. If they need further cooling, they can do it through their ears, which act as radiators oriented at precisely 17 degrees from due north, the coolest part of the sky.

Beyond avoiding heat, desert creatures reduce moisture loss. Most do not sweat, although evaporative cooling does occur. Coyotes, for example, like dogs, cool themselves by panting, which does involve moisture loss. Unless they have ready access to drinking water, it's important for coyotes to avoid heat.

Urine is another matter. Urine is the body's vehicle for cleansing itself of toxic wastes and salts that build up from metabolic processes. These are mostly nitrogen solutes derived from digestion of proteins. Kidneys function as filters to remove the toxins and produce the liquid concentrate called urine. For mammals, this usually means urea, a somewhat poisonous compound that has to be diluted with relatively large amounts of water — not the best solution for desert creatures. Birds and reptiles have an advantage because they excrete uric acid, which is essentially nontoxic and can be passed in a nearly dry, crystalline state. It takes extra energy to produce uric acid, but in the desert this is evidently a worthwhile tradeoff.

> ## Some Animals of the Lower Sonoran Zone
> Black-throated Sparrow
> Costa's Hummingbird
> Ladder-backed Woodpecker
> Greater Roadrunner
> Gambel's Quail
> Say's Phoebe
> Bighorn Sheep
> Rock Pocket Mouse
> Longtail Pocket Mouse
> Spotted Skunk
> Gray (Desert) Shrew
> Tree Lizard
> Painted Desert Whiptail
> California Kingsnake
> Western Chuckwalla

The degree of concentration and the tolerance for buildup of wastes vary with the organism. Some desert animals can store wastes in the bloodstream until they have sufficient water to flush their systems. Others produce urine that is concentrated almost to the point of being a solid. Chuckwallas (the canyon's largest common lizard) excrete excess salts into their nasal passages and blow it out through their nostrils!

Among mammals, human beings are some of the least well equipped for desert life. Had God meant us to live in the desert, you might say, he'd have given us rat kidneys.

Kangaroo rat kidneys, to be specific. This and other members of the genus *Heteromyid* are the champions of water conservation. While many desert animals get sufficient water from the food they eat, the *Heteromyids* don't need even that. They can survive indefinitely on metabolic water — that is, the moisture resulting from the digestion of food. All animals produce such moisture as a natural product of the energy cycle, but few creatures could survive on such a small amount. These capable little rodents do it by virtue of extra-efficient kidneys, the ability to excrete virtually dry droppings, nasal passages that condense water before it leaves the body, and by moving about only at night.

The mammals are nothing compared to the insects and arachnids. Black widow spiders, for example, can survive 200 days in a burrow without food or water. Scorpions have a special waxy layer in their exoskeleton that seals in moisture. Beyond that, they have very slow metabolisms and are capable of shutting down their breathing pores for a time to prevent transpiration. It's as if we could hold our breath to keep from losing water.

Plants use similar strategies, including retreat underground. Desert vegetation looks pretty sparse, but it's been said that if you reversed all the plants so everything normally underground were above ground, the desert would be as densely vegetated as a rain forest. Like an iceberg, most of a desert plant is beneath the surface. Extensive root systems collect more water, and wring the maximum from what is available.

It's a popular notion that desert plants have long taproots that drill deep into the soil for subterranean water. Some do, but most desert plants have shallow root systems, because water is more often available in the top few feet of desert soil. You can drill a long way down beneath the hot surface and find nothing but dry, dry rock. As desert dwellers have long understood, the better strategy is to collect rainfall when it comes and store it in a safe place. Ranchers build check dams for this purpose, gathering water in tanks. In the Southwest, a tank is simply the pond behind a small dam; it fills during winter from snowmelt, which with luck lasts until midsummer, when thunderstorms replenish the supply. The ancient inhabitants of the canyon area did the same thing, except instead of watering livestock behind check dams, they planted gardens in the saturated soil.

A desert plant is a vegetative tank. It collects water from a large area (explaining partly why there's so much bare ground out there — it's a

Grand Canyon National Park

collection surface kept clear by the competitive action of surrounding plants) and stores the moisture in its highly specialized body. Plants conserve what moisture they have by a number of mechanisms. They grow small leaves and drop them in times of drought. Waxy coatings help prevent loss. Breathing pores shut tightly during the day and open only in the cool of the night. Hairy surfaces shade the leaves and cut down on air movement.

The hardy barrel cactus, spiny survivor of intense drought and searing heat, puts out one of the most lovely flowers in the desert.

Unlike human beings, who need to sweat to stay cool, desert plants can adjust their rate of water loss. In dry soil, they give off less moisture than if the soil is wet. Presumably this affects their rate of growth, but the important thing is that they can survive long dry spells.

Certain succulents have an amazing internal recycling ability. Like all plants, they need carbon dioxide for photosynthesis during the day and produce waste carbon dioxide from metabolic processes at night. Unlike most green plants, cacti and other succulents are able to store the waste from the night, and use it for growing during the day. This means they do not need to open their stomata (breathing pores) to the dry desert air — a big advantage when water is scarce.

Especially cacti. Cacti have a singular ability to hunker down and get through tough times. Even after being removed entirely from the soil, they can last for years. Saguaros (not present in Grand Canyon) live for about two years out of the soil. In surrendering finally to the lack of water, they pinch out their lower parts first, sending all resources to a single branch that stays green when all else has gone dry; the last act of this last branch is to produce flowers, which in turn produce seeds. Its life is ended in a defiant act of reproduction.

In laboratory experiments, a barrel cactus removed from the soil and kept without water survived six years before curious scientists ended the experiment by cutting it apart. After all that time, it had lost a third of its weight at a steadily decreasing rate. On its first day out of the soil, it lost one two-thousandth of its weight; on its last day, it lost only one seventeen-thousandth. But it was still alive after six years without water.

One thing is clear: Cacti are perfectly adapted to the life they live, as content in the canyon's aridity as kelp in the ocean. Don't feel sorry for the prickly-pears.

John Wesley Powell named Marble Canyon for its water-polished limestone, which resembles the material of fine sculpture.

Rock layers in the canyon weather differently. Deer Creek has cut a slot through the Tapeats Sandstone to the underlying Vishnu Schist—a resistant rock that here produces one of the canyon's more beautiful waterfalls. *(David Edwards)*

Dana Butte reveals the mixed consistency of Supai Group rocks overlying the more homogeneous, cliff-forming Redwall Limestone.

As seen from the top of the Echo Cliffs near Lees Ferry, Marble Platform is a broad plain incised by the sharp gorge of Marble Canyon.

Right: The relatively soft rocks of the Grand Canyon Supergroup have eroded to form a broad valley below Desert View. Cliffs of harder stone provide a strong contrast.

Monarch butterflies commonly use the Grand Canyon as a migration corridor.

A light autumn snow dusts the mixed fir and ponderosa forest just below the North Rim. The vegetation in this area resembles that of northern Utah mountain ranges.

The walls of Transept Canyon, near Bright Angel Point, are lit by the twin glow of sunrise and the bright colors of mountain scrub foliage in autumn.

Aspen leaves turn golden in the fall and drop like bright coins to the forest floor.

Aspen trees are encased with smooth bark, cool to the touch. The name quaking aspen comes from the tendency of the leaves, at the ends of long stems, to quiver in the slightest breeze.

Right: The Kaibab Limestone of the North Rim is riddled with caves and underground channels, which explains why so few ponds and streams are found on the Kaibab Plateau. One exception is Greenland Lake, on the North Rim's Walhalla Plateau; caused by a sinkhole that became plugged with debris, it was enlarged by cattle ranchers before the park was established.

The Great Basin gopher snake is found predominantly north of the river in desert scrub, pinyon-juniper woodland, and ponderosa pine communities. Gopher snakes are nonpoisonous; they kill by constriction.

Several years after a fire swept through the Muav Saddle area on the North Rim, the plants of the mountain scrub community have begun to recover.

Seen at close range, a juniper tree is a nearly impenetrable tangle of sharp twigs and scaly leaves that provides shelter for a variety of animals. In marginal conditions, junipers give protection to pinyon pine seedlings, allowing them to grow where they might otherwise perish.

On the South Rim, the canyon is most often viewed through a frame of weathered juniper branches; on the North Rim, the same views are framed by fir and ponderosa.

A lone juniper overlooks Hermit Canyon at sunset.

Despite its gnarled and desert-hardened appearance, cliffrose produces one of the showiest displays of flowers in the canyon's desert scrub community, suffused with the fragrance of spiced honey.

Apache plume is easily confused with cliffrose except when in bloom or going to seed; its flowers are white instead of yellow and develop into dense tufts of feathery, purple "plumes."

Left: There is no mistaking the western collared lizard, a brightly colored and conspicuous inhabitant of desert scrub habitats. When fleeing danger, it sometimes stands up and runs on its hind legs.

Right: Utah agave is one of the canyon's more widespread plants, thriving from the rims all the way to the river. It lives 15 to 25 years before sending up a spectacular flowering stem; after the blossoms die, so does the plant.

Below: Engelmann hedgehog cactus produces delicate purple flowers that rise during April and May from an unapproachable tangle of spines.

The weaksteam mariposa lily blooms in spring throughout the inner canyon; a perennial, it grows from a bulb that lies as much as 6 inches below the ground.

Prickly-pear cacti are not always prickly. When the pads are new, soft growth surrounds what will become sharp spines.

Right: In the canyon, life zones are often stacked directly on top of each other like the rock layers. On this wall, conditions are different among the pinnacles of Coconino Sandstone than on the rubble-covered slopes of the Supai Group or at the base of the Redwall Limestone cliff.

One of the canyon's more dramatic views can be had at Toroweap, where the river flows about 3,000 feet below nearly vertical cliffs.

Three deserts—the Mojave, the Great Basin, and the Sonoran—influence vegetation at the western end of the canyon. Plants include ocotillo, barrel cactus, catclaw acacia, and honey mesquite.

Bighorn sheep are well adapted to desert conditions. Although they occupy the canyon's most remote corners, they are a common sight for river runners in the western end of the canyon.

Even the sure-footed bighorn sometimes slips. This ram's skeleton was found at the base of an overhanging cliff, suggesting that the animal had fallen to his death.

Left: Havasu Canyon, homeland of the Havasupai tribe, is known for a series of elegant waterfalls, including Mooney Falls.

Permanent sources of water in the canyon are precious; springs always seem to appear in beautiful surroundings, often framed with water-loving plants like maidenhair fern.

Left: Elves Chasm, a treat for boaters or hikers in search of shelter from the sun and heat, is one of numerous riparian grottoes hidden deep within the canyon.

Right: A young great horned owl finds shelter from the glaring midday sun in the shadows of a narrow side canyon.

Below: A canyon treefrog clings to reeds beside a desert stream. Treefrogs are conspicuous creatures in riparian areas.

Sacred datura, or jimsonweed, is a poisonous beauty with large, trumpet-shaped flowers. It blooms at night; the blossoms last only until the sun hits them.

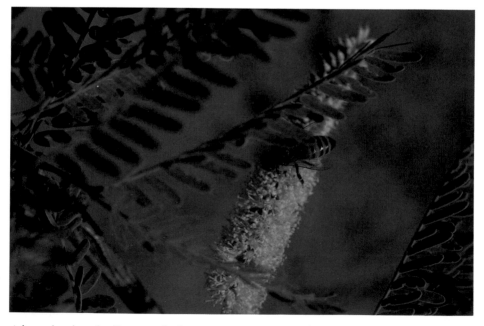

A bee plunders the flowers of a honey mesquite tree, a plant associated with the warmer regions of the canyon.

Looking like plants from another world, joshuatrees are not common in the canyon, but they grow in a virtual joshuatree forest in the area of Pearce Ferry on Lake Mead.

Boaters pause beneath the
enormous arch of Redwall
Cavern, a natural cavity in
the Redwall Limestone that
was exposed by the river
as it cut downward.

Canyon weather is ever-
changing. In late summer,
heavy storm clouds cast an
eerie light on the river, and
sudden rains often bring
flash floods.

Since Glen Canyon Dam was built, the Colorado often runs clear. But when rainstorms and melting snow carry sediment into the river, it regains its old red-brown color. Here, boaters negotiate Lava Falls in waves of different colors.

An early autumn snowstorm dusts the south Rim at Mather Point. On such a day, it might be raining over Marble Canyon near Lees Ferry, where the elevation is several thousand feet lower. Snow does fall, though rarely, at the bottom of the inner canyon; the cold spells that come with snow play a role in limiting the survival of many southern-desert plants.

Erosion has separated Wotan's Throne from adjacent Cape Royal. It stands now as an island surrounded by a sea of space.

Tamarisk thrives in moist areas throughout the canyon. An exotic plant that originated in the Middle East, it colonizes the unstable flood zones of river banks. It produces fragrant purple flowers in spring and turns bright yellow in autumn.

Several hundred feet above the river, the remains of an Anasazi bridge mark the spot where an ancient trail crossed a difficult section of cliffs.

An Anasazi basket lies in the shelter of an overhanging rock, where it was left centuries ago. In the canyon's dry environment, such artifacts survive indefinitely unless stolen.

Anasazi granaries, or storage structures, occupy a ledge above the river near Nankoweap Creek. These are well known and easily reached from the river. Others have been found in seemingly inaccessible locations high on canyon walls and pinnacles. The reason for such remote locations remains a mystery.

Two photographs taken from the same location near Moran Point illustrate air quality fluctuations. The top picture was made on a clear day in November 1986; on February 10, 1989, conditions were extremely hazy. On excellent days, a visual range of 243 miles has been measured.

8
Treefrogs and Flycatchers
Hidden Canyons

Several miles from the Colorado River, in a side canyon of a side canyon, there is a grotto. You can walk to it from the river, or down from the rim. Either way, it feels like a very deep place, far beneath towering walls, a long way from roads and a long way even from trails. Deep and protected and very well hidden, it lies at the end of a narrow gorge —a cold green pool of water the size of a large bedroom. It feels as private as a bedroom, tucked away in a cul-de-sac with no way out except the way you came in. No one who comes here is ever in a hurry to leave.

On one side of the pool is a ledge where several people can sit on smooth rock beneath an overhang. On the other side, a sheer slope of stone, layered in travertine, rises to an opening in the wall, above which lies the unknown; no way for a person to get up there and have a look. Shooting down that slope comes a narrow ribbon of water, only a few inches wide, half an inch deep, and 30 feet high. The water splashes into the pool with a gurgling sound that mixes and echoes with the hissing of its passage down the rock slide. For a ceiling there hangs a small patch of sky, but rarely if ever does the sun shine directly into this hidden chamber.

Ask anyone who has run the Colorado River, or any hiker who has spent enough time in the canyon to know something of its variety, to name his or her favorite places, and side canyons will be near the top of the list. Especially the small ones, the shaded grottos where little streams flow beneath high arching walls. These are the real jewels of the Grand Canyon, made more precious by the surrounding aridity and overwhelming size of the landscape. Their intimacy makes them pleasant. Water gives them magic.

The first time I saw the grotto described above was on a hiking trip. There were four of us. We parked our cars on the broken limestone of the rim, shouldered our packs, and set off down a long rubble slope. There was no trail, and without a trail, getting into the Grand Canyon takes some routefinding. It's not like a big hill that you can just walk down. To get through the cliffs, you have to follow its lines of weakness. We had only a general description of where to go, but even that was enough, because we knew we could find a way down.

The first night we set our camp on a flat rock ledge 3,000 feet below the rim, buried in the silence of the desert. There was no water burbling in the hollows. We heard no birds. No wind. No insects. We spoke in whispers to avoid the profanity of noise.

How different it was the next day. Dropping down a series of ledges like giant steps, we entered a small canyon whose walls rose steadily above our heads the farther we went. A stream appeared, flowing intermittently at first, then strong and unbroken. As it tumbled through house-sized boulders and slid through tiny pools, it sang a canyon song that rose and filled the narrow space. It was a canyon full of echoes — not just the sound of water and frogs and birds and insects and our still-hushed voices, but also the echoes of light, and air currents.

And something more, a cultural reverberation. We found it near a spring lined with maidenhair fern and gently bobbing scarlet monkey flowers. It was a panel of petroglyphs — animals and geometric patterns and human figures pecked into the rock by people drawn like us to the mysterious presence of water in the desert.

The stream vanished again. We walked on a bed of dry gravel and boulders, knowing that if we were thirsty enough we could dig a few feet down and find water. It was obvious from the plants that grew so well here that water still flowed through the stream bed beneath our

The Grotto, with its unusual waterfall and deep crystalline pool, is one of dozens — perhaps hundreds — of similar hidden riparian jewels in the Grand Canyon.

feet. There were still cottonwoods and willows, which do not survive without ample moisture. There were birds also. Mourning doves, white-throated swifts, several kinds of swallows, black phoebes hawking insects from the air, broad-tailed hummingbirds doing their spring mating display (superb aerial acrobatics), and one of my favorite canyon creatures, the police-whistle bird. The books call him an ash-throated flycatcher but I've always recognized him by his call, which sounds like an old-fashioned police whistle: *Chee-beeer!*

We found deer tracks in the sand, and that made me think of mountain lions. I've never seen one in the canyon, but their tracks haunt my thoughts. I began paying attention, looking for the big four-inch pugmarks on the soft sand and clay of the stream bank.

Soon there was water again, and from there all the way to the Colorado River we walked beside a permanent stream. In places, vegetation grew in dense tangles, forcing us to thrash our way through branches and hanging vines. Beneath overhung canyon walls, seeps painted the stone with patterns of algae and alkali and other minerals.

There were hanging gardens of maidenhair fern, monkey flower, and columbine.

Since it was springtime, everything was in bloom, bursting and building. The flowers included those of tamarisk, that alien beauty. Sometimes I cursed the tamarisk because it was hard to move through. Its rough bark scratched my arms and legs. The tips of broken branches were sharp enough to cause puncture wounds. But I admired the tamarisk for its persistence.

Tamarisk is native to the Nile River valley, where it stabilizes river banks and serves other functions regarded by humans as useful. Back in the '30s, someone thought it would be a good idea to plant it along the Colorado River. It became a project of the Civilian Conservation Corps. Like many exotic species, it was too successful. It escaped into the wild, out of control of the engineers, up into side canyons throughout the Southwest, where it now defies attempts to round it up and deport it. The engineers are trying to destroy it because someone decided after the fact that tamarisk uses too much of the water that should be going into growing lettuce and other irrigated crops. They won't succeed. Tamarisk is here to stay. It's gone wild. Every spring, it bursts with purple blossoms and fills the canyons with delicate perfume.

The walls grew ever higher. On bends, great cliffs were undercut by the stream, forming huge amphitheaters like band shells for choruses of male treefrogs. The frogs sounded like sheep. Demented sheep. But to the females lured by the bellows, it must have been beautiful music.

At stream level, everything was lush. I thought of Hawaii and New Zealand. Yet only 50 feet above the canyon bottom, on baked rocky ledges, conditions were as dry as old bones. Catclaw acacia shared space with cacti and grasses that had already gone brown, their foxtail seeds clinging to our socks when we ventured among them.

At wide places, the streambed cut through benches of sand and gravel where huge boulders had come to rest after falling from the walls above. The stream flowed 10 or 15 feet below these benches, leaving them high and dry. Nonetheless, vegetation here was as thick as a midwestern orchard, although instead of apple trees there were acacia trees. Around them grew blankets of wildflowers and grasses, and this was unusual because so often in the Southwest, anything that can be grazed has suffered from generations of cattle. One of the great values of a national park is the way it preserves a semblance of wild conditions. In Grand Canyon, we have a chance to experience natural conditions without the overwhelming influence of human industry. Once you've seen meadows like these, where the grass grows to its full height and is eaten only by native herbivores, it is possible to understand what we have done to most of our land.

Always the light! Reflecting and reverberating, rarely direct, warmed by its impact with the canyon walls. In that light, skin glows, water shimmers. Shadows are never harsh because there is so much loose light running around.

One of my friends walks across a shallow pool. Riffles from her passage gleam in gold light showering down from a bright cliff above her. She stands in a pool of gold, and I am reminded of the scatters of glitter that followed Tinkerbell in the Disney version of *Peter Pan*. If there was ever a never-never land, this is it. A secret garden in the desert where water flows clear and clean. Crouching on a boulder one evening, staring into a pool of water so clear it was nearly invisible, I was startled by a river of minnows. Hundreds of them. A silver hallucinatory flow. They passed without causing so much as a shiver on the calm surface.

The days melted into one another. There wasn't much value in counting either time or distance. Somewhere along the way, I think perhaps on the fifth day, we came to a narrow side canyon. It led us to the grotto with the green pool and the ribbon waterfall. The canyon's sanctum sanctorum. A tiny chapel dedicated to the liturgy of water.

Desert Water

Water. Without it, none of this would exist. No ferns, no frogs, no fish. Not even the canyons themselves.

Water in most of Grand Canyon's tributary streams comes from the high country. Rather than pouring over the edge, it percolates through caverns and fissures in the Kaibab Limestone and underlying strata until it hits an impermeable layer and emerges as springs. These are most common on the north side of the river, where rock strata dip toward the south, into the canyon. Springs occur less frequently on the south side, but nonetheless some do exist. Some springs are seasonal, and some are

David Edwards

Vasey's Paradise, named for a botanist on the Powell Expedition, is watered by a series of fountains that burst from the canyon wall several hundred feet above the river.

permanent. Some appear as damp spots in the sand or on canyon walls, and never produce enough flow to fill a cup, much less a stream. Others are live-born rivers, bursting entire from solid rock like Old Testament miracles.

The stronger springs manage to flow from their sources all the way to the Colorado River. Among them are Tapeats Creek, Bright Angel Creek, Shinumo Creek, and Clear Creek.

Others begin strong and die; or they vanish underground, only to reappear where underlying rock layers force the water back to the sur-face. A typical North Rim creek, for example, begins as a seep in the Hermit Shale, picks up enough volume to gurgle over tiny waterfalls, and soon becomes a small stream. It might sink beneath rubble for a while, but eventually the Redwall Limestone emerges from the debris to form a smooth pavement where the water has no place to hide. But it can erode, and some creeks slice deeply into the Redwall, carving slot canyons with vertical or overhanging walls. Emerging from the Redwall, the water makes its way across the Tonto Platform, a mile or more in width. Here again, weaker streams go underground or dry up entirely. They might reappear at the Tapeats Sandstone, which forms narrow canyons like the Redwall. Beneath the Tapeats lies the Vishnu Schist, and unless there is sufficient overburden to allow water to flow underground, this hard, impermeable rock forces to the surface whatever flow might exist.

Side canyons of the Grand Canyon fall into four distinct zones, each one defined by local geology and weather. The first is Marble Canyon zone, where the canyons are short and angled toward the northeast. Next comes the Chuar zone, where the Colorado River makes its big curve toward the west. This zone is characterized by long canyons on the north side, fed by heavy runoff from the high North Rim. Because the South Rim is so much lower at this point (as much as 3,000 feet lower) it receives much less precipitation, resulting in short or nonexistent canyons on the south side. The Little Colorado River is the only exception to this, but for a reason. Its source is hundreds of miles away in northeast Arizona, so it is not greatly affected by local conditions.

Then comes the Kaibab zone, which includes the developed areas, and is therefore the section most people see. On the north side, canyons are fed by runoff from the Kaibab Plateau and flow with the dip of strata. South side canyons are short because there is less moisture to begin with, and what does fall must run against the dip to reach the river — a more difficult erosional task. Finally, there is the Esplanade zone with some long, straight canyons reflecting deep fault lines. Each of these zones is distinguished by geologic and climatic differences that determine how side canyons develop.

Some side streams never flow except during occasional flash floods. They might remain dry for years at a time. Their beds are normally as dry as the surrounding desert, and they support the same plants or animals that are found in the general area. These are called ephemeral streams — here one day, gone for the next few months. Others are labeled intermittent. This means you can count on finding water in these only at certain seasons or in certain sections; for example, April and May are good water months for the intermittent streams because of snowmelt. Also, no matter what time of year it is, water is more likely found at the base of the Redwall than, for instance, out on the sun-drenched surface of the Tonto Platform.

Still other streams flow throughout the year, all the way from their sources to the river, bountiful and achingly beautiful — the largesse of the desert. There are perhaps a dozen of these major perennial streams in Grand Canyon. Each one supports a thin ribbon of riparian vegetation including cottonwoods, willows, and a host of other water-loving creatures.

Riparian Plants

You could take the flowing water out of all the Grand Canyon's tribu-taries — dry up the creeks and let their dusty beds blow off on the desert winds — and almost no one looking down from tourist viewpoints on the rim would notice the difference. Even floating on the river, you might not discern the change unless you knew to look. The Colorado River gets by far most of its flow from mountain ranges hundreds of miles away in Colorado and Wyoming. It doesn't need the puny contribution of Grand Canyon tributaries to keep it alive. But what a different place the canyon would be without them.

Of the plants, the most noticeable is that reliable beacon of desert water, the Fremont cottonwood. Its bright green leaves show up from miles away, a flamboyant color amid the subdued greens and browns of other arid-land vegetation. In autumn, cottonwoods turn brilliant yellow for a few weeks, glowing as if someone turned on an electric sign adver-tising water. The water might be underground, it might not be standing cool and limpid, but where even a single cottonwood tree can grow, there must be water within reach of its roots.

Along perennial streams, cottonwoods form linear forests lining both banks — trains of cottonwoods, caravans of cottonwoods. Half in the water, their big gnarled roots create little pools and eddies. They are joined by smaller trees and shrubs including redbud, several species of willow, and the non-native but pervasive tamarisk.

Common in the lower elevations is horsetail, or scouring rush. Sometimes called snakeweed, it has a hollow, segmented stalk, like short straws joined end to end. The segments pull apart with a popping sound that children love. They grow in thick stands along the sandy banks of streams and seem to do well in full sun. Maidenhair fern, in contrast, prefers shade and indirect light. Its favorite growing sites are cliffside

The stream orchid graces springs, seeps, and the banks of permanent streams.

seeps. It grows well beneath overhangs, with its roots anchored in hairline cracks, where it forms luxuriant clumps of small green leaves on black stems. If you ever think the air in a canyon is calm, look closely at the maidenhair, which never seems to stop moving.

Because they propagate from spores, neither horsetail nor maidenhair fern produces flowers. But other plants do, in often spectacular profusion: red and yellow monkeyflower, golden columbine, the deep scarlet of Indian paintbrush and cardinal flower, the yellow of Hooker's evening primrose, more red from columbine and blue from monkshood, blue from yet another species of columbine, and the sky blue of bluebells. Only orchids could make brown flowers look exquisite, and the stream orchid does just that.

There are many other flowering plants that I associate with side canyons but not necessarily with water. This is one of the most interesting things about these water-rich places — the moisture is extremely local. It can be a matter of inches between riparian abundance and Sonoran aridity. The most miserly, water-pinching cacti grow practically root-to-root with delicate little numbers like monkeyflower. You can put your feet in the stream and, if you're not careful, sit smack on a desiccated old prickly-pear.

In larger tributaries (Kanab Creek is a good example) the streams meander through sand and gravel benches that are high above the water table, too high to benefit plants that need abundant water. Then you find fields of globemallow glowing a pale Tuscan orange, and the poisonous but beautiful white trumpet flowers of sacred datura. Depending on its position in the canyon (usually this means the elevation and surrounding rock unit), the dry areas of tributary canyons support mesquite, acacia, sagebrush, cliffrose, and other shrubs, along with a full complement of the appropriate cacti, anything from hedgehog to prickly-pear to cholla.

Walking through such a canyon, a hiker continually switches from the blinding heat and soft sand of the benches to the fragrant lushness of the creek. Lizards skitter across the hot sand a few feet from where fish hide in shady pools of water. A few paces take you from the odor of hot sand to the old basement smell of dank clay.

This is not to say that the two worlds are entirely independent. Intermittent streams (which flow and dry up with the seasons) and ephemeral streams (which rise and fall according to storms) provide enough extra moisture that desert-hardy plants like mountain-mahogany and scrub oak grow more strongly and in greater numbers than do the same species outside the watercourse. They can get along without the added moisture, but they do better with it. Of course, if it becomes too wet, true riparian plants such as cottonwoods replace the nonriparian species. It's all a matter of balance.

Riparian Animals

Of all the animals that live in riparian areas, none seems more at home than canyon treefrogs, engaging little creatures with Pavarotti voices. No more than one and a quarter inches long, they are easily found clinging to smooth rock walls or boulders above pools of water. They sit in the sun with their legs tucked under their bodies, forming neat ovals. Their color varies from light brown to gray and olive, often with a silvery or bronze sheen and with yellow patches on the undersides of their hind legs. Against the dark water of a deep pool, they look almost white. They aren't easily spooked. Often you can touch them before they leap for underwater safety, and even then they are easy to catch. After a calming minute cupped in your palm, they will sit still for examination.

Despite the name, canyon treefrogs don't spend much time in trees. But they are excellent climbers. Like many of their cousins, they have toe pads that resemble suction cups, helping them scramble up smooth surfaces. It's impressive to watch them work their way up a glistening wet overhanging rock surface.

The toe pads help distinguish them from the only other Grand Canyon animal with which they could be confused, the red-spotted toad. The toad is a bit bigger, covered with red and orange warts, and lacks the round toe pads. The really striking difference, however, is that the toad can live away from water, apparently in all zones of the Grand Canyon, even out on the Tonto Platform.

During breeding season, which lasts from early spring to midsummer, canyon treefrogs sound like a badly orchestrated chorus of sheep. From one group you might hear

Canyon treefrogs breed in the spring. Their mating calls echo through any side canyon with permanent water or other lasting sources of water.

Ringtails, or ringtailed cats, are common throughout deeper parts of the canyon but are seldom seen because of their nocturnal habits.

Arizona Game and Fish Dept, Bob Miles

any number of voices — tenors, altos, sopranos blending in a comic medley. A sure sign of water, their calls are a welcome sound to thirsty canyon hikers who otherwise might blunder through thick underbrush for some time before finding a hidden pool.

Rivaling treefrogs as symbols of side canyons is the canyon wren. You hear him first. His call is a piercing whistle, the notes beginning high and rapid, then descending and slowing, ending sometimes in an impassioned buzz. A good whistler can easily imitate the sound well enough to bring a determined, pugnacious male flitting in for a close look. It's amazing that such a voice can burst from such a tiny vessel.

No one walking a side canyon can ignore the lizards skittering about on the dry walls. The commonest is the small, chameleonlike tree lizard, a lovely, agile creature often seen dashing up vertical and overhanging walls as if gravity pulled them in a direction other than down. Sometimes they do fall, and if it happens to be into water, they swim like experts.

In general, places like this are alive with animals. Water striders and water beetles cruise the pools. Water ouzels, or dippers, nest beside sparkling cascades. The desert striped whipsnake hunts lizards, other snakes, birds, and small animals. Up to five feet long but less than three-quarters of an inch in diameter at midbody, these fast-moving snakes thread the densest brush and zip across open areas with astonishing agility. They are harmless to anything but their prey, and because they hunt during the day they are seen relatively often.

Raccoons need water and love to eat fish and frogs, so you would expect to find them along permanent streams. It's odd, then, that although they do live in the canyon they are not often reported and seem not to be widely distributed. It's possible to mistake them for ringtails, or ringtailed cats, which are common throughout the canyon, not limited to riparian zones. Ringtails are the size of house cats but seem to have gotten mixed up with foxes and raccoons somewhere along the line. They have furry banded tails, prominent ears, and big eyes. They are nocturnal, so these field marks show up as often as not in the light of a camper's flashlight. Ringtails are anything but shy. They eagerly dig into packs and food bags and have no qualms

Some Riparian Animals

Desert Striped Whipsnake
Grand Canyon Rattlesnake
Yellow-backed Spiny Lizard
Canyon Treefrog
Red-spotted Toad
Blue-gray Gnatcatcher
Ash-throated Flycatcher
American Dipper
Black Phoebe
Common Yellowthroat
Yellow-breasted Chat
Belted Kingfisher
Canyon Wren
Rock Pocket Mouse
Spotted Skunk
Raccoon
Ringtail
Beaver

about walking through the door of a tent while people are sleeping inside. It was a ringtail that repeatedly tried to steal a loaf of bread from me one night. The first time or two, I was asleep and woke up in time to chase him off. Later, I was fully awake when he walked up, bold as a 300-pound bully, grabbed the bread bag and started pulling. Had the bag not torn, I'm not sure what it would have taken to make him let go. At least I got a good look at him, a handsome animal.

In the most intimate side canyons, owls can be found, particularly great horned owls. They nest in the shadows and perch on ledges beneath deep overhangs. Several times I have encountered juveniles on a canyon bottom. Not quite flying yet, and innocent of fear, they allowed me to approach closely with only a slight widening of their already wide eyes. Of adults, the only thing you usually see is a flash of feathers around the next dusky bend.

Mexican spotted owls, which are known to nest on the North Rim, are rumored to also live in narrow canyons of the sort that occur in the Redwall Limestone. Spotted owls need cover, whether in a forest or beneath overhanging canyon walls. Ironically, their chief enemies are great horned owls. How they manage to live in these hidden places, if they do at all, is a matter of speculation.

So much lies below the surface of the Grand Canyon, unseen and unknown — animals not counted, plants not studied, relationships not understood. There is a secretive little snake called the western ground snake. Because it is known only from several specimens found along tributaries in the central part of the Grand Canyon, it is considered unique to the canyon. Its length is 10 to 12 inches. Its color is red or orange with black bands. It burrows in the ground, is oviparous, laying eggs rather than giving birth to live young, and feeds on ants, small invertebrates, and invertebrate larvae. Or so it is thought. By and large, the life of the western ground snake is a mystery, carried on in its own private way under the surface in side canyons of side canyons deep in the heart of the Grand Canyon.

It should continue that way, for ground snakes and every other creature in the park. It shouldn't matter that some details escape the range of human knowledge. One of the guiding purposes of a national park is to provide wild animals and plants with enough protection to carry out their lives in a natural manner. If we know about them and how they live, that's nice for us. If we don't, at least we can be confident that whatever exists out there will carry on as it always has. A national park is meant to protect a system, which in turn will protect all its constituent parts, even the secrets. Maybe especially the secrets.

Would that it were true. Would that the old Colorado River had survived with its ancient secrets. But that is another story.

9
The River

The river. El Rio Colorado. Eventually, everything comes down to the Colorado. All the rocks in all the talus slopes, the shales and limestones, all the weathered, jewellike teeth of mice, the spines of cacti, the skulls of bighorn sheep, the rank and rotting trunks of cottonwood trees — the river takes it all, embraces it, and carries it away.

In the Grand Canyon's 277 miles, the river bed drops 2,220 vertical feet. It begins at Lees Ferry (3,090 feet) and emerges from the canyon at Grand Wash Cliffs at an elevation of 870 feet. The last 43 miles of the river channel, however, are currently submerged beneath the head of Lake Mead, which has a surface elevation of about 1,200 feet. This means that its effective drop is actually about 1,900 feet.

The river lowers itself into the canyon like a hiker on a well-graded trail, down through the layers of rock that rise above the water and move past in a panorama of geologic history. The journey begins at the base of cliffs made from Navajo Sandstone, the light-colored, smooth stone that characterizes most of Glen Canyon. Lees Ferry itself is located on the Moenkopi Formation, soft and red, easily eroded, and not generally seen on the canyon rims. The Grand Canyon officially begins immediately

Lees Ferry

Pearce Ferry

below Lees Ferry, where the Kaibab Limestone outcrops at a gentle angle. The tilted strata give the impression that the river is sliding steeply beneath the surface of the desert, but this is an illusion. Its average gradient is approximately 7.7 feet per mile, which is steep for a large river (25 times steeper than the Mississippi) but not steep enough to explain the fast-rising height of the canyon walls.

Soon the Toroweap Limestone makes its appearance, and after that, the Coconino Sandstone. Together, these three layers form the high vertical walls of Marble Canyon, which becomes deeper and deeper as the miles go by. Less than five miles from Lees Ferry, Navajo Bridge, which is level with the rim, stands 467 feet above the river.

After the Coconino comes the Hermit Shale, a red slope several hundred feet high, littered with boulders from the harder cliff-forming members above. Below that, only 11.2 river miles from Lees Ferry, the Supai Formation comes into view, lifting its rough, broken cliffs above the water line. About 10 miles later (mile 22.6), a smooth, gray ledge appears beneath the shaley Supai. This is the Redwall Limestone, namesake of Marble Canyon. Where the river meets the Redwall, it smoothes and polishes the limestone, revealing subtle internal colors, and producing one of the most beautiful stone surfaces found anywhere on earth. It resembles marble, but it has not yet undergone sufficient metamorphosis for geologists to classify it as such.

Down then, deeper in the canyon, past Vasey's Paradise, where springs burst from the sheer canyon wall and support a lush hanging garden; and on to Redwall Cavern, a solution cave at river level — a deep hollow dissolved out of the limestone before the Colorado exposed it to view, in the same way that a knife exposes a cavity in Swiss cheese. The Redwall is riddled with caves and solution pockets.

At mile 33, Redwall Cavern is scarcely past the beginning of a float trip through the Grand Canyon. So much more lies below — rapids to run and hot sand beaches to camp on, intimate side canyons, waterfalls, and warm nights filled with the music of the river. Where Marble Canyon ends, the river emerges into a relatively open bottomland eroded from the Grand Canyon Supergroup. But not for long; suddenly up rears the hard old core, the Vishnu Schist, beginning what Powell called the Granite Gorge. The first outcrop is at mile 77.4. On average, the river's width is several hundred feet. This is the narrow part. The walls are dark and close. Entering, it feels like you're being poured down a drain, swallowed into the gut of the canyon. From up ahead comes the thudding rumble of Sockdolager Rapid, dropping 19 vertical feet through a series of mighty constriction waves, only the first of many rapids within the gorge.

If you float every day you can get through the canyon in about two weeks. If you go by motorized raft, you can do it in five or six days. Either way, it will feel like a rush trip. The canyon has a way of altering the tallying of time. The days pour together and mingle their affairs until only the flow has meaning. Never mind the miles or the hours or even the names of things. The canyon and its river become the only world you care to know.

Not so long ago — the 1920s would be far enough back — it was possible to put your boat into the Colorado River somewhere in its upper reaches, wherever it looked attractive and big enough to float an expedition-sized boat, and float without the interruption of dams and reservoirs, and hardly a highway bridge, all the way to the Gulf of Mexico. The journey would end on the salty side of a vast delta, beneath the wings of herons, egrets, pelicans, and clouds of seabirds.

A dream trip: Emery and Ellsworth Kolb, who ran a photo studio on the South Rim for many years, made the run in 1911–12, from Green River, Wyoming (on the Green River), through Grand Canyon to the sea. You can still make the journey, if you're willing to traverse hundreds of miles of still water in the chain of reservoirs arrayed down the length of the Colorado, and if you keep in mind that the river, sucked dry providing water to thirsty western cities and farms, rarely makes it to the delta any more. (Not all the water is used in the Southwest; there

Entering the Granite Gorge

Heretofore hard rocks have given us bad river; soft rocks, smooth water; and a series of rocks harder than any we have experienced sets in. The river enters the gneiss! We can see but a little way into the granite gorge, but it looks threatening.

After breakfast we enter on the waves. At the very introduction it inspires awe. The canyon is narrower than we have ever before seen it; the water is swifter; there are but few broken rocks in the channel; but the walls are set, on either side, with pinnacles and crags; and sharp, angular buttresses, bristling with wind- and wave-polished spires, extend far out into the river....

As we proceed the granite rises higher, until nearly a thousand feet of the lower part of the walls are composed of this rock.

John Wesley Powell, *The Exploration of the Colorado River and its Canyons* are at least 22 major diversions of the river in the state of Colorado alone.)

Nowadays, boaters divide the river into segments. Powerboaters take to the reservoirs. River runners in kayaks, dories, and rafts (some with motors) stick to the places where the water still moves. This means that river trips usually end at Mile 227, where a road provides access to a landing at Diamond Creek. It is the first road to reach the river since Lees Ferry.

Mountain Water in the Desert

The Colorado rises in the Never-Summer Range on the west side of Rocky Mountain National Park in the state of Colorado. Among its major tributaries it counts the Green River, pouring out of Wyoming's Wind River Range, and the San Juan River, which starts in the San Juan Mountains of southwestern Colorado. All three rivers begin among melting snowfields at about 14,000 feet elevation and fall through white cascades and icy blue pools to the soft red world of the Colorado Plateau. They start among the hard Precambrian granites of their respective mountain ranges and join their waters in the Paleozoic and Permian sediments of a much more recent time.

It's like hitting chalk — soft, friable, soluble rock that turns to mud and clay. Having arrived free of any sediment, still exhaling the cold of alpine snowfields, the rivers are made over by their contact with the desert. They go red as if sunburned. Their water turns warm and lazy, flowing indolently in graceful loops through one canyon after another. In a few places, their pulse quickens. Westwater and Cataract canyons have whitewater on the same scale as the Grand Canyon. The Green River sees some action in Grey and Desolation canyons. But generally speaking all is peaceful until the rivers, combined into one master stream, drift into the Grand Canyon at Lees Ferry.

Mountain water in the desert. By the time it reaches the Gulf of California, the Colorado River has traveled 1,400 miles. All told, its drainage area measures 244,000 square miles. Average annual flow tops eight million acre-feet. Most of the water, of course, never gets to the gulf. It ends up in irrigation networks and urban water systems. There

Michael Collier

Glen Canyon Dam, 710 feet high, closed its gates in 1963, causing dramatic environmental changes along the river corridor.

are those who believe water flowing into the ocean is a waste.

The name means red. Red River. Red for the sediments it carries. Sandstone, shale, especially clay that pours like red paint into the water from surrounding drainages. During summer thunderstorm season, the water's density is astonishing. It doesn't exactly splash; it blurps. It coats everything with which it comes in contact — boats, paddles, skin, floating driftwood, boulders along the shore.

Or rather, it did, until the Glen Canyon Dam was built. Lake Powell now intercepts most of the sediment that used to flow through Grand Canyon. It settles out in growing deltaic deposits that will someday turn the sparkling reservoir into a great winding mud flat. Probably excellent wildlife habitat.

I never saw the Colorado in Grand Canyon before the dam. My image of the early river comes from time spent floating on it and its sister rivers above Lake Powell.

The difference between those upper rivers and the Colorado in Grand Canyon is like night and day. The summer temperature of the Green

River in Desolation Canyon is 70 to 75 degrees. I've spent hours drifting in a life jacket beside the raft, up to my neck in the slow-moving embrace of gentle water. That same water, emerging from the frigid depths of Lake Powell, is as clear as spring water and too cold for swimming. It has a hard, polished, wintry beauty. It takes your breath away. Because they are continually doused by waves, kayakers wear waterproof paddling jackets even on hot days. I knew a scientist whose work required that he stand up to his waist in the river for hours at a time. Having his lower half immersed in 48-degree water and his upper half in 110-degree air was too much for his body's temperature regulatory mechanism to handle. He complained of splitting headaches and dizziness. It was unnatural.

An unnatural contrast. That isn't a bad analogy for what the dam has done to the Grand Canyon's river environment. Ecological headaches. The dam has produced cold water, clear water, wildly fluctuating flows on a day-to-day basis, and reduced fluctuation on a seasonal basis. We'll look at these one at a time.

Cold Water

First, the cold water. Drawn into the dam 200 feet below the surface of Lake Powell, it drops through penstocks to turn the mighty turbines of the electric generators, and emerges at the foot of the dam with a nearly constant temperature of 48 degrees, winter and summer, an unnatural condition that has wreaked havoc with native fish.

It's not the cold itself that has done the damage, but rather the unvarying cold. During winter, when its flow commonly dropped to around 1,000 cubic feet per second (the lowest on record being 700 cubic feet per second in December of 1942), the old river would chill to near freezing. Then in summer it would warm up to 75 and even 85 degrees. Native fishes were accustomed to this range of temperatures. Their life cycles were tied to it. They could survive winter conditions, but they needed the summer's warmth for successful hatching of eggs and the growth of young. The new river is never warm.

Native fishes in the pre-dam river included bonytail, roundtail, and humpback chubs; also flannelmouth, bluehead, and razorback suckers;

speckled dace; and Colorado squawfish. All but the suckers are of the minnow family, and all but the dace grow larger than what we think of as minnows. Humpback chubs get to around 18 inches in length. The bonytail chub reaches 15 inches. But the squawfish was the champion of the Colorado, approaching six feet in length.

No more. Squawfish and roundtail chubs are extinct from the Grand Canyon. The razorback sucker was once thought to have vanished, until five individuals showed up in electroshock surveys. They still face oblivion; these were old fish that might have survived since before the dam was built. At least two alien fish have also been affected by the new river — carp and channel catfish.

With the river denied them as a spawning ground, native fishes are left with isolated pockets where tributary streams, unaffected by the dam, still provide limited original habitat. The only place known for certain to be used for spawning is the Little Colorado River. Because humpback chubs are found far downstream, it is surmised that other small areas (Shinumo Creek, for example) serve a similar function. But this is hard to say. Chubs can live a long

The humpback chub, once common in the canyon, is in danger of extinction.

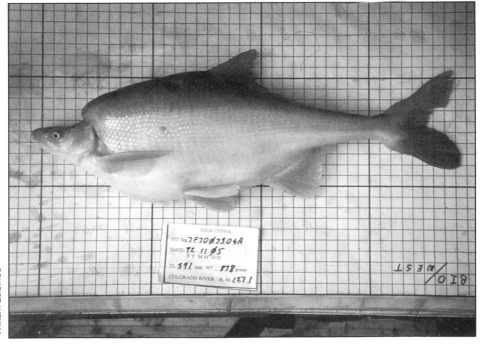

William Leibfried

David Edwards

The Grand Canyon begins at Lees Ferry. Four miles downriver from this picture, the canyon walls are nearly five hundred feet high.

time, perhaps as long as 40 years. Their presence does not confirm that they are spawning.

Is the remaining humpback chub population, estimated at 15,000 fish, in trouble? It's possible that humpback chubs could continue indefinitely with only one spawning area. The adults do all right in the river as long as they have a place to spawn.

On the other hand, it would take a relatively small disaster to devastate the Little Colorado spawning grounds. A toxic spill at the Cameron highway bridge and... who knows? It is not good for the entire Grand Canyon population of humpback chubs to rely on a short stretch of a small river as its only spawning grounds.

Other threats to the population include striped bass. Voracious predators, bass are a popular (exotic) game fish in both Lake Powell and Lake Mead. They enter the Grand Canyon either by swimming upriver, or being drawn through the penstocks of Glen Canyon Dam. Also, the 1983 flood transported large numbers past the dam.

Very little is known about pre-dam conditions on the river. Not even the humpback chub was recognized as a distinct species until 1942, when a visiting biologist took a close look at the single preserved specimen in the natural history collection.

Recently, a new threat has appeared — the Asian tapeworm, a species introduced with carp on the East Coast many years ago, which now presents an undetermined peril to native species in the Grand Canyon. It affects primarily the minnow family, including carp and chubs. How it got to the canyon is a matter of speculation, but it could easily have moved downstream from Lake Powell, carried by a species of copepod that serves as an intermediate host. Unlike some tapeworms, this species does not attach to the stomach lining. It lives loose, as a bolus in the stomach, in some cases nearly filling the stomach. Its effect on humpback chubs is not fully known, but Arizona Game and Fish personnel studying the problem believe it to be chronic and not acute; that is, it would tend to reduce growth rates and affect the storage of fat, which in turn could affect mortality rates but would not kill the fish outright. When parasites and their hosts evolve together they usually strike some sort of balance that allows both to survive. But these are exotic parasites, which can be devastating to host populations that have not had the opportunity to develop evolutionary protections. Whatever is going on, it seems to be happening fast. In 1989, no tapeworms were found in a total of 14 humpback chubs that were examined. A year later, 100 percent of 15 mature chubs subjected to autopsies carried the worms.

Clear Water

The old river never ran clear. Its job as an agent of erosion was to transport sediment and, as the Grand Canyon well demonstrates, it has performed well. The pre-dam river carried sediment loads calculated to average around 380,000 tons per day past Phantom Ranch. The biggest recorded flow was reached on one spectacular day in 1921 when the river rose to 200,000 cubic feet per second, carrying an estimated 27 *million* tons of sediment past Phantom Ranch.

Now the average daily sediment load measured at Phantom Ranch is on the order of 40,000 tons per day. All of this must come into the river below the dam, from tributaries including the Paria River at Lees Ferry, the Little Colorado River, and numerous small drainages. An

Grand Canyon N.P. Division of Resources Management

The erosion of Grand Canyon beaches is evident in comparison photos. Stone Creek campsite in May of 1981 (above) was broad and sandy. Eleven years later, in March of 1992 (opposite) the beach is smaller, studded with exposed rocks. The sand cliff in the foreground shows the result of rapidly fluctuating river levels.

unmeasured quantity of the river's load comes from the river bed itself—and this is a cause of concern.

The old river carried sediment out of the canyon but also replaced it with more from upstream. The new river does nothing but scour. It carries away first the fine material, then the sand. Beaches are shrinking; some have vanished altogether. The river bed, once buried in soft sediments, is now a hard, cobbled surface in its upper reaches, where the water has done the most thorough job of scrubbing away sand and silt. Generally the effects of clear water are most pronounced just below the dam; they diminish farther downstream, as the river picks up sediment and carries a more normal load.

In addition to scouring sediment, clear water is transparent. It allows light to reach the now-stony bottom. The old river bed was a murky place, fine for the chubs and suckers that evolved in just those conditions. The new river is best suited to new fish, and upon first hearing about this, few people shed tears. The new fish are trout. Big ones.

Long before the dam was built, rainbow and brown trout were released in canyon streams, notably Bright Angel Creek. Later, still thinking they might improve what Theodore Roosevelt said so prophetically could never be improved, the park service introduced amphipods (*Gammarus locustris,* also inaccurately called freshwater shrimp). A small crustacean and favorite food of trout, amphipods were also alien to the Colorado River system. They could not have survived in the seasonally warm and turbid river, but they did fine in the cool, usually clear streams. Then the gates of the dam were closed, the lake began to fill, sediment settled in the reservoir, and the river ran clear. Into this newly expanded world spilled trout and amphipods and other creatures from the side streams. They joined millions of their kind dumped into the river by Arizona Game and Fish personnel.

The new river resembles a Montana spring creek — with a cold, constant flow of water and a stony bottom rich in algae and food organisms. The dominant alga is *Cladophora glomerata,* which grows in long, bright green strands attached to the river bed. Cladophora forms dense clouds that billow in the current and provide a base for many other living things.

Grand Canyon N.P. Division of Resources Management

Among the smallest are diatoms, one-celled organisms capable of photosynthesis that attach themselves to the algae. Diatoms are a major food source for the amphipods and other creatures which in turn feed the trout. Actually, the conditions here are better than a spring creek, whose waters are pure; the water surging through the dam is loaded with nutrients (notably phosphorous, which is essential for Cladophora growth) and microscopic zooplankton which occur abundantly in the lake and add to the richness of the river.

The result is a world-renowned trout fishery, especially the 15.8-mile section of river between Lees Ferry and the dam. Rainbow trout weighing 18 pounds have been taken; also the state record brook trout, tipping the scales at 5.5 pounds. (Brown and cutthroat trout have also been taken here, but the trout are predominantly rainbows.)

Below Lees Ferry, the Paria River joins the Colorado and during wet times of the year, clouds it with silt. Much of the time, however, the Colorado remains green all the way to its junction with the Little Colorado River, which, if it is flowing, can add significant amounts of sediment. Of course it's not always flowing, and then the Colorado picks up only small amounts of sediment from its own bed, or from small tributaries, and retains its clarity for many miles. This means trout fishing for almost the entire length of the canyon — a recent development that delights many people. Besides providing fish, the clear river is gorgeous to look at, despite being an unnatural color in the desert.

If they could state their feelings, bald eagles would agree. In the mid- to late '80s, eagles began to discover a winter spawning run of trout in and around the mouth of Nankoweap Creek, in the eastern canyon. The number of eagles spending time here in the winter has increased to over a hundred. The creek has apparently become an important source of food for them, providing fuel for their long northward migrations.

No one disputes that trout are a noble and much-desired species. But this is a national park, not a zoo or a fish farm that we manipulate to suit the current fashion. Some might think that the loss of some extra-large minnows is a price worth paying for trophy trout, without taking into account the larger issues involved. These include such weighty matters as biological diversity and the integrity of national parks. The biggest loss — and it goes back to well before the dam was built — is one of knowledge. We have no clear picture of the river, and many of its tributaries, in their natural states. There is no baseline against which to measure changes, and this makes management of the river a bigger challenge than it might otherwise be.

The End of Floods

Spring floods once roared through the canyon, depositing sediment, clearing out driftwood, moving rocks, rearranging rapids and sweeping the banks clear of vegetation. Fed by snowmelt from the high Rockies, the floods typically came in late May or early June and were gone by early July. The flows would subside for a month or so, to be replaced in August by summer flash floods brought on by the region's annual monsoonal thunderstorms. Early photographs of the river show broad sandy banks and rocky shorelines with few mature riparian plants.

During the big spring floods, the river rose 30 to 50 feet from its normal summer level, even 100 feet where the

Confluence of the Colorado and the Little Colorado rivers. Since the dam was built, the Little Colorado has become more significant as a source of sediment and as the last known breeding habitat of the humpback chub in Grand Canyon.

Department of Interior, Grand Canyon N.P.

channel was especially narrow. If we discount the extremes, we find an average annual fluctuation of around 4,000 and 90,000 cubic feet per second, with summer flows generally around 20,000 cubic feet per second. Since the dam was built, the maximum has been limited to around 30,000, except for the flood of 1983 and the high-water years that followed. Not to worry, say the water engineers, that will not happen again. (These are the same fellows who at one time said it would not happen at all.)

There could certainly be another flood similar to the one witnessed in 1923 by the Birdseye expedition. The result of intense summer thunderstorms, it came out of the Little Colorado River (mile 61) and raised the level of the river at Lava Falls (mile 179) by 12 feet in a matter of hours. The maximum flow from that flood reached 95,000 cubic feet per second (measured at Phantom Ranch). Because there are still no dams on the Little Colorado, a flood of that size could occur again, although it would be an unusual event and the subject of much excitement among river runners who happened to be in the canyon at the time. It is unlikely that we will ever see a flood on the scale of the spring runoff in 1921, when 200,000 cubic feet per second roared under the bridge at Phantom Ranch; or in 1884, when there was a flood, estimated from driftwood lines above the river, of 300,000 cubic feet per second.

What, then, are the effects of controlling the river within such a narrow range of flow?

First, from a river runner's point of view, the new Colorado lacks the power to rearrange its rapids. One of the most interesting aspects of canyon rapids is that they are all runnable. There are no impassable waterfalls, no horrendous, river-blocking hydraulics. The river has always been able to keep up with the job of removing material dumped into it. But what happens now that the river lacks its old seasonal punch? It is likely — perhaps inevitable — that a flash flood or debris flow or rockslide will someday create a new boulder dam, squeezing the river into a channel too narrow to navigate, with water too wild for any boat. This could happen in numerous places, not just one. The river channel would become choked with increasingly dangerous rapids. What is now the most challenging rapid on the river — Crystal Rapid — was raised to its current level of difficulty by a post-dam (1966) debris flow. The 1983 flood managed only to make it worse. At certain water levels, Crystal becomes so dangerous that passengers on commercial raft trips are told to walk around. Someday everyone might have to walk, and carry the boats to boot.

Meanwhile, the lowered flows have had a far-reaching impact on streamside plants. Before the dam, there were two distinct belts of riparian vegetation. One was in the area affected by flooding; the other was just above the flood line, which was often 30 feet (or more) higher than normal summer flows.

The lower belt was an unstable environment that swung from one extreme to the other — from inundation to desiccation, from underwater (and battered by strong currents) to high and dry. Floods wiped the slate clean. Except in occasional protected niches, only the quick-growing plants could put down roots, mature, blossom, and set seed before the next flood. This meant annuals for the most part — grasses and fast-growing herbaceous plants.

The upper belt was a thin line of woody, riparian plants perched on the top of the flood line where they were safe from scouring currents but could periodically get enough water to live. Generally these were shrubs and small trees. In the canyon's upper reaches, they included redbud, Apache-plume, scrub oak, and netleaf hackberry. In its lower parts, where warmer conditions prevailed, honey mesquite and catclaw acacia were predominant.

Above both belts, providing the sort of radical juxtaposition that the canyon does so well, were the desert plants, independent of the river. Like the others, they varied from one end of the canyon to the other, from the low, warm western end to the cooler eastern end. This belt has not been affected by the dam, except that it might have moved down into places that the water no longer reaches. Generally, the variety of desert vegetation is richer in the western canyon, where ocotillo, barrel cactus, creosote bush, cholla cactus, and even a few Joshuatrees are found.

The two lower vegetation belts were dramatically changed by the dam. The new high water line is on average about 30 feet lower than the old one. No longer do floods scour the areas previously affected by flows above 30,000 cubic feet per second. As a result, plants from the upper belt have moved down into once-hostile territory. What had been a thin (in places nonexistent) green line became an ebullient, almost impenetrable thicket. At the same time, the lower belt has been

David Edwards

A large open beach in 1987, this sandbar was mostly covered with grasses, cattails, and tamarisk by 1992.

considerably narrowed, pushed toward the river by the expanding tangle of coyote willow, seep-willow, desert broom, arrowweed, and tamarisk.

Particularly tamarisk. A vigorous colonizer, tamarisk produces large numbers of seeds throughout the summer months. It grows in dense stands, crowding out other species, occupying even formerly bare sandbars. Being an exotic plant, tamarisk is officially unwelcome in the national park, and for a time it was feared that tamarisk would overcome and replace native species. But its primary native competitor, coyote willow, turns out to have one important advantage: It reproduces by root cloning, not by seedlings. Lacking floods at the right time of year, tamarisk has trouble reproducing. Its seeds fall on dry ground. At the same time, willow (and other clonal species, including arrowweed) are able to invade tamarisk stands and gradually outcompete the alien plant.

The old floods did more than wipe out vegetation; they also performed a nurturing service. By saturating ground that otherwise remains dry, the floods gave mesquite seeds, for example, a chance to become established. Once mesquite puts down roots and reaches the water table, it can live high above the river. But it needs help getting started. Without floods, no seedlings replace old plants, and the roots of the highest plants find themselves above the lowered water table. Thus the old flood line, which once stood at the 100,000 cubic feet per second level, marked by mesquite and acacia and others, is liable to vanish. It will retreat to lower, wetter ground or disappear entirely, according to local circumstances — just as it must have done throughout the history of the canyon, following the river ever deeper.

The increased riparian vegetation provides habitat for a host of animals, beginning with insects and working up to deer. There have been dramatic increases in the populations of nesting birds, who find in the dense thickets their three essentials — cover, food, and nest sites. In turn, peregrine falcons nesting in cliffs above the river are provided with more of their primary food source, small birds. Rodents, lizards, snakes, amphibians, and arachnids have moved into the new vegetation, eating and being eaten in larger numbers than ever before.

Some species are still problematic. Although otters have been sighted occasionally in the past, no one knows their status at present. Certainly they are rare. Perhaps the sightings made years ago were of transient animals, or maybe the population has always been so low that years can pass with no reliable observer noticing one. The same is true of muskrats. For either animal, it would seem that conditions have been enhanced by the dam. The increase in riverbank vegetation provides cover for both, and nesting materials and food for the muskrat. Otters would find the trout-hunting good. Spring floods would no longer wipe out nesting grounds or young animals.

River otters, which are abundant elsewhere, could be reintroduced and would likely do very well, but the park is hesitant in case there remains a native population, perhaps genetically distinct, that would be harmed by an influx of non-native animals.

Changes in the river environment have certainly improved life for beavers, the one aquatic mammal known to inhabit the canyon. Beavers have apparently been here all along, in small numbers, living on the river and in major side streams. Obviously the increase in vegetation has provided them with more of their favorite foods — primarily coyote willow, the common shrubby willow found wherever there is abundant ground water. It grows well on riverbanks and sandbars, as long as the ground that supports it is not swept away or rearranged by periodic floods. Besides coyote willow, beavers in the canyon also eat Goodding willow, cottonwood, tamarisk, catclaw acacia, mesquite, cattails, and various riparian roots, most of which benefit from the new conditions.

Fluctuating Flows

We've just seen that the river flow rate is more stable than it was before the dam was built. But fluctuations on a smaller scale create their own havoc. The problem has to do with peaking power, the production of electricity to meet times of high demand. When people in Phoenix and Los Angeles start up their air conditioners on hot summer days, power demand lurches upward. Hydro facilities like Glen Canyon Dam have an advantage in meeting these sudden needs because they can be turned on and off at a moment's notice, literally changing by the minute. Coal-fired plants have a long warm-up period and cannot respond so quickly.

The demand for electricity fluctuates daily, according to a predictable cycle. In summer, air conditioners go on in the morning and off at night. So did the dam, once it began operating for peaking power in the early '80s. In doing so, it generated not only electricity but tremendous profits as well. And it wreaked havoc on the river, which fluctuated between less than 3,000 cubic feet per second to a maximum of 31,500 cubic feet per second (33,200 after changes made in the mid-1980s). The river rose and fell 10 feet or more in a matter of hours. Trout were left high and dry, trapped by the rapid retreat of the river. Sandbars, suddenly exposed, collapsed as the water contained within them rushed out. Gently sloping beaches became toppling sand cliffs. The river was being flushed like a toilet.

The politics and history of Colorado River water management — from start to finish, through all its various dams and diversions and pork barrels — could supply the plot line for a thick Russian novel. It's a story that goes way back to John Wesley Powell. It involves seven states, two countries, and a welter of federal and state bureaucracies. Opinions are always divided; objectives are contradictory; one group's values are another group's curse; but always, it seems, the river and its natural systems are the last interests served.

The story makes for fascinating reading — in some other book. The point worth making here is that according to long-standing western (and national) tradition, water is regarded as the servant and tool of society. How much is stored, where it is stored, how it is used, and when it is allowed to flow are decisions that have almost always been guided by political and economic considerations.

As for natural environments, the dam builders buried Glen Canyon, a place unique on the face of the Earth, without so much as a backward glance. The same interests had planned two more dams in the Grand Canyon itself (these were stopped by an energetic conservation battle in the mid-'60s). People eager to build lakes in the canyon could hardly be expected to consider the effect of the dam's operation on the river and its creatures. The river that once rose and fell with the mysterious and profoundly beautiful circle of the seasons has been reduced to a reflection of business cycles and the tides of commerce.

That might be changing. The preeminent position of power generation and water storage over all other values has at last been shaken. As usual, the politics have followed a dark and winding course through an opposition emplaced like Precambrian bedrock (the Russian novel plot again). The heroes go unnamed because they do not make the official announcements, but it must be said that the announcements were encouraging for the future of the river. In August of 1989, Secretary of the Interior Manuel Lujan reluctantly ordered an Environmental Impact Statement on the operation of the Glen Canyon Dam. There had been other studies, some ongoing, but they lacked the political punch of an EIS. Two years later, Lujan announced a period of experimental "interim flows" on the Colorado River below the dam. These flows, designed to limit the damage done by rapid fluctuations until research was finished, were limited to a maximum of 20,000 cubic feet per second and a minimum of 5,000. Moreover, daily fluctuation rates would be held between 5,000 and 8,000 cubic feet per second. After a 90-day test period, the interim flows would remain in effect until the EIS was finished in late 1993.

In October, 1992, President George Bush signed the Grand Canyon Protection Act. This law was based on a new principle: Glen Canyon

Dam must be operated in a manner that protects and enhances the natural environment of Grand Canyon National Park and Glen Canyon National Recreation Area. It required that interim flows be maintained until completion of the EIS and mandated a long-term monitoring program to ensure that the canyon's resources are protected. In the end, decisions regarding the actual operation of the dam would be made by the Secretary of the Interior based on the findings of the EIS and the monitoring program.

Considering the former reluctance of the Bush administration to act on these matters, there was much relief among supporters of the river when the 1992 elections guaranteed a new Secretary of the Interior. There was positive enthusiasm when Bruce Babbit, former governor of Arizona, a man not only familiar with the river but inclined toward backpacking trips in the canyon, was confirmed as interior secretary.

Depending on how it is administered, the law could mark a significant turn of policy. At least in principle, the ecological health of Grand Canyon National Park has been given priority over the profits of the dam. This is not to say that the river's problems are over. How to protect the canyon's resources is still very much a matter of interpretation.

Wilderness River

In 1911-12, when Emery and Ellsworth Kolb ran the river, they must have felt a bit like Apollo astronauts visiting a world beyond the reach of all but a select few. They made the trip in wooden boats not very different from those used by Powell and produced a film telling the story of their adventure. They knew that thousands of tourists who could never hope to do the same would at least want to see how it was down there in the hidden, turbulent gut of the Grand Canyon. They were right. For years afterward, in the auditorium of their combined home and studio on the South Rim, they entertained visitors with tales of perilous adventure and daring among the mighty rapids of the Colorado.

It was indeed a great challenge to run the river in the early days. Only a few had gone before them, and while Powell had demonstrated that there was no great waterfall lurking around some blind corner, a point of no return and certain death — in short, that it could be done at

David Edwards

Snowy egrets do not breed in the canyon but use the river corridor as a migration route.

all — no one had removed the essential danger from the enterprise.

As late as 1949, only 100 river runners had traversed the Colorado through Grand Canyon. By 1954, only 200. But gradually a new attitude toward outdoor adventure was taking hold. Places like Grand Canyon were no longer considered the special domain of explorers and scientists only. Other people had reasons for being there — reasons that were as legitimate as any science. They were personal reasons. Reasons of the heart. We call it recreation, but it is much, much more than simply having fun.

Aiding the nonspecialist was an array of new equipment — perhaps most important, inflatable rubber boats and bridge pontoons left over from World War II. Practically indestructible, and in their larger sizes nearly impossible to tip over even in the biggest rapids, the "baloney boats" (as they were disparagingly called by the wooden-boat oldtimers) opened the river to just about anyone who wanted to go. Hundreds did, and after word got out, thousands more floated the Colorado as paying passengers or independently with groups of friends.

There were still hazards to face. There are hazards even today. But the biggest lesson was not one of adventure and risk. Rather, the canyon proved to be a much friendlier place than many had imagined. Far from a gloomy abyss, it was a place of light and natural richness.

The popularity of the river boomed, until in 1972 over 16,400 people ran the river. Concern developed over the impact of so many people camping on the beaches, burning driftwood, burying their garbage, scattering their waste, and tramping through side canyons. That year, the park service began limiting permits. Studies were conducted on human impact along the river, and new regulations were drawn up requiring clean camping techniques.

The new regulations worked. Of all backcountry users, river runners have the least impact per person. Their boats leave no tracks on the water. They carry out all their solid waste, even toilet waste. Commercial guides are among the most devoted to keeping the canyon in a pristine state. In some ways, they have a better grasp of canyon conditions than the uniformed personnel who oversee their operations. They know the place intimately, care about it passionately, and try their best to pass on these values to their passengers.

Even so, there's no denying that 15,000 people per year floating down the river have an impact on the inner canyon, if only because they walk the same trails to the same beauty spots. Inevitably, campsites and major attractions acquire a worn look. Worn by affection to be sure, but worn nonetheless. There's talk of more regulation, more stringent limits.

But it's worth pointing out a paradox. Compared to the violence done the canyon and its river system by the Glen Canyon and Hoover dams, and compared to the mood-shattering noise of sight-seeing aircraft and commercial jets in the air overhead, and compared to the scenic degradation caused by air pollution from any number of sources — and most of all, compared to the potential effects of the dams that some would still like to build in the Grand Canyon itself — the impact of hikers and boaters is very small indeed.

Clearly the river is a highly altered place. If it were possible to do so, and the park's objectives were the primary factors to consider, the ultimate goal would be to return the river to its natural condition, the way it was before the dam was built and before carp and catfish found their way into the system. This, of course, is impossible for a variety of reasons, not the least of which is the lack of information about pre-dam conditions.

Among the suggestions for alleviating the impact of the Glen Canyon Dam is a proposal to modify the dam's intake structure, in effect raising the point of intake from its current location 200 feet below the top of the dam, and causing it to draw water from the sun-warmed surface of the lake instead of from the frigid depths. The warmer water, of course, makes a warmer river below the dam and might provide suitable spawning temperatures for the native fish during four months of summer. That seems like a reasonable and simple answer to the temperature problems. However, there are always complicating biological factors in these matters, and this one is no different. First of all, if warm water is taken from the surface of Lake Powell, that could disrupt systems within the lake with unforeseen results. Furthermore, it might not work. Is it really possible to skim large quantities of warm water off the surface of the lake without bringing cold water up from below? Beyond that, what other effects would warm water have on the river below the dam? Would it benefit exotic catfish, therefore increasing their population? Would it encourage the copepods, which among other things serve as intermediate hosts for the Asian tapeworm? What would it do to the *Cladophora* algae? Simply warming the river might create more problems than it solves.

The whole business could be depressing. But I keep one thing in mind. I remember those big lava dams that formed over a million years ago in the western canyon. They were catastrophic events. The biggest ones must have dried up the river completely for years at a time. Their reservoirs were immense; the largest was much bigger than Lake Powell. Imagine how people would react if it happened today.

The river can take care of itself. It most certainly will. And the canyon — well, it's a big old place that has seen worse than anything we can ever do to it. That doesn't stop us from being sad about the self-induced impoverishment of the natural world in our own time. Our only time. But it's some small comfort nonetheless.

Western collared lizard

Where to Find Wildlife

Mammals

It has been said that the most abundant mammals at the canyon are white-footed mice. This might be true, but you'd never guess it by looking. Like so many other canyon creatures, mice are secretive, shy, and nocturnal. We have to accept, almost as a matter of faith, that they exist at all. Yet some mammals are easily seen. Rock squirrels, Uinta chipmunks, and cliff chipmunks frequent both rims, where some of them have learned to beg for scraps (they should not be fed). Small bands of mule deer roam throughout the canyon, even in the developed areas. Elk are present on both rims, although sightings are rare on the North Rim and not common on the South Rim. One of the best places to find elk is in the area of Grandview Point, early in the morning or just at dusk. Bighorn sheep, reputed to be among the most reclusive of all wild animals, are in fact rather common along the river corridor and easily spotted by boaters. Recently, a small band of sheep has been frequently seen by hikers along the Bright Angel Trail between Indian Garden and the South Rim.

Among predators, mountain lions have never been common but are reported on a regular basis. They prefer rocky, broken country along the canyon rims or in larger side canyons. After a light snow on the North Rim, a hiker stands a good chance of finding tracks, if not the animal itself. The same goes for bobcat and coyote tracks. The meadows of the North Rim are a likely place to find coyotes hunting mice. They do it with a grace and skill that cats might envy.

Kaibab squirrels, recognized by their flamboyant white tails, are a pleasure to see. Look for them wherever there are ponderosa pines, but only on the North Rim. The large tree squirrels on the South Rim (lacking white on their tails) are their close relatives, Abert squirrels. Also among the conifers, and usually but not always nocturnal, are porcupines. You can sometimes hear them before you see them. They make strange, unexpected sounds — high-pitched, like babies crying, or singing to themselves, *doo doo dee doo doo*. Many a spooky story of haunted forests ends with the hilarious discovery of an unassuming little porcupine.

Below the canyon rims is a whole different world, especially at night. Backpackers become all too familiar with creatures like ringtails and spotted skunks, both of which are inveterate camp robbers. However, the biggest nighttime nuisance comes from members of the genus *Peromyscus*, white-footed mice, of which the canyon enjoys five species — the deer mice, cactus mouse, canyon mice, brush mouse and pinyon mouse. The species vary with

location, but just about anywhere you choose to camp, you can scan the area with a flashlight shortly after dark and pick out a few mousy marauders, among other nocturnal creatures.

Birds

Fortunately for birders, there is an excellent guidebook to the canyon's birds, *Grand Canyon Birds* by Bryan Brown. The book lists 303 species found in the Grand Canyon and surrounding area. Brown gives expert and thorough advice on where to find birds and what to expect in the various vegetative zones. For general advice, he points out that areas of mixed vegetation are richest in bird life. At Grand Canyon, these are often places with water — along the river or near streams, springs, and ponds. They also include edges of meadows and the shrubby areas along and just below either rim. One of the most rewarding techniques for birdwatching is to sit quietly at some point on the rim, especially in spring and early summer, and keep a sharp eye (and ear) peeled. It is a birding axiom that you can chase some flitting feathery bundle all day and not get a close look at it; but if you sit still and think about other things, that very bird will soon enough come to you. In birding, patience is everything.

Without running down the list of all 303 species, it is worthwhile to point out the birds most visible along the rims. White-throated swifts and violet-green swallows fly together, cruising exuberantly along the edge of the precipice. Both catch insects on the wing and can be hard to tell apart. Swallows fly a little slower on wider wings; swifts are sometimes called "flying cigars" because their tails are about the same size as their heads. The better identifier is the wing pattern of swifts; their wings seem to alternate left and right.

Ravens and vultures live throughout the canyon. Vultures can be told from other soaring birds by their wobbly flight, with wings held in a dihedral, a wide V; eagles, in contrast, soar with their wings held flat. In the forest and woodland of the South Rim, common birds include mountain chickadees, white-breasted and pygmy nuthatches, Steller's jays, pinyon jays, and black-chinned hummingbirds.

The canyon wren claims the affection of all who meet one. Its clear, lilting call is hard to describe but easy to imitate, and once heard is never forgotten. Listen for it anywhere near high cliffs, but especially in narrow side canyons. No other creature evokes the feeling and aroma of being in canyon country like the canyon wren.

Arizona Game and Fish Dept, Bob Miles

Ringtails are common in the canyon but are rarely seen because of their nocturnal habits.

Amphibians and Reptiles

As with birds, the reptiles you see vary with the habitat. Along the South Rim, look for eastern fence lizards (identified by the bright blue patches on their sides), northern whiptails (long tails and fast movements) and mountain short-horned lizards (also called horny toads). Despite their reputation, rattlesnakes are not common. If you see a snake on the South Rim, it is likely to be a Sonoran gopher snake; on the North Rim, a Great Basin gopher snake. If it does prove to be a rattler, it will probably be one of three subspecies of *Crotalus viridis* on the South Rim, the Hopi rattlesnake; on the North Rim, the Great Basin rattlesnake; and below the rims, the Grand Canyon rattlesnake.

In riparian side canyons like Bright Angel Canyon, hikers stand a good chance of seeing desert striped whipsnakes. Long and very thin, these agile snakes are colored brown to olive. They hunt during the day, taking lizards and other small animals. If not disturbed, they tolerate observers. Few snakes move with such grace.

Among lizards, the western collared lizard is conspicuous. Living only south of the river at all levels in the canyon, it can be 14 inches long. It has a double black "collar," a brown to green back with yellow speckles, and sometimes an orange throat patch. The colors vary, but the most colorful can seem as bright as tropical birds. Chuckwallas, by comparison, are drab creatures with what seems to be too much skin. The reason for the excess becomes apparent when they are threatened. Retreating into crevices in the rocks where they prefer to live, they wedge themselves by inflating their bodies with air, so that not even a snake can get them out.

In riparian areas, the numerous chameleonlike lizards that skitter over the smooth rocks are tree lizards *(Urosaurus)*; with bright eyes and a habit of cocking their heads when you approach, they seem almost personable. Not so the larger, robust-looking fellows with prickly scales, the yellow-backed spiny lizards. Where there is water, there are usually canyon treefrogs — small, bronze- or silver-colored frogs with voices like sheep; and red-spotted toads, whose song is a high-pitched trill.

CHECKLIST OF SELECTED ANIMALS

MAMMALS

Merriam Shrew	*Sorex merriami*
Dwarf Shrew	*Sorex nanus*
Gray (Desert) Shrew	*Notiosorex crawfordi*
Leafnose Bat	*Macrotus californicus*
Yuma Myotis	*Myotis yumanensis*
Little Brown Myotis	*Myotis lucifugus*
Long-eared Myotis	*Myotis evotis*
Fringed Myotis	*Myotis thysanodes*
Long-legged Myotis	*Myotis volans*
California Myotis	*Myotis californicus*
Small-footed Myotis	*Myotis leibii*
Silver-haired Bat	*Lasionycteris noctivagans*
Western Pipistrel	*Pipistrellus hesperus*
Big Brown Bat	*Eptesicus fuscus*
Red Bat	*Lasiurus borealis*
Hoary Bat	*Lasiurus cinereus*
Spotted Bat	*Euderma maculata*
Lump-nosed Bat	*Plecotus townsendii*
Pallid Bat	*Antrozous pallidus*
Mexican Freetail Bat	*Tadarida brasiliensis*
Big Freetail Bat	*Tadarida molossa*
Blacktail Jackrabbit	*Lepus californicus*
Eastern Cottontail	*Sylvilagus floridanus*
Mountain Cottontail	*Sylvilagus nuttalli*
Desert Cottontail	*Sylvilagus audubonii*
Spotted Ground Squirrel	*Citellus spilosoma*
Rock Squirrel	*Citellus variegatus*
Golden-mantled Squirrel	*Citellus lateralis*
Yuma Antelope Squirrel	*Ammospermophilus harrisi*
Whitetail Antelope Squirrel	*Ammospermophilus leucurus*
Least Chipmunk	*Eutamias minimus*
Colorado Chipmunk	*Eutamias quadrivittatus*
Uinta Chipmunk	*Eutamias umbrinus*
Cliff Chipmunk	*Eutamias dorsalis*
Tassel-eared (Abert) Squirrel	*Sciurus aberti aberti*
Kaibab Squirrel	*Sciurus aberti kaibabensis*

Red Squirrel	*Tamiasciurus hudsonicus*
Valley Pocket Gopher	*Thomomys bottae*
Northern Pocket Gopher	*Thomomys talpoides*
Silky Pocket Mouse	*Perognathus flavus*
Apache Pocket Mouse	*Perognathus apache*
Little Pocket Mouse	*Perognathus longimembris*
Arizona Pocket Mouse	*Perognathus amplus*
Great Basin Pocket Mouse	*Perognathus parvus*
Longtail Pocket Mouse	*Perognathus formosus*
Rock Pocket Mouse	*Perognathus intermedius*
Merriam Kangaroo Rat	*Dipodomys merriami*
Ord Kangaroo Rat	*Dipodomys ordi*
Great Basin Kangaroo Rat	*Dipodomys microps*
Beaver	*Castor canadensis*
Western Harvest Mouse	*Reithrodontomys megalotis*
Canyon Mouse	*Peromyscus crinitus*
Cactus Mouse	*Peromyscus eremicus*
Deer Mouse	*Peromyscus maniculatus*
Brush Mouse	*Peromyscus boylei*
Piñon Mouse	*Peromyscus truei*
Northern Grasshopper Mouse	*Onchomys leucogaster*
Southern Grasshopper Mouse	*Onchomys torridus*
Whitethroat Woodrat	*Neotoma albigula*
Desert Woodrat	*Neotoma lepida*
Stephens Woodrat	*Neotoma stephensi*
Mexican Woodrat	*Neotoma mexicana*
Longtail Vole	*Microtus longicaudus*
Mexican Vole	*Microtus mexicanus*
Muskrat	*Ondatra zibethica*
Porcupine	*Erethizon dorsatum*
Coyote	*Canis latrans*
Red Fox	*Vulpes fulva*
Kit Fox	*Vulpes macrotis*
Gray Fox	*Urocyon cinereoargenteus*
Black Bear	*Ursus americanus*
Ringtail	*Bassariscus astutus*
Raccoon	*Procyon lotor*
Longtail Weasel	*Mustela frenata*
Badger	*Taxidea taxus*
Spotted Skunk	*Spilogale putoris*

Striped Skunk	*Mephitis mephitis*
River Otter	*Lutra canadensis*
Mountain Lion	*Felis concolor*
Bobcat	*Lynx rufus*
Elk	*Cervus canadensis*
Mule Deer	*Odocoileus hemionus*
Pronghorn (Antelope)	*Antilocapra americana*
Bighorn Sheep	*Ovis canadensis*

AMPHIBIANS

Arizona Tiger Salamander	*Abystoma tigrinum nebulosum*
Utah Tiger Salamander	*Abystoma tigrinum utahensis*
Red-spotted Toad	*Bufo punctatus*
Woodhouse Toad	*Bufo woodhousei woodhousei*
Great Plains Toad	*Bufo cognatus*
Great Basin Spadefoot Toad	*Scaphiopus intermontanus*
Northern Leopard Frog	*Rana pipiens*
Canyon Treefrog	*Hyla arenicolor*

REPTILES

Desert Tortoise	*Gopherus agassizii*
Arizona Night Lizard	*Xantusia vigilis arizonae*
Desert Banded Gecko	*Coleonyx variegatus variegatus*
Utah Banded Gecko	*Coleonyx variegatus utahensis*
Great Basin Skink	*Eumeces skiltonianus utahensis*
Southern Many-lined Skink	*Eumeces multivirgatus epipleurotus*
Southern Desert Horned Lizard	*Phrynosoma platyrhinos calidiarum*
Mountain Short-horned Lizard	*Phrynosoma douglassii hernandesi*
Banded Gila Monster	*Heloderma suspectum cinctum*
Desert Iguana	*Dipsosaurus dorsalis*
Western Chuckwalla	*Sauromalus obesus obesus*
Yellow-backed Spiny Lizard	*Sceloporus magister uniformis*
Northern Sagebrush Lizard	*Sceloporus graciosus graciosus*
Southern Plateau Lizard	*Sceloporus undulatus tristichus*
Northern Plateau Lizard	*Sceloporus undulatus elongatus*
Long-nosed Leopard Lizard	*Gambelia wislizenii*
Desert Collared Lizard	*Crotaphytus insularis*
Western Collared Lizard	*Crotaphytus collaris baileyi*
Painted Desert Whiptail	*Cnemidophorus tigris septentrionalis*
Desert Side-blotched Lizard	*Uta stansburiana stejnegeri*

Northern Side-blotched Lizard	*Uta stansburiana stansburiana*
Tree Lizard	*Urosaurus ornatus*
Western Brush Lizard	*Urosaurus graciosus graciosus*
Western Blind Snake	*Leptotyphlops humilis*
Grand Canyon Rattlesnake	*Crotalus viridis abyssus*
Great Basin Rattlesnake	*Crotalus viridis lutosus*
Hopi Rattlesnake	*Crotalus viridis nuntius*
Mojave Rattlesnake	*Crotalus scutulatus scutulatus*
Northern Black-tailed Rattlesnake	*Crotalus molossus molossus*
Southwestern Speckled Rattlesnake	*Crotalus mitchellii pyrrhus*
Mojave Patch-nosed Snake	*Salvadora hexalepis mojavensis*
Sonoran Gopher Snake	*Pituophis melanoleucus affinis*
Great Basin Gopher Snake	*Pituophis melanoleucus deserticola*
Wandering Garter Snake	*Thamnophis elegans vagrans*
Long-nosed Garter Snake	*Thamnophis angustirostris*
Red Coachwhip (Racer) Snake	*Masticophis flagellum piceus*
Desert Striped Whipsnake	*Masticophis taeniatus taeniatus*
Utah Black Headed Snake	*Tantilla utahensis*
Western Long Nosed Snake	*Rhinocheilus lecontei lecontei*
California Kingsnake	*Lampropeltis getulus californiae*
Utah Mountain Kingsnake	*Lampropeltis pyromelana infralabialis*
Western Ground Snake	*Sonora semiannulata gloydi*
Desert Night Snake	*Hypsiglena torquata deserticola*
Spotted Night Snake	*Hypsiglena torquata ochrorhynchus*
Sonoran Lyre Snake	*Trimorphodon biscutatus lambda*
Arizona Glossy Snake	*Arizona elegans noctivaga*
Desert Glossy Snake	*Arizona elagans eburnata*

FISHES

Native Species

Humpback Chub	*Gila cypha*
Speckled Dace	*Rhinichthys osculus*
Razorback Sucker	*Xyrauchen texanus*
Flannelmouth Sucker	*Catostomus latipinnis*
Bluehead Sucker	*Catostomus discobolus*
Roundtail Chub (extirpated)	*Gila robusta*
Bonytail Chub (extirpated)	*Gila elegans*
Colorado Squawfish (extirpated)	*Ptychocheilus lucius*

Introduced Species (selected)

Rainbow Trout	*Salmo gairdneri*
Brown Trout	*Salmo trutta*
Brook Trout	*Salvelinus fontinalis*
Carp	*Cyprinus carpio*
Channel Catfish	*Ictalurus punctatus*
Fathead Minnow	*Pimephales promelas*
Rio Grande Killifish	*Fundulus zerbrinus*
Striped Bass	*Morone saxatilis*

BIRDS

Eared Grebe	Mourning Dove
Western Grebe	Great Horned Owl
Double-crested Cormorant	Common Night-hawk
Great Blue Heron	Common Poorwill
Snowy Egret	Black-chinned Hummingbird
Canada Goose	Costa's Hummingbird
Mallard	Calliope Hummingbird
Bufflehead	Broad-tailed Hummingbird
Common Merganser	Rufous Hummingbird
Turkey Vulture	Belted Kingfisher
Northern Harrier	Lewis's Woodpecker
Sharp-shinned Hawk	Acorn Woodpecker
Northern Goshawk	Yellow-bellied Sapsucker
Red-tailed Hawk	Williamson's Sapsucker
Ferruginous Hawk	Hairy Woodpecker
Rough-legged Hawk	Northern Flicker
Golden Eagle	Olive-sided Flycatcher
American Kestrel	Western Wood-Pewee
Blue Grouse	Gray Flycatcher
Wild Turkey	Black Phoebe
Gambel's Quail	Say's Phoebe
American Coot	Ash-throated Flycatcher
Killdeer	Cassin's Kingbird
Solitary Sandpiper	Western Kingbird
Spotted Sandpiper	Horned Lark
Common Snipe	Purple Martin
Band-tailed Pigeon	Violet-green Swallow

Ravens are ubiquitous canyon residents, thriving at all levels among all plant communities.

David Edwards

Steller's Jay
Scrub Jay
Pinyon Jay
Clark's Nutcracker
Common Raven
Mountain Chickadee
Plain Titmouse
Bushtit
Red-breasted Nuthatch
White-breasted Nuthatch
Pygmy Nuthatch
Brown Creeper
Rock Wren
Canyon Wren
Bewick's Wren
House Wren
American Dipper
Golden-crowned Kinglet
Ruby-crowned Kinglet
Western Bluebird

Mountain Bluebird
Townsend's Solitaire
Hermit Thrush
American Robin
Northern Mockingbird
Sage Thrasher
Cedar Waxwing
Phainopepla
Loggerhead Shrike
Bell's Vireo
Solitary Vireo
Warbling Vireo
Orange-crowned Warbler
Nashville Warbler
Virginia's Warbler
Lucy's Warbler
Yellow Warbler
Yellow-rumped Warbler
Black-throated Gray Warbler
Hermit Warbler

Grace's Warbler
MacGillivray's Warbler
Common Yellowthroat
Wilson's Warbler
Yellow-breasted Chat
Western Tanager
Black-headed Grosbeak
Blue Grosbeak
Lazuli Bunting
Indigo Bunting
Green-tailed Towhee
Rufous-sided Towhee
Rufous-crowned Sparrow
Chipping Sparrow
Brewer's Sparrow
Vesper Sparrow
Lark Sparrow

Black-throated Sparrow
Song Sparrow
Lincoln's Sparrow
White-crowned Sparrow
Dark-eyed Junco
Red-winged Blackbird
Yellow-headed Blackbird
Brewer's Blackbird
Brown-headed Cowbird
Northern Oriole
Cassin's Finch
House Finch
Red Crossbill
Pine Siskin
Lesser Goldfinch
House Sparrow

10
Amberat Chronicles

A cold wind blows across the canyon, whistling through the trees on the South Rim. Shivering, you move back a few steps, into the shelter of an alpine fir. At least it's warmer than the North Rim. Over there, the plateau rises to timberline; the highest trees are bristlecone pines, wind-blasted veterans of the snow zone.

A huge bird cruises along the rim. Hooked bill and naked head: a condor. Then, stranger still, an even larger bird riding a 12-foot wingspan. This one is a Merriam's terratorn, not to be found in any field guide to the birds. Nor will a field guide to North American mammals help to identify some of the animals living here. Down on the Tonto Platform, those specks moving through the juniper forest aren't mules. They are camels. They share the canyon with Shasta ground sloths, Harrington's mountain goats, and an unidentified horse- or burrolike animal.

This you might have seen if you had visited the canyon 15,000 years ago during the last Ice Age. It is a picture from the past revealed to us through the amazing archival qualities of amberat, a natural and little-known substance found in the Grand Canyon. Amberat — a pleasant sounding word. It brings to mind precious materials like amber, the jewel made from pine resin, or ambergris, the base of fine perfume. And truly, to aficionados, amberat is a treasure, however facetiously they might smile when pronouncing its name. Kenneth Cole, an amberat expert, defines it as "various debris collected by [packrats]... and packrat fecal pellets, all sealed into a mass of solidified packrat urine." Lest this highly esteemed material begin to lose its cachet with readers, Cole quickly points out that older amberat (the good stuff) has only a mild resinous smell. It is the younger, less valuable matter that tends "to smell as one might expect for a deposit of feces imbedded in urine."

Packrats, also called woodrats, live throughout the Grand Canyon. There are five species present, all members of the genus *Neotoma*. Differences among the species are subtle. Generally, they all have furred tails about three-fourths as long as their bodies, rounded ears, and long whiskers. They build large nests from just about anything — sticks, grass, stones, pieces of cactus, leaves, feathers, bones, teeth, and whatever else catches their interest. It seems that packrats can be interested in just about anything small enough to carry.

The sheer volume of material used in construction can be impressive; in many cases, the collection effort has been the work of many generations of packrats all living in the same place. They homestead in buildings (abandoned or not), in rock walls, at the base of juniper trees, beneath large shrubs, in rock crevices, and in caves. Being tidy creatures, they periodically clean house, ejecting trash and producing a sort of packrat landfill — a midden. Trampled flat and cemented with urine into a hard mass, the midden provides a stratified record from the lives of thousands of packrats over thousands of years. If left undisturbed and protected in a dry or well-ventilated cave, it becomes a sizable quantity of (sweet smelling, they tell us!) amberat.

By analyzing and dating the contents of amberat, scientists are able to discern what lived and died at different periods of time going as far back as 30,000 to 40,000 years.

Because packrats rarely forage more than 100 feet from their dens, whatever is found in them must have occurred in the immediate area. This is important in trying to put together data on local vegetation. One of the other methods, widely used all over the world, studies the layers of pollen found in lake beds and bogs. The pollen indicates very well what was growing in the area surrounding the lake. But because pollen

The white-throated woodrat, or packrat, is one of five species found in the canyon. The habit of all woodrats to build elaborate houses from a huge variety of materials has proved invaluable to scientists studying prehistoric conditions in the Grand Canyon and other arid environments.

Courtesy of Arizona-Sonora Desert Museum

is borne on the wind and can travel many miles, it is harder to distinguish the plants that were growing on neighboring mountain slopes from the ones that grew on the lakeshore.

On the other hand, a stick or a bone found in a packrat midden is likely to have fallen very close to the den. So if juniper twigs show up in amberat from the canyon's inner gorge, it means there must have been junipers growing nearby. And if that was the case, it's fair to say that the climate was different back then — probably analogous to the areas where we now find juniper trees, which rarely grow below 4,000 feet elevation. In general, Cole found that during the last Ice Age (lasting from about 22,000 years ago to 14,000 years ago), juniper grew about 2,400 vertical feet lower than it does today.

It should be added that packrat middens are not the only source of such information. Other animals live and have lived in Grand Canyon caves. They also hauled in things that became buried in dung and dust to tell the tales of ancient times. Among the more important of these were ground sloths, whose dung deposits were discovered in 1936 by a park service team. The discovery, made in a place called Rampart Cave at the far western end of the Grand Canyon, kicked off a search for similar deposits throughout the Southwest. Also useful are caves found high in the canyon walls — notably the Redwall Limestone — that had once been nesting and resting sites for condors and other large birds of prey. The bones they brought home millennia ago remain there still, awaiting further analysis.

Packrat nests can be as much as four feet high and many feet in circumference. The ones that last longest and are of most interest to paleoecologists are built not in the open, like this one, but in caves or beneath rock overhangs.

These old remains reveal a surprising lesson: the so-called eternal canyon, this monument to timelessness, turns out to be a quick-change artist putting on and taking off different cloaks of vegetation in the blink of a geologic eye.

Fifteen thousand years ago the climate was cooler and perhaps wetter. Precipitation fell mostly in winter and was unreliable or unevenly distributed in summer. The

Grand Canyon had the same shape as today, but the plants were different. Forest and woodland species extended well below the rims into
areas that now support only desert scrub. The summit of the Kaibab
Plateau was near timberline, perhaps an area of alpine tundra with no
trees at all. The highest forest consisted of bristlecone and limber pines.
On the South Rim, there were alpine fir and spruce trees, a forest was
inhabited by ruby-crowned kinglets and mountain chickadees. Juniper
trees, now found only above about 4,500 feet, grew along the river two
or three thousand feet below their current range. There is no evidence
that pinyon pines were yet present in the area.

Where there is now desert scrub, there were junipers. Where there
are now junipers, there was Douglas-fir. It was as if the land had shifted
upwards several thousand feet or drifted northward to a higher latitude.
Fifteen thousand years ago, plant cover in the canyon above 5,000 feet
resembled the flora found today in mountain ranges of northern Utah:
spruce, fir, and limber pine instead of ponderosa pine. Below that level,
the canyon vegetation resembled what now grows in the high volcanic
desert of southern Idaho: big sagebrush, Utah juniper, shadscale, and
Douglas-fir.

The evidence can be made to work in the opposite direction through
time. Thus, 1,650-year-old middens in Idaho were compared with middens 10 times that old from the Tonto Platform. The species aren't
precisely the same (agave, for one, is missing in the Idaho middens) but
the major components turned out to be the same — even in their relative
proportions.

In trying to picture the Pleistocene Grand Canyon, it is tempting to
imagine that the vegetation we see today, in all its modern complexity,
was simply pushed to lower elevations. In this view, juniper trees extend
their range downward, and with them come all or most of the plants
and animals we associate with junipers today. At the same time, desert
scrub communities move lower, as if making room for the juniper woodland.

Midden data show otherwise. As it turns out, there were different community types during the Ice Age, different mixes of plants and animals.
Woodland species occurred with low desert species in juxtapositions that
are unusual today. It seems that individual plants responded to Pleistocene
conditions differently — some were strongly affected by it, others hardly

at all. Around Rampart Cave, where the juniper forest did indeed move downward two or three thousand feet, other plants stayed put. During the Ice Age, barrel and hedgehog cacti grew around Rampart Cave, and today they still do. The junipers, for their part, have retreated to higher ground. One interpretation for this could be that Pleistocene summers were cooler and wetter, allowing junipers to survive at lower elevations, but winters remained relatively mild, allowing barrel cacti to stay where they had been before it started getting chilly. The climate wasn't just colder; it followed different patterns.

One of the bigger surprises to come from midden analysis has to do with moisture. We think of the Ice Age as being relatively wet, but this was apparently not the case in the Grand Canyon. Arthur Phillips, one of the amberat fellows (*paleoecologist* is the correct term) noted in 1977 that areas in the western canyon were unexpectedly dry during the Pleistocene. Two side canyons where he thought he would find evidence of permanent water (riparian species in the middens) turned out to have been dry, supporting only desert plants. This suggests that precipitation from year to year was locally unreliable then, just as it is today.

A Warming Trend

It's hard to put a date on the end of the last Ice Age. Apparently the climate began to warm between 13,000 and 16,000 years ago, starting the break-up of the great Laurentide ice sheet. The change was not immediate. There is evidence of a temporary warming, followed by a return blast of cold. Probably the presence of so much ice had an effect on the North American climate. Yet the movement toward a warmer climate was inexorable.

In general, the region became drier (although new summer weather patterns over Grand Canyon brought monsoonal flows and huge summer thunderstorms). From much of the inner canyon, forest and woodland vanished, yielding the ground to more drought-tolerant species. Thinking about it, I get a mental image of forests evaporating like rain puddles after a storm; of animals moving in opposite directions, some headed for the cooler canyon rims, others making their way downhill to the new warmer zones, both groups shaking their heads, saying,

"You can have it." The trouble with this image is that it requires creatures of the warm desert to enter the canyon the way most visitors do — over the rims and down. Except for a few very mobile species, it would not have happened this way.

A more accurate view might be that as squirrels and pine trees retreated upward, the desert flowed in, moving up the river corridor from the west, pushing in from the spreading southern deserts. Of course individual plants don't migrate, and in many animal species the individuals themselves are slow to leave their accustomed home ground. Species, on the other hand, do it all the time. Even plants as securely rooted as junipers migrate with changing conditions. They colonize new worlds and retreat from old ones. They send scouts across frontiers, and if the scouts find favorable conditions, the species marches on in the form of airborne seeds, bird- or critter-borne seeds, probing rootlets, and even bits of adult plants, like willow fragments carried on the river.

This did not happen all at once. The climate change was gradual, and the movement of plants usually lagged behind; in the case of juniper, these hardy trees seem to have held on for perhaps a thousand years in places where the climate had turned unfavorable. More commonly, Ice Age residents departed or died out well before replacements arrived, leaving the canyon with relatively few species during the time of greatest change (10,000 to 12,000 years ago). One effort to describe the changing of the vegetational guard envisions the quick disappearance of Ice Age species from marginal habitats where even slight changes would make their lives untenable. Meanwhile, in the best parts of their former distribution range, the same species hung on for as much as 3,000 years, slowly losing the battle to an inhospitable climate and competition from those better suited for life in the new conditions.

Natives and Non-natives

The Grand Canyon is no stranger to change. As we have seen, the canyon itself is one of North America's youngest major geographical features. Big lava dams and the lakes they created have come and gone. In the last 12,000 years or so, the climate has changed dramatically. And still the evolution of this landscape and its wildlife continues.

Native to the Middle East, burros are tough, desert-adapted creatures that survive quite well in rough, arid environments.

Consider the birds. Since 1900, seven species of birds have invaded the canyon: indigo buntings, vermilion flycatchers, great-tailed grackles, magnificent humming-birds, hooded orioles, summer tanagers, and red-faced warblers. All of these are regarded as natural events, not the cause of human activities — at least not in the canyon itself. On the other hand, it's hard to discern what allows birds to extend their range. The advance of irrigated farming, the planting and watering of trees in formerly treeless areas, the growth of leafy suburbs across the plains — even the placement of bird feeders and bird houses — all these could have an impact on, for example, the indigo bunting's ability to colonize the Southwest, as it did after the turn of the century.

Seven other birds were clearly introduced by human activities. Three came from Europe: starlings, house sparrows, and rock doves (pigeons). Three were planted as game birds: chukars, wild turkeys, and ring-necked pheasants. Before 1949, wild turkeys were native to the South Rim only. That year, birds trapped in southern Arizona were transplanted to

Grand Canyon National Park

national forest land on the North Rim. They prospered and are now a common sight along the backroads of the plateau. Ring-necked pheasants, however, did not find conditions favorable and did not survive in the canyon area. One other, Gambel's quail, is native to the western end of the canyon, but introductions have also been made.

Several species have vanished in the near past. California condors were present as recently as 1924, the time of the last sighting. Burrowing owls also lived here, until the prairie dog colonies in which they lived were wiped out by overzealous government officials intent on making the range safe for cattle. There were jaguars at Grand Canyon as recently as 1906. Wolves lived on the North Rim until they were eradicated by government hunters. There might also have been grizzlies on the North Rim. And a few otters have been seen in the river, but none recently.

Not all these vanished animals were done in by human opposition. Some were already on the edge of survival, or on the margins of their

The heavy impact of an expanding burro population raised concern not only for the plant life of the Grand Canyon but also for native animals forced to compete for limited forage and water. There are reports that a few burros have returned to the far western end of the canyon, but for most of its length, they are absent.

range. But clearly the arrival of people bearing guns and saws and branding irons did them no favors.

At one time, burros were a big issue. Originally from the deserts of south and southeast Africa, the burro was introduced to North America by the Spanish. Later they became a favorite pack animal of southwestern prospectors and miners, who exploited their toughness and ability to cope with desert conditions. Those same characteristics allowed burros to survive and prosper in the desert when the prospectors turned them loose, or when they escaped.

In spite of their long ears, friendly ways, and fuzzy, rumpled appearance, burros are astonishingly tough. They can survive for several days without water. They can withstand dehydration amounting to 30 percent of body weight, because most of the water loss comes from body tissues instead of from their blood plasma. Their sweat is low in chlorides, meaning they retain enough salt to permit quick rehydration. When really dry, they can drink up to 30 liters in a few minutes. They reproduce at a rate that could almost be called scandalous. Females become sexually mature at an age as young as 10 months and can produce two foals every three years. At Bandelier National Monument in New Mexico, the park service tried in 1975 to reduce a population of burros by killing 52 animals, about one-third of the herd in question. Eighteen months later, the population was back to its former level.

Burros are smart. In Death Valley, they learned how to open campground water spigots. In captivity, they figure out gate latches.

It's hard not to admire these sturdy, personable little animals. On the other hand, they have been accused of terrible environmental crimes — stripping the desert of vegetation, trampling the ground and causing erosion, scaring other animals away from water holes. Being nonruminants, their digestive systems are not particularly efficient, and they need large quantities of forage. Both browsers and grazers, they eat almost anything from tender herbs to old sticks. One report from western Arizona described ocotillo reduced to stubs and paloverde trees all but extirpated by a resident herd of burros.

As of 1980, there were about 350 feral burros in the Grand Canyon and thousands more in the desert areas of Arizona, New Mexico, Nevada, and California. Until the late '70s, the park service had engaged in periodic control work, shooting what they regarded as the excess population.

But a new federal law protecting wild horses and burros, along with vociferous public opinion, put a stop to shooting as an option.

In the canyon, the major concern was that burros were causing a decline in desert bighorn sheep by eating them out of house and home and keeping them from water holes. As good as the sheep are at surviving in an arid environment, the burros are better. There was general (but not unanimous) agreement even among those opposed to shooting as a control measure that burros were wreaking havoc on the range. The park service wanted not just to control burros but to eliminate them from Grand Canyon National Park. Eventually an animal protection organization called the Fund For Animals mobilized a small army of wranglers, river boats, and helicopters to round up every burro in the canyon and ship all of them out for adoption.

That was done in 1981 and was declared a success: all the burros were gone, down to the last bray. (There *have* been reports recently of burros moving back into the western end of the canyon.) So how have the sheep done? Astonishingly, after all the fooforaw, there's been no detailed followup research. It is assumed that the sheep are doing well. Occasionally an Arizona Game and Fish Department airplane flies over to do some counting, and river runners see them frequently. The sheep perch on outcrops above the water and watch the boats go by.

Then there is the case of the willow flycatcher, a bird that was once more common in Glen Canyon than in Grand Canyon. The dam changed that in a paradoxically compensatory way. While it destroyed Glen Canyon's riparian habitat, it allowed the expansion of new riparian zones downstream in the national park. The flycatcher remains rare; it is on Arizona's list of endangered species, and although the canyon population averages somewhere around 10 breeding pairs, this represents the largest breeding population in the state of Arizona.

The birds are here largely by benefit of that enormous artificial alteration, the Glen Canyon Dam. By stopping the big spring floods, the dam allowed a dense riparian growth of willow and tamarisk to occupy that part of the riverbank that was previously scoured every year or so by floods. It also cleared the river of sediment, allowing light to penetrate, algae to grow, and all sorts of small organisms to prosper, among them the insects that are the flycatcher's primary food. Other birds could tell a similar story. At least 10 species have increased their breeding populations by a factor of 5 to 10 times since the dam was built.

This seems appropriate for a national park. Flycatchers are rare and lovely creatures. Native creatures. We should protect them, monitor them, and hope they live long and multiply. The dam, whatever its other failings, has provided them with food and shelter in an amiable environment. Isn't that a wonderful thing?

Yes and no. Most people would agree that non-native species should be kept out of the park. No cows. No tulip gardens. No burros. No rhinoceroses. Let the Grand Canyon remain in its natural state, the way it would be had we never entered upon the scene. According to some views, we humans should experience the canyon as if from another dimension; we should see and smell and feel but let not the slightest vibration of our presence mar the exquisite and complicated workings of the natural system.

Ahem. The sound of throats clearing. Such a philosophy might serve well as an ideal to strive for. But as a practical matter, what is the park to do about such exotic species as tamarisk and trout? What is the park to do about the entire massively altered river corridor?

National parks attempt to preserve the natural scene (to quote from the 1963 Leopold Report, which guides park service policy in these matters) "as nearly as possible in the condition that prevailed when the area was first visited by white man. A national park should represent a vignette of primitive America. . . . If the goal cannot be fully achieved it can be approached. A reasonable illusion of primitive America could be recreated."

For a moment let us pretend that everyone agrees to return the river to its primitive state — that is, to the condition that existed when John Wesley Powell first saw it. Remove the dam, clean up the accumulated silt in Glen Canyon and its tributaries, eliminate trout, tamarisk, amphipods, and other exotic species, bring back the bonytail chub, the river otter, the squawfish, and sit back to watch the stately progress of nature. Would that be good?

I suppose the willow flycatchers could move back to their old Glen Canyon haunts. Perhaps other species would follow them, including the peregrine falcons who find the hunting so good on the river as it now flows. But I wonder about the eagles.

Like many other species, bald eagles range too widely to be contained, or sustained, by a few patches of protected land. They need the entire continent, and there is no better explanation of why this is so than recent

Peregrine falcons are among the native species that have benefited from changing conditions along the river since construction of Glen Canyon Dam. Increased vegetation has enhanced nesting opportunities for the smaller birds that provide food for peregrines.

Arizona Game and Fish Dept., George Andrejko

events on one of their major feeding grounds: McDonald Creek in Glacier National Park. For decades, there was an annual fall gathering of eagles along the creek. Hundreds of eagles were drawn by the autumn spawning run of kokanee salmon from Flathead and Whitefish lakes. The fish moved into the clear, shallow waters, and the eagles feasted.

No more. Efforts by Montana state game officials to enhance the local kokanee fishery backfired. They introduced to Whitefish Lake an organism called opossum shrimp (actually a crustacean, like the amphipods introduced to the Colorado River to feed trout), which they hoped would provide a better food source for the salmon than the plankton they were already getting. The same thing had been tried in the Kootenay Lakes of British Columbia with great success — the average size of the salmon there had risen from around one pound to as much as six or seven pounds.

Indeed, the "shrimp" did well in Whitefish Lake, and spread down-stream to Flathead Lake, where they also flourished. At the same time, the salmon population collapsed. The famous run diminished from about 150,000 fish to fewer than ten. Why? What went wrong? Someone apparently did not understand the feeding habits of the crustaceans. As it happened, they settled to the lake bottom at night, rising during the day to prey on the salmon's main food source, zooplankton. The salmon followed the reverse schedule, feeding at night. So they did not eat the crustaceans, but the crustaceans ate what had been sustaining the salmon. The salmon starved and the eagles lost an important food source. (The difference in the Canadian lakes was that there springs circulate the water, forcing the crustaceans off the bottom where night-feeding salmon can get to them.) The eagles, by the way, were the only natives in this equation. Kokanee salmon were introduced to Flathead and Whitefish lakes around the turn of the century.

What an irony, then, that eagles would discover trout running in Nankoweap Creek at about the same time the salmon disappeared from McDonald Creek. It seems almost poetic, but it's really just one more hard luck story for eagles. During the winter of 1991–92, only about a half dozen eagles showed up. It was a dry year, and as one biologist put it, Nankoweap is a great place for catching trout, but not if the stream is dry. When Nankoweap fails to run, as it did that year, so do the salmon, and the eagles are forced to look elsewhere.

Nonetheless, that event was anomalous. The run usually occurs, and when it does, Nankoweap Creek provides eagles with a critical food sup-ply. The fat they put on during the winter has much to do with the success of their nesting efforts the next summer.

The Grand Canyon was made a national park mostly because of its unique and inspiring landscape, just as Yellowstone was set aside for its geysers and hot springs and Glacier for its high peaks. Yet all of the parks represent a much more significant effort than the mere preservation of scenic highlights. Taken together, as a system, they are meant to pre-serve and represent the full range of American biota and landscapes, along with all the abstract, intangible values that accompany wild lands. To retain a sufficient sample of the nation's natural wealth to last not 10 years, or a century, but forever — this is an inspired sentiment for a nation to espouse, and a noble goal.

But it cannot be done within the park system alone. Increasingly we are made aware of how small the parks are, how easily affected they are by changes beyond their borders — indeed, how strong are the interconnections even between such distant places as Grand Canyon and Glacier national parks.

In the Southwest, riparian habitat is disappearing at a frightening rate. The canyon is one of the few places where it has increased; and depending on how the dam is operated, it could expand further. In this case, habitat lost elsewhere is being compensated for by human-caused changes within the park. It seems to me that "correcting" those changes becomes a more complicated issue when the park is viewed in its regional or national context.

Barring some unforeseen geologic event, Glen Canyon Dam is here to stay at least until Lake Powell fills with silt, at which time it will become useless for water control and electrical generation, and if people are still around to care about it, some decision will have to be made. In the meantime, there are things that could be done to alleviate the dam's impact — that is, return the river corridor to a "reasonable illusion of primitive America." For one, silt could be pumped into the river below the dam, giving it back its color. That would take out most of the trout but it wouldn't bring back the native species, whose main problem is the cold water. Warm water might be successfully drawn from the lake for several months each summer, but as we have seen in the previous chapter, the effect on the river is still unknown. The dam could release enough water in the spring to re-create the old cycle of annual flooding, which might cut out some of the dense new riparian shrubbery. On the other hand, tamarisk is more resistant to floods than native vegetation, so it might cut back the wrong plants. Yet another consideration: The 1983 flood (and subsequent high-water years) had a devastating impact on beaches, nesting birds, and other elements of the river environment. Floods alone, without the addition of sediment, would be worse than useless.

How will the park deal with these complex issues? The case of burros and bighorns was relatively simple. The matter of tamarisk is not. The burros were perceived as doing damage to native species with no counterbalancing benefit. Their removal impaired the survival prospects of no native creatures and probably benefited dozens. This cannot be said of tamarisk.

The problem is as thorny as a jumping cholla and as difficult to get away from. Currently the park service has no philosophical umbrella under which to fit this new situation. Considering all the agencies involved with the river corridor (the National Park Service, the Bureau of Reclamation, several Indian Reservations, the Western Area Power Administration, the seven states that draw water from the Colorado, the Mexican government, and the U.S. Fish and Wildlife Service, among others) it would be a large, oddly shaped umbrella to construct. If the Grand Canyon Protection Act truly marks a sea change in policy (that is, if it does put the ecological welfare of the river corridor above the demands of power generation), it will at least help establish priorities. It is hoped that decisions made by the Secretary of the Interior after the EIS is finished in 1993 will resolve some of the river-related issues.

One thing we know for certain. The canyon will continue to evolve, whether by natural causes or not. And however it turns out, whatever events occur on the river or the rims or anywhere in between, packrats will continue with their archival chores, busily collecting the history of Grand Canyon and storing it away in the amberat chronicles.

11
From Anasazi to Aircraft

He is a small man with coppery brown skin wearing a loincloth of woven cotton. It is early summer; he needs no other clothing. In one hand, he carries a carefully chosen piece of Vishnu Schist. He chose it for the way it felt in his hand, heavy and oblong, easy to grip. He improved it before setting off up the canyon by breaking bits of rock from one end, making the end a point. In his other hand he carries a small clay pot that he filled at the last flowing water, more than a half mile down-canyon. Just last week, the stream fell strong and clear without interruption all the way from the forest on the distant rim. He brought the pot because he knew it would be dry here and he would need water to drink.

It is time, he knows. He has waited long enough since he had the dream. It came to him early one morning, in the half-awake time, and the image remains strong in his mind. He knows he should put it on the rock.

When he gets to the right place, he climbs above the dry streambed to a flat expanse of sandstone covered with desert varnish, a natural patina of minerals. The rock gleams gunmetal blue in the desert sun but when he chips away bits of the varnish, the reddish yellow of the sandstone shows through. Setting down his pot of water, he picks up a second piece of rock — this one to use as a mallet against the base of his pointed stone — and starts to work, tapping, pecking, ever so carefully. First a general outline, just the important points of the figures he has in mind. He wants to be sure it looks right. This is important work and should not be hurried.

He will be in good company here. Others before him have pecked figures into the sandstone cliff — figures of animals and people, geometric designs, and other-worldly shapes, like the one from his dream. All the figures express inner imperatives. None are placed here capriciously. He must know — anyone living in a place like the desert Southwest, where time stretches toward an endless horizon, must know — that a thousand years from now other people will stand in this canyon, along the trail that runs from the rim to the river, and contemplate his work. All the more reason to do it well. Plan it out. Take tiny chips. Make the lines clean and deep.

As the day wears on, his son wanders up the canyon, drawn by the constant tapping and a five-year-old's curiosity. He sits for a while watching, marveling at the pictures on the wall. Some are from stories he has heard around winter fires, and seeing them etched in stone gives them reality. But soon the canyon draws his attention elsewhere. There is so much to do here. He makes a game of shooting with his toy bow and arrows at his father's water pot. The pot is empty by now. Having drunk from it, his father set it safely on a rock ledge caused by a deep horizontal crack in the cliff. It makes an appealing target but one impossible to hit with the pretend weaponry of a child. All three of the boy's arrows rattle harmlessly off the rock, but one of them stays up on the ledge. Putting down the bow, he climbs up the easy steps, collecting his arrows, proud that at least one came so close. There it is, just inches from the pot. And... ah ha! A chuckwalla! One of those big brown lizards, back in the tight crack, wedged in the way chuckwallas do when escaping predators. Maybe he can jab it out with arrows.

The chuckwalla proves resistant. The crack is too deep. If only his father would help — but his father is intent, tapping away, and after a while, the boy chases after tree lizards. If you are really quick, you can catch them. If you are only half-quick, you get nothing but a wriggling tail that the tricky lizard leaves behind.

When the man finishes the petroglyph, it is nearly dusk. His son is still here, played out and lying asleep on the warm sand. The figures look good, just as he had imagined. He sits for a few minutes, wrapped in the peaceful stillness of the canyon, watching the glow of post-sunset light fade on a high red pinnacle. The shapes of bats flick across the narrow strip of sky, and the canyon walls grow black. Time to go. Satisfied, he scoops up the yielding body of his sleeping son and starts for home. Not until the next morning, when his boy misses his bow and the arrows he jammed into the chuckwalla's refuge, does he remember the pot.

Had the arrows been his own adult arrows, carefully fletched and spirit-empowered, he would go back for them immediately. But a child's toys are easily replaced. As for the pot, it was an old one. He will pick it up some other day. If he remembers.

Centuries later I think about that pot, and the arrows. I heard about them because I know who found them. A hiker was following a side canyon toward the river when she came to a smooth ledge at the base of a cliff. There were petroglyphs etched in the canyon wall, and she decided it was a good place to stop for lunch. Lying back on the cool rock beneath the shade of the overhanging cliff, she let her eyes trace the shelves and alcoves on the canyon wall, until something caught her attention — it looked like the chipped rim of a pot. She scrambled up to see and sure enough, there it was, along with three small arrows.

The rest is speculation. She could only guess how they got there. I thought of the little boy because I've poked at a few lizards myself, and because she said the arrows were small, without stone points. I like the story. I've thought about it for years, letting the details change according to what feels right. I also like knowing that unless someone else moved them, the pot and the arrows are still there, just as she found them, untouched and shining with the mysterious allure of lost relics.

As for the petroglyphs and the motivations behind them, no one can say for sure. When I see how carefully the best of them were made, how much effort went into their making, it seems obvious that they were taken seriously. Was it art? Communication? Perhaps both.

I recognize the unscientific nature of my imagining. I know I run the risk of misrepresenting the feelings and actions of ancient people. But at the same time, I regard such musings as the most significant value of archaeological sites in a place like the Grand Canyon. It requires nothing

A row of Anasazi granaries, once used to store corn, beans, and other food items, was built high above the river near Nankoweap Creek. In and around such structures, some of the original corn cobs have survived the centuries.

more than being human to imagine the personal details of ancient lives. There are thousands of petroglyphs in the Grand Canyon, and while their direct meaning is a puzzle, the human voice speaking to us over the centuries is unmistakable.

There are not many places in America where you can find ancient history so immediately present. So tangible. The ghosts of America, as represented in our oldest settlements and artifacts, generally go back only a few hundred years. Here they are as old as Choeps. Knowing that ancient people inhabited the Grand Canyon is important to our experience of the place in the way birds, plants, and rocks are important.

Through the simplest of artifacts, we can make a connection across the gulf of centuries and cultural differences. It takes only a hand print in the dried clay of a 10th-century wall; a warm place in the sun where you know someone sat; a fragment of pottery delicately formed, appealing to us across the centuries with the quality of its craftsmanship. Through these things there comes to us a flash of recognition. These people were real, cut from the same cloth as we. And with that recognition, the flash goes the other way, back in time. From our knowledge of ourselves and how we would react to such conditions, we can imagine things for which we have no physical evidence. We can hear the sounds of voices, children laughing, mothers calling, adults talking quietly. We don't know the language those ancient people spoke, but the music of human voices is everywhere the same.

Having felt the ghosts of ancient people in some hidden spot deep in the canyon, you can feel them from anywhere else you go. Having made the connection once, you never view the Grand Canyon quite the same again.

To know more, however, to go beyond speculation (and into details like cotton loincloths), we must listen to the professionals — the archaeologists who study these things in a disciplined manner, who correlate artifacts from one area with those of another, establish dates, note the passage of time and document the growth of cultures. Only the archaeologists are able to answer specific questions like: How did these people live? Where did they come from? What did they eat? Did they trade with other cultural groups? When were they here? Without the efforts of scientists, we would have only the mystery. Thanks to them, we know more. The picture, in brief, is as follows:

There have been people living in the Grand Canyon more or less continuously for at least 4,000 years. Although the earliest people left very little behind to mark their passing, what they did leave are some of the most evocative and lovely of all artifacts: split-twig figurines, effigies of four-legged animals resembling deer and bighorn sheep, sometimes pierced by small twigs as if in imitation of a spear or an arrow. They were set in the dim recesses of caves and covered with rocks in what seems to have been a ceremonial placement — perhaps to bring good hunting.

No one knows for sure who these people were. The figurines discovered so far have been dated by carbon-14 analysis at between 3,000 and 4,000 years ago. There is evidence connecting them with a desert culture first described in California. Most likely, they were hunter-gatherers who moved with the seasons, perhaps visiting the canyon at a specific time each year. Their shelters would have been simple structures, not liable to endure for centuries. Below the canyon rims, where rock overhangs provide ample protection from the elements, they might not have had to build anything.

Not long ago, archaeologists lacked evidence for Grand Canyon habitation between about 1000 B.C. and A.D. 500. This seemed to indicate that the canyon was deserted for all those centuries. But new evidence is surfacing all the time, and it now appears the people have indeed lived here more or less continuously. What the earliest ones left behind was just not as readily seen and dated as what came later.

Around 2,500 years ago, a new culture made its appearance on the southwestern scene — the culture now referred to as *Anasazi*. Derived from a Navajo term meaning "ancient ones," Anasazi can also be interpreted in the more negative sense of "enemy ancestors." That Anasazi would become the best-known name for these ancient people is ironic because they were never ancestors of the Navajo, who come from a different, northerly cultural background. The Navajo weren't even in the region at the time. The Anasazi were the ancestors of the modern Hopi (among other Pueblo tribes), who have a different, more honorific name for them: *Hisat Sinom*.

The Grand Canyon was at the edge of their world; they lived mostly to the northeast in Four Corners country, where they built the famous cliff dwellings on Mesa Verde in Colorado and many others scattered throughout the region. When the term "Indian ruin" is mentioned, it usually refers to an Anasazi structure. For many centuries, however, and in most places, they built on a much smaller scale, beginning with simple brush structures and moving up through pit houses to large stone pueblos. The cliff dwellings came toward the end of their occupation in the late 13th century.

The Anasazi were possessed of a revolutionary idea: agriculture. Someone learned how to cultivate food plants; or, as seems more likely, people arrived who already knew horticultural techniques. However it developed, the idea spread quickly, and brought a new way of living for people who had previously wandered with the seasons. Growing crops meant staying in one place, improving the ground, building check dams to hold water, guarding the fields against raiders, whether human or animal. It also led to more permanent structures and new tools and appurtenances. All of these things result in the artifacts that inform us, through archaeological study, about ancient ways of life.

The canyon hides innumerable treasures. Hikers found this collection of pottery tucked away in the rocks just yards from a popular trail. The photo shows the pots just as they were found, except for the two small pots in the upper center; they were found inside the large gray pot.

Grand Canyon National Park

Over time, the Anasazi culture matured. Archaeologists have identified several distinct stages of development, as defined by changes in the tools and dwellings of these people. The earliest are called Basketmakers, named for their splendid yucca-fiber baskets, the best of which were woven tightly enough to hold water. They applied similar skills to their woven sandals and carrying bags. Later, they learned to make pottery. They hunted with bows and arrows, replacing the spears and atlatls (spear-throwing tools) of their predecessors. They built increasingly substantial dwellings that were more elegant than the modern name for them, pit houses. Set partway into the ground, they were circular or rectangular in shape. Roof beams were held up by four wooden posts, while the roof itself was made of smaller sticks covered with clay. The entrance was an opening in the top. They were easy to build and comfortable in all seasons.

Split-twig figurines are among the canyon's most evocative and delicate ancient artifacts. Made from willow twigs split length- wise, then bent and twisted into the shapes of animals, they resemble deer and bighorn sheep and are thought to have had ritual significance for the people who left them in canyon caves some 4,000 years ago.

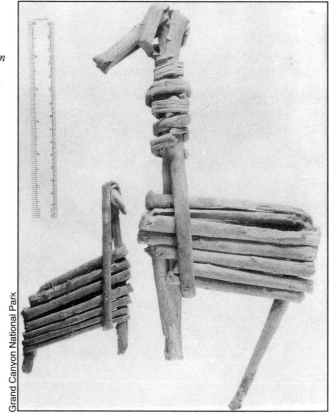

Grand Canyon National Park

An important change occurred around A.D. 750 or 800, when the people began to live in villages — first as clusters of pit houses, then as larger structures with joined living and storage rooms. This marked the beginning of the Pueblo period, the height of Anasazi culture. Things were particularly good in the years from around 900 to 1130, a time of relatively abundant summer rainfall. The farming was good, and the population swelled in formerly marginal country at lower elevations — including the Grand Canyon, which saw its maximum habitation around A.D. 1100.

A different cultural group, the Cohonina, moved into the western end of the canyon around the year 600. They adopted techniques from their Anasazi neighbors and lived in a similar manner.

There were no large pueblos in the Grand Canyon, but there are hun- dreds — maybe thousands — of archaeological sites from the Anasazi period. They include farm sites with irrigation terraces; grain storage structures, often set beneath protective overhangs; stone pits where the hearts of agave plants were roasted; numerous petroglyph and pictograph panels; and some small cliff dwellings. Two settlements are noteworthy: Tusayan, on the South Rim, and Walhalla Glades on the North Rim. The latter was a summer farming outpost of a settlement located on the Unkar Creek delta, beside the river, 5,000 feet below.

Early people did little to change what we see of the canyon today. Looking down from the rims, you might never guess that anyone ever lived down there. Walking along the rims, it takes an educated eye to pick out the old home- and farmsites. But they are there, in surprising numbers, and in their time, and in certain places, the Anasazi must have been highly visible. They had gardens, built houses, cut trees, and burned wood. Back then, you would have seen campfires winking in the night. Walking down any major side canyon, you would have encountered people, smelled the smoke of cooking fires, and heard children's laughter echoing from the cliffs.

How many lived in the canyon at any one time? No one can say. Around A.D. 1100, there were hundreds of occupied sites. After that, the population dropped off steeply, until by 1150 the Grand Canyon was essentially abandoned. The people headed east and south, to the Hopi mesas and beyond to the Rio Grande. There is growing agreement that it was the climate that drove them out — a long drought that made life in an already marginal land impossible. The dry conditions affected Anasazi throughout the Southwest, although it's interesting to note that their most spectacular developments — the cliff dwellings like those at Navajo National Monument and Mesa Verde National Park — were built around the turn of the 13th century and abandoned some time after 1250.

There is much still unknown of that time in the Grand Canyon. Every fact learned about the canyon's prehistory seems to raise another set of intriguing questions. Although much activity centered on springs and other sources of permanent water (where we would expect to find signs of people), there are numerous structures in more remote, waterless areas — for example, on mesa tops standing separate from the canyon rims. Why were they there? Some structures appear to have had a defensive purpose, but no evidence of warfare has ever come to light. If they *were* built as forts, what a strange and turbulent time it must have been. Even stranger are the food storage structures located in places that are seemingly inaccessible. One archaeologist says a helicopter is the only way she knows that anyone could build such a structure. Why so remote? So apparently hidden? Was it customary to build your private food stash in some secret place to guard against lean times?

The Anasazi lived by moving when necessary. Such was survival in an uncertain land. They moved, and they survived, and they still do in Pueblo communities from the Hopi mesas to the Rio Grande Valley. They never came back to live in the Grand Canyon, but at the same time they never totally left it. The Hopi, as they always have, regularly visit sacred sites within the canyon; it remains very much a part of their world. Since around 1300, the Hualapai and Havasupai people (a redundancy; *pai* means people) have lived on the western South Rim and its canyons.

On the North Rim, Paiutes hunted deer and other animals. The name for the Kaibab Plateau comes from two Paiute words, *kaiuw* (meaning mountain) and *a-vwi* (lying down). "Mountain lying down" describes very well this high, alpine area with no clear summit and no defining pinnacle, as if a large mountain were lying on its side. In summer, Navajos would come here to trade for deer skins. From the beginning, Indians used the obvious travel routes: Bright Angel Trail began as a route to the springs now called Indian Garden — once a Havasupai farming site. The North Kaibab Trail began as an old Paiute trail down Bright Angel Creek. It was used and sporadically maintained by mapping crews, miners, and tourism operators in the early part of the century and remained in an undeveloped state until 1928, when the park service completed the cross-canyon Kaibab Trail.

Scientists and Miners

This brings us to the arrival of Europeans, the first of whom were Spanish soldiers brought to the South Rim by Hopi guides in 1540. The Spanish looked the place over and saw nothing of the gold they were seeking, so they left it alone. So did the first Americans, who blanched at the rugged country, called it by all sorts of awful names, and dismissed it as useless.

Courtesy of Fred Harvey

John Hance, a miner, guide, and famous spinner of tall tales, came to the Grand Canyon around 1883. He established an asbestos mine deep in the canyon but soon learned that tourism was more profitable and, in his inimitable style, much more fun. His "ranch," set near Grandview Point, was the canyon rim's first hotel.

John Wesley Powell popularized the canyon to some extent but in a scary sort of way; the account of his river expeditions was hardly an advertisement for Grand Canyon adventure tourism. Yet it was Powell who recognized and promoted the scientific potential of the region. Behind him came explorers and scientists, some of whom fell deeply under the spell of the place. They returned again and again, most of them in search of nothing more profitable than knowledge.

Miners were another matter — usually on their own or with a few comrades, they came ostensibly looking for wealth, but their desires proved to be more complicated. Perhaps it was the canyon's doing. Perhaps the canyon worked its magic on them. Perhaps this is nothing more than my romantic notion, but I get a sense that some of these fellows weren't dedicated so much to mining as to finding a way to survive in this area. I like to think of them as resourceful people motivated by an attraction to the place more than to a specific career.

They included John Hance, William Bass, Louis D. "the Hermit" Boucher, Ralph Cameron, and others whose names are now part of the landscape. They built trails, and when they gave up mining they made their livings guiding tourists to camps they constructed at favorite sites in the canyon. For the most part, their impact below the rims was transitory. Hance's mine can still be seen at Horseshoe Mesa. His hotel, situated on the rim near Grandview Point, is long gone. At Bass's camp there are still tools and other relics that are old enough to seem attractive in an archaeological sense (sadly, vandals agree, and try to make off with whatever they can carry). Boucher's camp is gone but for the outlines of the foundations. Dave Rust's camp, now called Phantom Ranch, still stands, the only commercial tourist facility below the rim.

It's a good thing that miners never found much of mineral value. Imagine how the place would look if its rock had been riddled with precious ore. Imagine what a mess the river would be, reeking with the contamination of wastes from a time when there were no controls whatsoever on the techniques of mining. I picture tramways, roads, tailing piles, rusting corrugated mills, hydro plants, and power lines. Some of the best wild country in America has been saved by its lack of exploitable, removable wealth.

Here's a John Hance story: There was this big snowstorm one night, and he woke up to a field of white. He strapped on his snowshoes and went for a walk. Walked a long way, across the blinding snow. It was awfully soft, fluffy stuff, and awfully deep. He was thinking about heading home when he started seeing the ground beneath him. Three thousand feet below! These were clouds! He'd walked right off the snowy rim and out onto the clouds that filled the canyon. Now they were clearing, and he was darn near to getting dropped. He had to step fast, jumping across the gaps, and barely made it back to the rim.

I don't know about his snowshoes, but the part about the clouds is true. It happens in winter. A solid cloud layer stretches from one rim to the other. It is an undulating sea of mist, beautiful to look at. I once stood at Mather Point on a day like that, when a pair of ravens came rocketing out of the cloudbank like porpoises leaping from the waves. In the presence of magic like that, I wouldn't have been surprised to see old Hance come walking through on his snowshoes, kicking up little streamers of cloud, ready to tell some wild story about where he'd been.

After a while, as the old miner said they would, the clouds part. Shafts of sunlight spill through the openings, splash across the mesas and gorges, and suddenly there stands the Grand Canyon playing its old spectacular role, revealed to its public. Bravos and applause.

Too bad clouds aren't the only things filling the canyon these days. It's become a crowded place — this empty space, this void, this vast nothingness, as early romantic writers were inclined to describe it. Modern writers would never think such a thing, not because we are more hardheaded practical folk, but because most of the time now the canyon looks anything but empty. The air is a soup. During summer, it can be so thick that you can't see from one rim to the other, or from the rim to the bottom.

I don't want to overstate the case. Grand Canyon air is still relatively clean. On only 10 percent of summer days does visual range fall below 89 miles. (Visual range is a measurement that considers not only distance at which an object can be seen but also qualitative factors such as contrast, sharpness, and color.) In most places, that would be considered quite good.

On the other hand, when you see a truly clear day at the canyon, a day when visual range extends to 155 miles and more (up to 243 miles), you realize what you've been missing. It's as if you have been driving behind a dusty windshield all day, and someone finally washes it clean. The mountain that was just visible a hundred miles away is now smack in your face. Colors are vibrant. Edges are sharp. Red rock against deep blue sky: this is the air for which the Southwest desert is famous.

If you want to see the canyon under these conditions, the best time is in winter, when the air comes from the northwest. It pours down cold and clear and puts a shine on the entire landscape. Unfortunately, winter can also be a time for inversions. The air stagnates and fills up with pollution from local sources, and then the canyon can look pretty dirty.

In summer, air comes from the southwest and southeast, bringing pollutants from a variety of industrial and urban sources. The big one, as you might expect, is the Los Angeles basin, which sends up a rich yellow-orange stew of urban exhalations. Observers are actually able to track its progress as it moves, oozing eastward as a shapeless haze that eventually shrouds the canyon. It travels long distances: Los Angeles air has been detected as far away as the Dakotas.

Robert M. Butterfield

Under certain conditions that happen in winter, dense fog fills the canyon from rim to rim. By descending several hundred feet on a day like this, hikers can pass through the clouds into a shady world below.

In a park where gazing into the distance is the primary activity of visitors, clean air is of vital importance. Congress has recognized this in the Clean Air Act as amended in 1977 and 1990. Among other provisions, the act defines classes of air quality, with national parks and wilderness areas at the top of the list — *Mandatory* Class I areas. These are not by definition the places with the country's cleanest air (though many do fit that category).

The goal is to keep them from becoming polluted or to clean up existing pollution. The law requires "the prevention of any future and the remedying of any existing impairment of visibility in Mandatory Class I federal areas which impairment results from man-made air pollution."

As it applies to the Grand Canyon, the Clean Air Act requires protection of the good winter air that comes down from Nevada. It also requires the cleanup of bad air sources.

There are two problems when it comes to enforcement. First, what entails impairment? To know whether visibility has decreased, there has to be an established baseline. Unfortunately, no one was monitoring air quality in 1870. Or 1900. Systematic measurement did not begin at the Grand Canyon until 1978, several years after the Navajo Generating Station in Page, Arizona, began burning about 10 railroad hoppers of coal per hour.

The second problem is this: When the haze curtain drops, how much of the pollution comes from human sources? There are numerous natural substances that cause haze — anything from dust to forest fire smoke to the ejecta from volcanic eruptions. Of course no one would argue the case of volcanoes, but dust and forest fires are not always the product of nature. Dust is raised by such things as construction, overgrazing, and wind or traffic on dirt roads. Forest fires can be set by arsonists.

The Navajo Generating Station provides a good illustration of the problem. There has never been any question about how much sulphur dioxide the plant emits (up to 10 tons per hour; 40,000 to 70,000 tons per year). Rather, where does it go? The plant is visible for miles around the town of Page. You can see its plume on most days, a dirty yellow scrawl across the blue sky. Because of prevailing weather patterns, emissions would generally head northeast. But when the air stagnates around the Grand Canyon, as it does in winter, a sizable quantity of sulphur dioxide ends up between the rims. This was shown by a study conducted throughout the region in 1987. It was called the Winter Haze Intensive Tracer Experiment, during which chemical tracers were added to the smokestack emissions from the power plant and picked up with monitoring equipment around the Colorado Plateau. According to park service analysis of the data, the Navajo Generating Station is responsible, on average, for 40 to 50 percent of human-caused haze during the winter months. On the worst days, the numbers are higher, up to 72 percent, with the highest levels recorded below the canyon rims. This means that the power plant is the single largest cause of poor visibility in the Grand Canyon during winter months.

But things should change. In 1991, the EPA mediated an agreement between the owners of the power plant and environmental groups on a sulphur dioxide control strategy. Emissions are to be reduced by 90 percent based on a rolling annual average, phased in over a period of three years from 1997 to 1999. In addition, the power plant has agreed to schedule its annual maintenance for winter months (during maintenance, parts of the plant are shut down and produce no emissions whatsoever).

These changes should reduce sulphur dioxide significantly, and that is a good thing. But more important, this is the first time in the history of the Clean Air Act that a source of industrial pollution has been forced to lower its emissions to protect the visibility in a Class I area. As a precedent, that could have real weight, affecting more than the huge areas of the Colorado Plateau that have suffered the plant's bad air. After all, there are Class I areas ringing the Los Angeles basin.

How ironic. On one hand, we find that the Grand Canyon is too small, that its environment can be degraded by pollution sources far beyond its boundaries. On the other hand, because of the Clean Air Act, and because Grand Canyon is among the world's most significant national parks, its very existence is having an impact on the lives of people throughout the country. It has always been hoped by supporters of national parks that these islands of wildness would exert an influence larger than their mere physical size; that they would provide standards for judging the effects of our activities in other places. Perhaps those hopes will be realized.

Then again, maybe not. The park is constantly in need of defense, and although a thorough review of the conservation issues threatening the canyon is beyond the purpose of this book, several other hazards should be mentioned in brief.

For one, there is the matter of uranium mining on the periphery of the park. The Colorado Plateau in general has been a hot spot for uranium prospecting since the 1940s. At the canyon itself, structures of the old Orphan Mine still stand on the South Rim just west of Grand Canyon Village. Established in 1893 as a copper mine, it produced uranium in the 1950s and '60s and is now inactive and belongs to the national park. In 1980, a Denver-based mining company struck a rich deposit of uranium ore outside the park on the Kaibab Plateau. The discovery was made in Hack Canyon, a few miles north of the park boundary, and it set off a flurry of prospecting activity; within a few years, hundreds of claims had been made on both sides of the canyon.

Although none of these claims is within park boundaries, concern for the park centers on two issues. First, the very existence of mines and mills, with all the attendant activity of road-building, ore trucks, and power lines, deals a blow to the wild integrity of land that should serve as a buffer around the park. Air quality, water quality, wildlife, and wilderness values all could suffer.

Second, there is concern about tailings, and for good reason. In 1979, contaminated water from a spill at a uranium mine in New Mexico poured down the Rio Puerco into the Little Colorado River. Radioactive material made it all the way to the main Colorado River. Since then, tighter controls are supposed to have been enacted. But in 1984, a flash flood in Hack Canyon came past the mine site and carried off 10 tons of high-grade ore. The clean-up as required by the EPA involved the removal of 1,500 tons of contaminated soil. Considering the power of erosion to rearrange the Grand Canyon landscape, there is real cause for concern about bringing piles of ore to the surface.

The question of aircraft overflights has been a hot issue from time to time and seems likely to arise again. The problem is noise — a factor that, like air pollution at current levels, probably does no documentable damage to park flora or fauna. However, it does change the feel of the place. Certainly the natural aural fabric of the canyon is an essential ingredient in the wilderness experience.

Before new regulations went into effect in 1988, helicopters and airplanes loaded with sightseers flew below the rims, buzzing from one beauty spot to the next. Under current regulations, aircraft are never permitted below the rim and must fly in specific corridors. Forty-four percent of the park is designated flight-free, which according to the park service protects most visitors, including 90 percent of backcountry users, from the intrusion of sight-seeing aircraft. Some would take issue with these figures. Even with aircraft kept above 14,500 feet (the flight-free zones), their drone is present; for that matter, jets flying above 30,000 feet are easily heard when the canyon is quiet. Anyone taking a walk down the Hermit Trail, which lies below one of the corridors, has experienced the constant parade of airborne engines. It is certainly an annoying and disruptive sound. It is also an enormously popular way to see the canyon: an estimated 750,000 people take scenic flights each year.

Another issue unlikely to die is "row versus roar" — the use of large motorized inflatables (motor rigs) on the river. These are the biggest craft plying the waters, carrying about 30 passengers per boat (compared to the smaller oar-powered craft that carry two to four passengers each). One is a bus; the other is a push-cart. Those who favor oars complain that the noise of motors disrupts the natural feel of the canyon; they contend that if the park's policy is to preserve a "vignette of primitive America," then motors do not belong. Those favoring motors argue that not everyone can afford the cost or the time of taking a slow-moving float trip. Motors can push rafts through the entire canyon in four or five days, and because the boats are so big, one boat with two or three guides can carry many more passengers at a lower price per person. Motors, they say, are more democratic.

Back in the canyon, a thousand years ago: The Anasazi petroglyph maker is older now, in his late 40s, a grandfather. He doesn't move as easily he did. His knees are stiff, but as an elder of the clan he has certain prerogatives. Old men are allowed time for contemplation. Today he sits on a flat boulder at the edge of the inner gorge, watching the endless river roll by, listening to the thunder of rapids. Earth power. Water spirit. The river is life. Never stopping, always flowing away, always coming back.

He is a man of simple possessions and limited experience with the wider world. But he has at least one great thing for which I envy him. He can look at this landscape, and the future, with confidence. He can imagine the grandson of his grandson sitting on this very rock thinking these same thoughts as the old river slides past. This is the way it is, and has been, and will be. Yucca will bloom in the spring. The river will rise in muddy torrents, and in the side canyon the stream will fall cold and clear past the petroglyphs where the pot he has now long forgotten still waits on the rock shelf. Maybe that grandson, generations in the future, will tap his own figures into the desert varnish beside those of his forebears.

This is the part I envy. It would be enormously reassuring to look down through your children's lives into the future, and have confidence in the world they will inherit.

Of course he was wrong. The world changed for his people. They left the canyon. But he never knew that, and what a fine feeling it must have been. He believed it. We can only hope.

Traveler's Information

Notes to Chapters

Bibliography

Index

General Information for Visitors to Grand Canyon

Visitor Centers

Grand Canyon National Park visitor centers and museums provide brochures, books, maps, and general information. A free park newspaper, *The Guide*, is distributed at entrance stations and lists services, seasonal schedules, and hours of operation. Separate editions are available for the North and South rims.

On the South Rim, the main visitor center is in Grand Canyon Village. Nearby, at Yavapai Point, the Yavapai Museum features geological exhibits, along with a panoramic view of the canyon. About 20 miles east, the Tusayan Museum has archeological displays adjacent to a prehistoric ruin. There is also a Visitor Information Center at Desert View, open seasonally. On the North Rim, a National Park Service information desk is located in the lobby of the Grand Canyon Lodge.

Correspondence and requests for general information may be directed to park headquarters: Grand Canyon National Park, P.O. Box 129, Grand Canyon, AZ 86023 (602-638-7888).

Entrance Fees

Entrance fees are $10 per private vehicle and all its passengers, with one permit valid for up to seven days. Individual travelers entering by other means (bicycle, motorcycle, foot, bus,

etc.) may obtain a $4 seven-day permit. A $15 permit allows unlimited visits to both rims for a calendar year; it includes the pass holder and immediate family or all passengers in a private vehicle. A Golden Eagle Pass, good in all national parks, costs $25 per calendar year. Finally, Golden Age Passports (for persons 62 or older) and Golden Access Passports (for handicapped persons) are free; these include not just park admission but reduced camping fees at National Park Service campgrounds.

Season

The South Rim is open all year, although some facilities close and hours are cut back during the winter. The North Rim is closed each winter, beginning with the first heavy snowfall (late October or early November) and lasting until mid-May. Early and late visitors should call ahead for conditions.

West Rim Drive

During summer, from about Memorial Day to September 30, the 8-mile-long West Rim Drive is closed to private vehicles (permits for disabled persons are available at the Visitor Center). Instead, free shuttle buses carry visitors back and forth. The buses make it possible to combine walking with riding. The Rim Trail (beginning to the east at Yavapai Point) is paved to Maricopa Point and extends all the way to Hermits Rest. Restrooms and drinking water are found only here at the end of the road, along with a gift shop and snack bar.

Hiking

Hiking here is very different from hiking in forests or mountains. There is little water and, in summer, the heat is intense. Going down is easy; coming back up is not. The canyon has a way of drawing hikers ever deeper, until they are tired and their water is gone, and then they face the long haul back to the rim. As a rule, even experienced walkers tend to be overambitious. It is best to set modest goals, consult with park rangers, and choose well-traveled trails (for example, the Kaibab or the Bright Angel) for one's first forays.

Permits are required for overnight camping in the Grand Canyon backcountry. The permits are free but limited. During the high season (April through October), backcountry campsites on the major trails are fully booked. Write to the park well in advance of your intended trip to request reservations. These may be obtained any time after October 1, covering the following calendar year. You may call for information and a backcountry planning kit at (602) 638-7888, or write to the Backcountry Reservations Office, P.O. Box 129, Grand Canyon, AZ 86023. Equipment can be rented at Babbitt's General Store in Grand Canyon Village.

Mule Riding

Mule trains are an old tradition in the canyon. They provide an alternative to hiking, but riding a mule can feel like a strenuous activity. Day trips are available from both rims. From the South Rim, two-day trips go all the way to the Colorado River, spending the night at historic Phantom Ranch; bookings should be made up to a year in advance. For information, call (602) 638-2631 or 638-2401.

River Trips

Seeing the canyon from river level provides a new, adventurous perspective on the deep wilderness that comprises most of the park. More than 20 companies operate trips taking five days to longer than two weeks. The only one-day trips run the smooth water of Glen Canyon above Lees Ferry, originating via Page, Arizona. A list of river companies is available at visitor centers.

Handicapped Access

Many overlooks and some trails on both rims are wheelchair accessible or accessible with assistance. An Accessibility Guide, with permits for parking and access to the West Rim Drive is available at the Visitor Center.

Lodging

Accommodations are found on both rims and in surrounding communities, including Tusayan near the South Rim and Jacob Lake 45 miles from the North Rim. To watch sunset or dawn over the Grand Canyon is one of the greatest pleasures of visiting the park. This means staying overnight, which requires advance planning. During much of the year, Grand Canyon lodging is usually full. Reservations, made as early as possible, are essential. If no rooms are available, it's a long drive back to neighboring cities.

All South Rim lodging (including Phantom Ranch,accessible only by foot and mule) is operated by Grand Canyon National Park Lodges, P.O. Box 699, Grand Canyon, AZ 86023 (602-638-2401). In Tusayan: Best Western Grand Canyon Squire Inn (602-638-2681); Moqui Lodge (602-638-2401); Quality Inn (602-638-2673); Red Feather (602-638-2414); and Seven-Mile Lodge (602-638-2291). For North Rim, contact TW Recreational Services, Box 400, Cedar City, UT 84720 (801-586-7686).

Campgrounds

Park service campgrounds on both rims provide basic services, including tent pads, picnic tables, toilets, drinking water, and trash collection. They include: Mather Campground at Grand Canyon Village. Fee, $10 per night. Reservations up to eight weeks in advance available through MISTIX, at P.O. Box 85705, San Diego, CA 92138-5705 (tel: 800-365-2267); no reservations between December 1 and March 1. Showers, laundry, and dump

station are located nearby. Desert View Campground, near the east entrance. No reservations, no hook-ups, and closed during winter. Fee, $8 per night.

North Rim Campground, on the North Rim. Fee, $10 per night. Reservations can be had through MIST-IX (see above). No hook-ups, closed in winter. Shower, laundry, and store located nearby. Hook-ups can be had at Trailer Village, on the South Rim near Mather Campground. Open all year, operated by Grand Canyon National Park Lodges, (602) 638-2401.

Outside the park, campsites are available at Babbitt's Camper Village in Tusayan. Open all year, hook-ups and other services. Call (602) 638-2887. The Kaibab National Forest offers simple camping at Ten-X Campground just south of Tusayan, Demotte Campground 16 miles north of the North Rim, and Jacob Lake Campground 45 miles north of the North Rim. Glen Canyon National Recreation Area operates a campground at Lees Ferry on the Colorado River.

Emergencies and Medical Facilities

Call 911; from hotel and motel rooms, dial 9-911. On the South Rim, the Grand Canyon Clinic (638-2551 or 638-2469) provides routine care during business hours and 24-hour emergency care. On the North Rim, a clinic is staffed by a nurse practitioner (638-2611).

NOTES TO CHAPTERS

Chapter 1 Pages From the Past
There is an enormous volume of published geological information available on the Grand Canyon. Much of this is written for professionals. One outstanding collection lies somewhere between popular and professional writing. It is *Grand Canyon Geology*, edited by Stanley S. Beus and Michael Morales, published in 1990 by Oxford University Press and the Museum of Northern Arizona. This book is a virtual compendium of current knowledge of canyon geology.
History of Geology: "The Development of Geological Studies in the Grand Canyon," by Earle E. Spamer. *Tryonia*, Miscellaneous Publications of the Department of Malacology, The Academy of Natural Sciences of Philadelphia, No. 17, June 1989.
Geology along the Colorado River: *Guidebook to the Colorado River*, by W. Kenneth Hamblin and J. Keith Rigby. Two volumes, published in 1969 by the Department of Geology, Brigham Young University. Especially useful for the river runner, although some of the information is dated.

Chapter 2 Old River, Young Canyon
Origin of the Colorado River: "Canyon Maker: A Geological History of the Colorado River," by Ivo Lucchitta, *Plateau,* Vol. 59, no. 2. The entire issue of the magazine is devoted to this subject; Lucchita's discussion is well written for the nonspecialist. A somewhat more technical version of the same article is found in *Grand Canyon Geology*, Chapter 15.
Lava Dams: W. K. Hamblin, "Late Cenozoic Lava Dams in the Western Grand Canyon," in *Grand Canyon Geology*.

Chapter 3 The Power of Erosion
Erosion: Richard Hereford and Peter W. Huntoon, "Rock Movement and Mass Wastage in the Grand Canyon," in *Grand Canyon Geology*.
Rotational landslides: Peter W. Huntoon, "The Surprise Valley Landslide and Widening of the Grand Canyon." *Plateau,* Vol.48, nos.1 and 2:1-12.
1966 Flood: M. E. Cooley, B. N. Aldridge, and R. C. Euler, "Effects of the Catastrophic Flood of December 1966, North Rim Area, Eastern Grand Canyon, Arizona," Professional Paper 980, Washington, D. C.: U. S. Geological Survey.
Debris Flows: Robert H. Webb, Patrick T. Pringle, and Glenn R. Rink, "Debris Flows from Tributaries of the Colorado River, Grand Canyon National Park, Arizona," Professional Paper 1492, Washington, D. C.: U. S. Geological Survey.

Chapter 4 The Distribution of Living Things
Grand Canyon rattlesnakes: Donald Miller, Robert A. Young, Thomas W. Gatlin, and John A. Richardson, *Amphibians and Reptiles of the Grand Canyon*, Grand Canyon Natural History Association Monograph No. 4, 1982.
Plant distribution: Peter L. Warren, Karen L. Reichardt, and others, "Vegetation of Grand Canyon National Park," Technical Report No. 9, Cooperative National Park Resources Studies Unit, University of Arizona. Also: Barbara G. Phillips, Arthur M. Phillips, III, and Marilyn Ann Schmidt

Bernzott, *Annotated Checklist of Vascular Plants of Grand Canyon National Park*, Grand Canyon Natural History Association Monograph No. 7, 1987.

Desert Microclimates: William McGinnies, *Discovering the Desert: Legacy of the Carnegie Desert Botanical Laboratory* (Tucson, Ariz.: University of Arizona Press, 1981).

Shiva Temple Expedition: J. Donald Hughes, *In the House of Light and Stone*. Kolb's involvement is described in Edwin Corle's book *Listen, Bright Angel* (New York: Duell, Sloan and Pearce, 1946).

Canyon Life Zones: This information is drawn from a variety of sources. One of the better discussions is included in the book *Grand Canyon Birds*, by Bryan T. Brown, Steven W. Carothers, and R. Roy Johnson.

Chapter 5 The Kaibab Plateau

Kaibab Plateau Ecology: D. I. Rasmussen, "Biotic Communities of the Kaibab Plateau, Arizona," *Ecological Monographs*, Vol. 11, 1941: 229-275.

Kaibab and Abert squirrels: David E. Brown, *Arizona's Tree Squirrels*, Arizona Game and Fish Department, 1984.

Kaibab Deer Herd: C. John Burk, "The Kaibab Deer Incident: A Long-persisting Myth," *BioScience,* Vol. 23, no. 2, February 1973. Also Graeme Caughley, "Eruption of Ungulate Populations, With Emphasis on Himalayan Thar in New Zealand," *Ecology*, Vol. 51, no.1, Winter 1970. Also Thomas R. Dunlap, "That Kaibab Myth," *Journal of Forest History*, April 1988.

History of the Kaibab Deer Herd, specifically of hunting: J. P. Russo, *The Kaibab North Deer Herd*, Arizona Game and Fish Bulletin No. 7, 1964.

Chapter 6 Blackbrush and Rattlesnakes

Rattlesnakes: Laurence M. Klauber's book *Rattlesnakes: Their Habits, Life Histories, and Influence on Mankind*. Also *Amphibians and Reptiles of the Grand Canyon*.

Pinyon-juniper woodland: Stephen Trimble, Chapter 11, *The Sagebrush Ocean*, University of Nevada Press, 1989.

Chapter 7 Wild West

Solpugids and other creatures: James Cornett, *Wildlife of the North American Deserts*.

Human body and water: E. F. Adolph and Associates, *Physiology of Man in the Desert*.

Plant adaptations: William G. McGinnies, *Discovering the Desert*.

Chapter 8 Treefrogs and Flycatchers

Types of Side Canyons: Andre R. Potochnik and Stephen J. Reynolds, "Side Canyons of the Colorado River, Grand Canyon," Chapter 20, *Grand Canyon Geology*.

Chapter 9 The River

The most comprehensive single source of information on the river's natural history is *The Colorado River Through Grand Canyon: Natural History and Human Change*, by Steven W. Carothers and Bryan T. Brown. Designed for river runners is Lawrence Stevens's *The Colorado River in Grand Canyon: A Guide*.

Effects of Glen Canyon Dam on the river and fisheries: Ron Harris, "A Lee's Ferry Tale: Power, Politics and Trout on the Colorado River," *Trout*, Autumn 1991. Also, there is a wealth of material in the files of Glen Canyon Environmental Studies (U.S. Department of the Interior, Bureau of Reclamation, Flagstaff, Arizona).

Chapter 10 Amberat Chronicles

Packrats: Donald F. Hoffmeister, *Mammals of Grand Canyon.*

Pleistocene conditions and packrat middens: K. L. Cole, "Late Quaternary Environments in the Eastern Grand Canyon: Vegetational Gradients Over the Last 25,000 Years" (Doctoral Dissertation, University of Arizona, 1981). Also by K. L. Cole, "Late Quaternary Zonation of Vegetation in the Eastern Grand Canyon," *Science,* Vol. 217, 17 September 1982; and "Past Rates of Change, Species Richness, and a Model of Vegetational Inertia in the Grand Canyon, Arizona," *The American Naturalist,* Vol. 125, no. 2, February 1985. With emphasis on the western Grand Canyon, Arthur M. Phillips, III, "Packrats, Plants, and the Pleistocene in the Lower Grand Canyon" (Doctoral Dissertation, University of Arizona, 1977). Also Jim I. Mead, "In Search of Ancient Pack Rats," *Natural History,* Vol. 89, September 1980: 40-45.

Tamarisk and willow in the river corridor: Lawrence Edward Stevens, "Mechanisms of Riparian Plant Community Organization and Succession in the Grand Canyon, Arizona" (Doctoral Dissertation, Northern Arizona University, May 1989).

Vegetation and birds: Bryan T. Brown and Michael W. Trosset, "Nesting-Habitat Relationships of Riparian Birds Along the Colorado River in Grand Canyon, Arizona," *The Southwestern Naturalist* Vol. 34 no. 2, June 1989: 260-270.

Burros and bighorn: S. W. Carothers, M. E. Stitt, and R. R. Johnson, "Feral Asses on Public Lands: An Analysis of the Biotic Impact, Legal Considerations, and Management Alternatives," *Transactions of the North American Wildlife and Natural Resources Conference,* Vol. 41, 1976: 396-406. Also Joseph Stocker, "Battle of the Burro," *National Wildlife,* August 1980; and Stephen Mills, "The Bighorn and the Burro," *New Scientist,* 4 June 1981.

Chapter 11 From Anasazi to Aircraft

Prehistoric people in the Grand Canyon: Anne Trinkle Jones and Robert C. Euler, *A Sketch of Grand Canyon Prehistory.*

Anasazi in the region: Gary Matlock, *Enemy Ancestors: The Anasazi World With a Guide to Sites;* and J. Richard Ambler, *The Anasazi.*

History of the Canyon: J. Donald Hughes, *In the House of Stone and Light.*

Air pollution: Carl Bowman, "Where Earth is the Floor of the Sky," a draft document summarizing air quality issues, available from the National Park Service, Grand Canyon National Park. The park's vertical files hold extensive information on air quality.

Uranium mining: Dan Dagget, "Yellowcake National Park," *Sierra,* July/August 1985.

Bibliography

Adolph, E. F. and Associates. 1969. *Physiology of Man in the Desert*. New York: Hafner Press.

Ambler, J. Richard. 1989. *The Anasazi*. Flagstaff, Ariz.: Museum of Northern Arizona.

Babbitt, Bruce. 1978. *Grand Canyon: An Anthology*. Flagstaff: Northland Press.

Beus, Stanley S., and Michael Morales (eds.) 1990. *Grand Canyon Geology*. New York: Oxford University Press, Museum of Northern Arizona.

Brown, Bryan T., Steven W. Carothers, and R. Roy Johnson. 1987. *Grand Canyon Birds*. Tucson: University of Arizona Press.

Brown, David E. 1984. *Arizona's Tree Squirrels*. Phoenix: Arizona Game and Fish Department.

Carothers, Steven W., and Bryan T. Brown. 1991. *The Colorado River Through Grand Canyon: Natural History and Human Change*. Tucson: University of Arizona Press.

Cornett, James W. 1987. *Wildlife of the North American Deserts*. Palm Springs, Calif.: Nature Trails Press.

Dodge, Natt N. 1985. *Flowers of the Southwest Deserts*. Tucson: Southwest Parks and Monuments Association.

Elmore, Francis H. 1976. *Shrubs and Trees of the Southwest Uplands*. Tucson: Southwest Parks and Monuments Association.

Grey, Zane. 1908. *The Last of the Plainsmen*. The Outing Publishing Co.

Hoffmeister, Donald F. 1971. *Mammals of Grand Canyon*. Urbana: University of Illinois Press.

Hughes, J. Donald. 1978. *In the House of Stone and Light: A Human History of the Grand Canyon*. Grand Canyon Natural History Association.

Jones, Anne Trinkle, and Robert C. Euler. 1990. *A Sketch of Grand Canyon Prehistory*. Rev. ed. Grand Canyon: The Grand Canyon Natural History Association.

Klauber, Laurence M. 1982. *Rattlesnakes: Their Habits, Life Histories, and Influence on Mankind*. Abridged ed. Berkeley and Los Angeles: University of California Press.

Krutch, Joseph Wood. 1957, 1958. *Grand Canyon: Today and All Its Yesterdays.* New York: Morrow Quill Paperbacks.

Matlock, Gary, and Scott Warren. 1988. *Enemy Ancestors: The Anasazi World with a Guide to Sites.* Flagstaff, Ariz.: Northland Press.

McGinnies, William G. 1981. *Discovering the Desert: Legacy of the Carnegie Desert Botanical Library.* Tucson: The University of Arizona Press.

Miller, Donald, Robert A. Young, Thomas W. Gatlin, and John A. Richardson. 1982. *Amphibians and Reptiles of the Grand Canyon.* Grand Canyon Natural History Association Monograph No. 4.

Olin, George, and Dale Thompson. 1982. *Mammals of the Southwest Deserts.* Rev. ed. Tucson: Southwest Parks and Monuments Association.

Phillips, Arthur M. III. 1979. *Grand Canyon Wildflowers.* Grand Canyon: Grand Canyon Natural History Association.

Powell, J. W. (1895 Flood & Vincent) 1961. *The Exploration of the Colorado River and its Canyons.* New York: Dover Publications.

Rasmussen, D. I. 1941. *Biotic communities of the Kaibab Plateau, Arizona.* Ecological Monographs, 11:229-275.

Schmidt, Jeremy. 1992. *The Grand Canyon: A Traveler's Guide.* Jackson, Wyo.: Freewheeling Travel Guides

Schullery, Paul (ed.) 1981. *The Grand Canyon: Early Impressions.* Boulder: Colorado Associated University Press.

Stevens, Lawrence. 1983. *The Colorado River in Grand Canyon: A Guide.* Flagstaff, Ariz.: Red Lake Books.

Whitney, Stephen. 1982. *A Field Guide to the Grand Canyon.* New York: Quill.

INDEX